Get Work as a
FANTASY ARTIST

I0473605

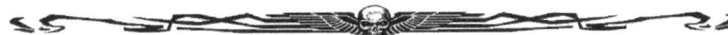

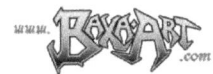

Why You Need This Book

I know that art is your passion. And I know you'd love to make a living painting heroes and monsters. You can! I know, because I've been a freelance fantasy illustrator for over 25 years!

I want to **give you an advantage over the other guy** by sharing **INSIDER STRATEGIES** that I use to connect with clients and get jobs!

Get Work as a Fantasy Artist makes it easy for you because it contains everything you need to get illustration jobs all in one place!

Everything to Guide you to a Successful Art Career
- How to build a powerful and *effective* portfolio
- Use critiques to catapult you to a professional level
- How to find fantasy art job opportunities
- How to solicit companies
- What Art Directors are looking for – and why they'll hire YOU!
- Conventions, agents, illustration directories, marketing yourself
- And so much more!

They don't teach these techniques in school. They can only come from years of working in the industry

Get valuable insight into Art Directors, and take the guesswork out of talking with them and asking for work

I know you have the drive and the passion; you just need some laser focused direction. Learn from my years of experience and super-charge your effectiveness and have the confidence to make your mark.

No matter where you are in your career, you will find something useful in this book. It's packed with information that you can apply right away.

**Take your career into your own hands!
READ THIS BOOK and boost your chances of living your dream as a fantasy artist!**

Published by:

Body Ritual Graphics, Los Angeles, CA
www.BaxaArt.com
www.BaxaArtAcademy.com

First Softcover Edition: August 2014
First eBook Edition: December 2013

10 9 8 7 6 5 4 3 2 1

ISBN-13: 978-0-9905077-0-3

Table of Contents

Book 1: Artistic Growth

Book 2: Breaking In and Staying In

TOM BAXA

Get Work as a Fantasy Artist:

Book 01
Artistic Growth

By
Tom Baxa

ABOUT TOM BAXA

I've been a professional fantasy illustrator for over 25 years! Phew, I can hardly believe it. Want to know my secret? Work your butt off! No surprise there, anything worth doing is worth doing with all your heart.

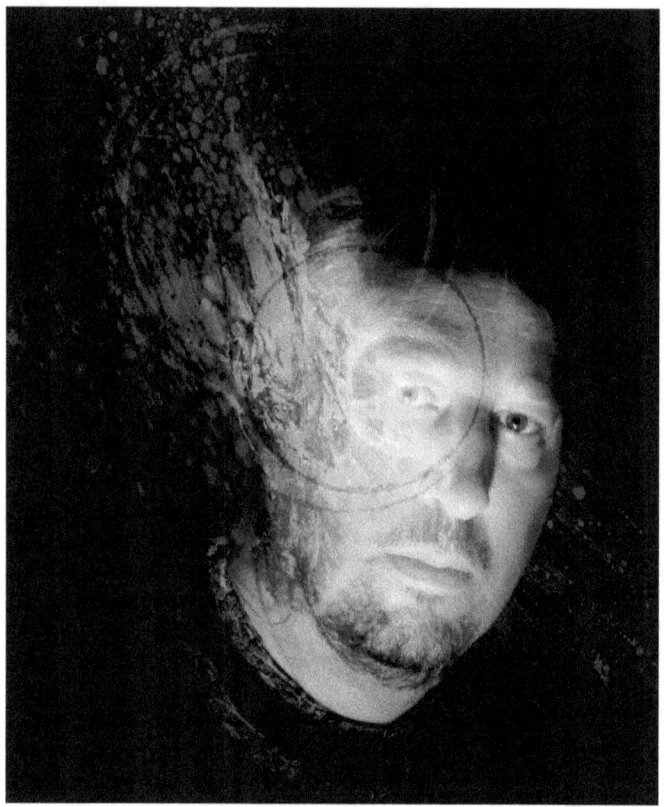

It starts with your artwork and whatever means you use to get good at your craft whether it be at school, a mentorships, or hours at the easel. I always try to create dynamic compositions with wickedly designed characters embroiled in emotionally packed events. I like to use at least three light sources to add drama and mood. And in addition to image making and story-telling, I love to indulge the artist in me and explore color, brushy paint strokes, and mark making. These are some of the things that make my work uniquely mine.

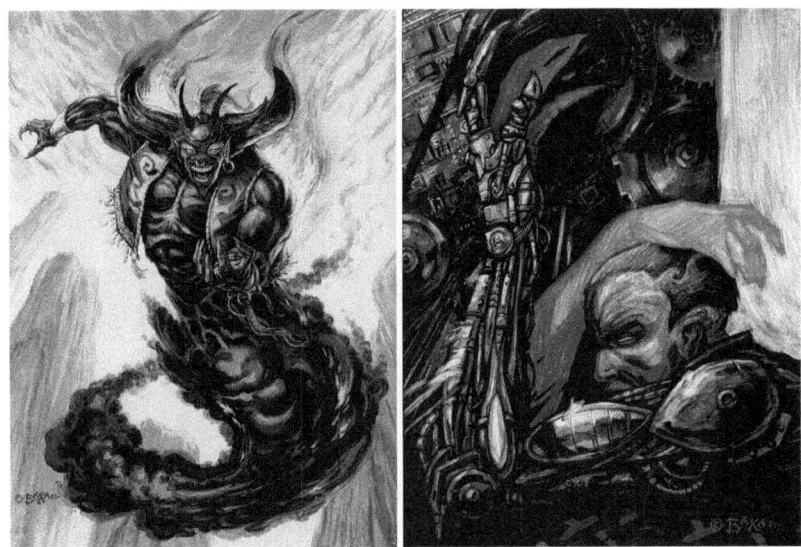

Dark Djinn © Thomas M. Baxa 2003 and *Phantom Limb* © Thomas M. Baxa 1997.

Before computers were in every home, companies mainly used black and white art for the interiors of books, so that's what I specialized in. Right out of college, where I got a bachelor's degree in Illustration, I inked comics for some indies and did spot illos for **Dragon** magazine. I soon worked my way into doing interior art for **Dungeons & Dragons**, and lots of it.

I also worked for other role playing game companies and eventually landed a primo staff position at FASA where I was granted a lot of leeway for experimentation and I did some of my best work while growing as an oil painter.

I continued freelancing and made an effort to go to conventions and connect with art directors in the fantasy RPG industry. As a result of my networking efforts, I landed my first **Magic: the Gathering** and **World of Warcraft tcg** cards.

My career has been filled with a wide variety of high end clients in the role playing game, collectible card game, miniatures, video game, advertising, and film industries. My work has appeared on the covers and interiors of countless books and magazines (including *Spectrum*), and my concept designs have contributed to many cool video game and movie projects.

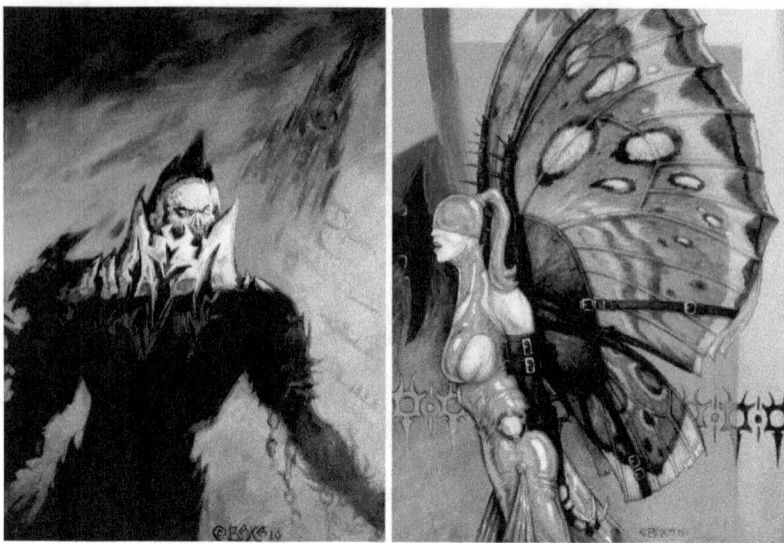

Armored Slayer © Thomas M. Baxa 2010 and *Cherry Gloss* © Thomas M. Baxa 2005.

I continue to freelance as an illustrator and concept artist, as I develop my own projects, both as an artist and an author, and continue to grow the BaxaArt brand including its newest addition BaxaArtAcademy.com.

Check out my website BaxaArt.com for great art, merchandise, prints, and paintings for sale, as well as my art book ***Blood Rituals: The Art of Tom Baxa***. My blog, ***BaxaArt Blog***, http://baxaart.blogspot.com, is full of updates about my work, helpful information, stories about my life as an artist, cool art by me and my friends and much more.

I still follow the strategies outlined in this book to grow as an artist, find new leads, and make contact with art directors in an effort to further my freelance career. And you should too!

BaxaArt Academy

Mission Statement

BaxaArt Academy's mission is to provide a virtual mentorship for artists of all levels through demos, tutorials, information, and professional experience. BAA will offer instruction through books, instructional videos, blog articles, online portfolio reviews, and painting instruction as a springboard to a fulfilling career as a fantasy artist and personal artistic growth.

BAA explores such topics as improving artistic skills, building a portfolio, finding work, and the business side of being a working illustrator. It's about sharing information about great artists, resources, supplies, gear, books, and more.

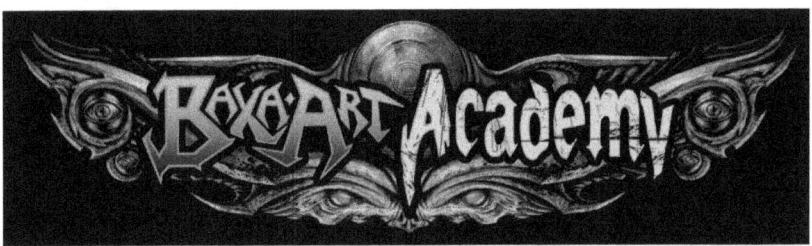

Expert Experience

I've been a professional fantasy illustrator with major clients for over 25 years. The experience I've gained over the years is invaluable, and BAA was formed to be a resource for artists to learn from my many experiences.

Artists Helping Artists

BaxaArt Academy was created as a means to pay it forward to up-and-coming fantasy illustrators. Early in my career, and still to this day, teachers and fellow artists have generously helped me navigate the ins and outs of being a professional artist. This is one of the ways I can return the favor.

Creating art can often be a solitary pursuit, but we artists need community to share ideas, learn from each other, and feed our artistic souls. BaxaArt Academy offers the opportunity to do so. Explore all that BaxaArt Academy has to offer at BaxaArtAcademy.com.

INTRO

Way To Go

Congratulations on taking the first step towards becoming a working fantasy illustrator! You've taken action by getting this book and I can tell that you're committed to improving your skills and your knowledge. Way to go!!

The information in this book is invaluable and could only be amassed through years of experience working in the field. Guess what? Because you've boldly stepped up - you will be rewarded with tips and strategies that will put you ahead of your competition and speed up your learning curve, bringing you that much closer to living your dream job.

Even if you have had some paying illustration jobs, the info in this book can give you insights to help you excel in your field.

Quick note: I often use the word "painting" in this book to describe making art, but I use it as a blanket term for all forms of art-making, whether you're a traditional artist or digital artist. It's all art, right? Also, for the purposes of this book, I will use the term "art director" (or AD) to mean *any* person who is in a position to hire you to do artwork for a company. And, because I'm a man, I refer to most people in this book with male pronouns. Women, please do not take offence – I know full well that women are fantasy artists and in creative positions of power.

Visit www.BaxaArt.com for full color versions of the art in this book.

Alright, let's jump in – and no matter what, never let anyone sway you from living your dream as an artist, whatever form that takes.

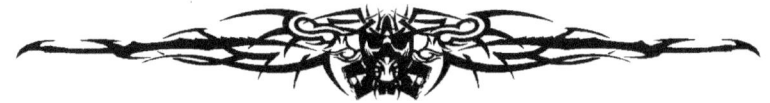

SECTION 1: Your Growth as an Artist

First Things First

Before you can get work, you have to get good. And that's a life long journey, believe me. First off, let's talk a little about the ways you can become a better artist – and this goes for everyone, no matter where you are in your art career. I know working pros that have gone back to school to get their masters, or learn different skills, study with one of their favorite artists, or learn digital tools like Photoshop, Painter and Illustrator.

This book has valuable information for EVERY artist, no matter where you are in your career.

What Do You Want to do With Your Life?

This may seem like a silly question, but so few of us take the time to consciously and concretely figure out what we really want. Not what you think you should do, not what others are doing, and not what your parents, friends, siblings, spouses, and society think you should do. What do *you* want to do?

What's your dream? I know you love making art – I do to. So what do you want to do with that passion? If your answer is to paint in your room just for yourself, that's totally ok. You can do anything you want. I'm assuming since you bought this book, you'd at least like to see your work in print and make some money doing what you love.

This is a practical guide with tools and insights into being a working fantasy illustrator. But you may want to step back for a moment and take a look at what you *really* want. Do you even know? A lot of people don't. And that's ok. You don't necessarily have to have it all figured out right this minute. Exploration is part of the fun, in your artwork and in your life.

But it can be helpful to think about some things that give you joy, that get your crank going, that feed your soul. Coming up with some answers will help give you direction. We seldom make a concerted effort to really examine what is truly important to us.

I'm not going to go into great detail about this topic in this book, but keep an eye out for a future book all about determining what moves you, committing to following your dream, and creating goals to live the life you are passionate about.

I strongly recommend you take a few minutes to explore what you want, even if you think you know. I know this sounds like fluff, but you'd be surprised what you will learn about yourself when you sit and write down your thoughts. And you must *write* them down. Make them real and claim them. And remember, dream BIG and don't worry, because nothing is locked in stone.

Here's a couple of things to think about:
- If you didn't have to worry about money, what would you do with your art?

- Think big! Don't limit yourself. Don't write "I want to get my first inking job"; write "I want to have my own creator owned comic that I draw."

- Be specific. Don't write "I want to make art," write "I want to live in Seattle with a job doing concept art for Valve Studios."

- Don't just write down what you think is possible for you achieve with what you know now

- You don't have to know exactly how it's going to happen. Trust that you will learn what you need to know, and make the connections you need to make on your journey to your goals

- Brainstorm a list of all kinds of ways to make money with your art, even if you're not sure how they work.

No matter what you come up with, never give up on your Dream.

Don't listen to the nay-sayers. You will constantly hear all kinds of reasons why you shouldn't be an artist. People may be negative for so many reasons, all of which hold no value for you, like: they're cranky that day, they're jealous, they're bitter because they're not following their dream, they had a bad professional experience, they don't really understand the art industry, etc. Take their input for what it's worth and plan strategies to **move forward despite all obstacles**!

Even people who care about you will try to tell you that you can't make a living as an artist (like your parents, your friends, your family, etc.). They mean well, they really do. And they're afraid for you; they love you and genuinely just want you to succeed in life. Just say "thank you for caring enough to give me your opinion," and hold true to what's in your heart.

It may take a little while to build your client list and do art full time but, do or die, live your dream. Supplement your income with a part time job, sell products related to your art, give art lessons, teach, etc. Do whatever it takes to get there - and do it with passion! Do the best art you can and keep going after what you want. You can make it happen! Go for it!

Your Art Education: College

We're all the same! Believe me, I was exactly where you are at some point in my career, wherever you are. In fact, I'm still working hard to follow *my* dream, just like you. And so are all the pros out there. So you're not alone!

One of the best things you can do for yourself, is to keep learning, however you can. There are many paths to the same goal and only you know where you want to go.

You've taken a major step by getting this book! You want to learn more and that's a good thing.

Everyone is at a different stage in their career. You may be in high school just thinking about what you what to do for a living. Or looking at colleges wondering what you should major in. Maybe you've done some illustrations for friends or even publications – just enough to tell you that you want to do more! Maybe you've been working in the industry for a while and are looking for some tips to help you to land that big fish you've always wanted to work for.

The point is that we can all benefit from more information.

So let's talk about formal education – like going to college or art school or a "trade" school focused on art.

Before we do, let me just say that if you're a self starter and didn't go to school for art, don't worry. In the art field, it's all about your artwork and your professionalism. It's extremely rare that someone asks if you have a degree or not.

That being said, I strongly recommend that you go to school, or alternately, study with someone. Getting *direct* feedback about your work or looking over someone's shoulder as they do a painting demo are a couple of the best ways to learn.

I was so fortunate to go to a public high school with an excellent and highly developed art program. That was a pretty rare thing, even in my day. Nowadays, with the arts being marginalized in public schools, it's almost non-existent. I feel so lucky to have been able to delve into my love earlier than most.

I also went to college and got a degree in Illustration at Northern Illinois University. I wanted to go to the Art Institute of Chicago, a full-on art school, but my dad wanted me to get a "well rounded" education, and since he so graciously paid the tab, I went to a state school about an hour away from home. No regrets. I learned a lot. And the art program was wonderful.

Even though I just said that that often sought after piece of paper is not that critical for a career in art, **what you learn during the process of getting your degree can be invaluable**!

One of the most important things you need to get better as an artist is spend hours and hours and hours making art. There is NO substitute for spending time drawing and painting. Period. That's where you learn how to manipulate the tools of the trade, learn about paint and light and color and structure and all the rest. You also start to get a feel for what gets you excited about art; what kind of subject matter you like; what kind of artist you want to be. That's the good stuff!! So make art, always. If fact, take a break from this book right now and go draw.

Welcome back. Continuing on...

In college you have classes and assignments and deadlines. You have to work. And that's a good thing. Some structure. It also forces you to work when you're "not in the mood." You can't fool me – I've been there – I still struggle with it: you only paint when you feel like it. Well guess what? That won't cut it when you have a job due tomorrow and you have to finish it to get paid. In school, you will start to develop work ethics that will carry you through to the professional world. And the good thing is that there is a bit less pressure than a job (although it may not feel like it at the time), so you can learn as you go.

One of the great things about a learning environment is that you are working side by side with other artists. You see what they are working on and it inspires you in your work. You get ideas, you learn new techniques, you collaborate on projects. You talk art, you compare notes, you give each other feedback and encouragement. All great stuff. And lots more fun than sitting in your room by yourself trying to learn by looking at jpegs of art.

Choosing a School
Ok, so you're thinking about schools. That's great. Before you choose, it may be helpful if you have some idea of what kind of art career you're interested in. If you're not sure, that's ok. But, again, sometimes it is helpful to have an eye on where you're going to help you make a better choice as to which school to go to. For example, if you're interested in doing concept art for films, I would say look into Art Center in CA; if you're interested in drawing comics, consider Joe Kubert's School in NJ.

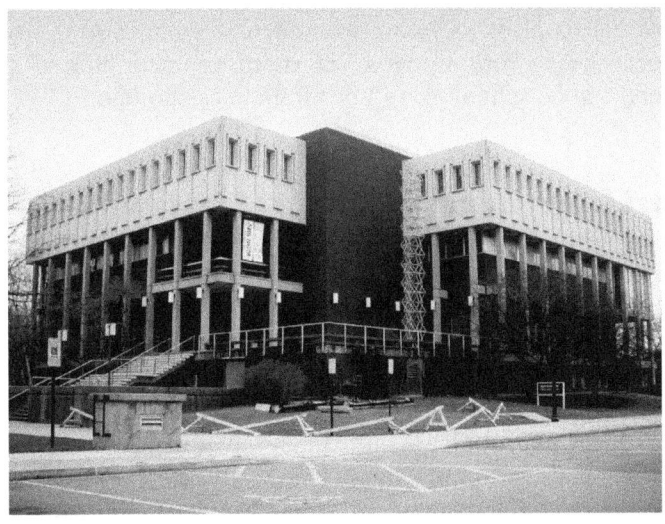

I spent many fun hours in the art building at NIU!
Photo © by Jost Situ aka C2.0

Art Programs and Instructors

Look for schools that have extensive programs in your area of interest and, most importantly, **check to see if they have professors who currently work in your chosen field of interest.**

When I started college, I wanted to draw comic books. When I was checking out colleges, I found out that a working professional comic book artist was teaching at Northern Illinois University (NIU), so I was able to study under him and learn a lot about the industry and how to tailor my portfolio to it. Turns out, he was also a fantasy gaming artist to boot. His name was Mark Nelson, and he's an amazing artist and person. (You can check out his work at www.GrazingDinosaurPress.com).

Mark gave me a lot of practical and artistic advice about the industry, opened doors for me at companies, and introduced me to a lot of people in the industry including working pros and art directors. He was very gracious that way, and I will always be eternally grateful.
That's what I'm trying to do for you with this book – help you get in with some sage advice.

A lot of pros are faculty members at schools and you can usually learn about instructors at a school's website. So it's up to you to do some research. There are tons of resources available to you. Start with your school councilor, college websites, and college admissions officers, etc. Call up colleges and ask about their instructors' backgrounds. Ask your friends on Facebook if they can recommend a college with a strong art department. Ask working pros via email or their blog if they can recommend a good school. Don't be afraid to ask around.

Fine Art Curriculum

Since you have to take a variety of courses to get your degree, you have a great opportunity to be exposed to other forms of art. Having a sculpture class can teach you a lot about drawing, and vice versa. You'll carry concepts and ideas from one discipline to another that will open your eyes to things you never considered, and it will make you a better artist.

No matter what your major, you'll likely have to take some "fine art" courses like painting and drawing. One word of caution: instructors in the Fine Art program at colleges will often steer you away from an "illustrative" approach to art. That could be good and bad.

It could be bad if you fight it. If you go into this situation knowing that fine art professors are focused on a different form of expressing ideas than illustrators are, and approach your fine art classes with an attitude of wonder and interest in learning new ideas – you'll get a *lot* out of it.

It could be disastrous if you let them discourage you. They are who they are and have their own ideas about what art should be, and you're you. You don't have to adopt their ideas – but you should try to learn from them, and apply them to your art when appropriate. Your instructors don't have all the answers that are right for you, but that shouldn't stop you from learning all you can from them.

At NIU, I had a fine art painting professor who hated illustration and narrative art. He thought it was sophomoric, maudlin, and an unsophisticated way of expressing one's ideas. At first I wasn't sure what to make of John F. McCarthy, but you know what? I ended up taking 4 semesters with him because he pushed me to find other ways of communicating through art, and I learned a lot. And actually I'm grateful to him for *not* letting me do illustration in his painting class. He and I still had different ideas about art, but he came to respect my position because he saw that I had a genuine passion for learning and I never gave up.

> **Definition: Narrative Art** is artwork that tells a story. It can be a single image or a series of images, like comic books. This is the opposite of something like abstract art where there is no story being told. A narrative artist often uses representational imagery and conventions of story to express the idea he wants to convey.

Besides fine art classes, try to take a digital photography class, Photoshop class, and also take as many classes you can that teach the business side of art. These will be extremely helpful as you move forward in your career.

Be open to all forms of art and see where the journey takes you – especially when you're in school. Who knows, you might even find that you don't want to be an illustrator and want to become an abstract expressionist.

Many Ways to Learn

Ok, I know college can be expensive, and it's not for everyone. That's ok. There are many ways you can become a better artist. Even if you did go to college, you should continue to expand your artistic toolbox with some of these resources. This list is by no means complete, but you might discover some things you never thought of.

Four Year College
> It's worth it!

Study Abroad
> Make art in a foreign country with private instructors or at a university. Many countries have generous financial help plans and artist in residence programs where you can get free tuition, room and board, or other amenities because they support the Arts. Imagine how amazing it would be to wake up every morning to paint plein air in the South of France! You may think living in a foreign country is expensive – you might be surprised to find that it can be cheaper than living here. You have to live somewhere, why not Italy!

Art Retreats to Exotic and Inspiring Locales
> Artist love to host retreats, either in their home town, at their studios, or at awesome and inspiring locales in other countries like Europe or Egypt. They are often all inclusive (food, lodging, and instruction – sometimes even art supplies) and much less expensive than you might think. You usually have to cover your airfare.

Artist Colony
> These are permanent locations that encourage artists to live there and to live and breathe art. They often offer seminars or weekend retreats as well. Artist colonies have a wonderful sense of community and connection; and are a nurturing environment with good people who have a love of all things creative and spiritual. How inspiring would it be to paint the incredible colors in the landscapes of New Mexico?

Ongoing Education
> Working for a living? Take night classes, also called "ongoing adult education," at a local community college or university.

Art School
> There are many excellent art schools where all you study is art. None of those pesky gen-ed classes like math and science.

Art "Trade" School

These schools often focus on a certain area of commercial art like 3D animation or graphic design and offer convenient class times in the evenings and weekends. They're a good way to focus on a particular industry you'd like to explore.

Private Art Lessons

Studying with a professional artist or private teacher is a fantastic way to grow as an artist. Nothing beats the kind of one on one feedback you'll get on your work at every step in the process. Your teacher can see some of the good, and bad, things you are doing during the early stages of a painting and steer you straight. It's also an opportunity to have someone to help you focus on what *you* want to do, without the constraints of grades or university requirements. Look around, your favorite fantasy artist might even be offering lessons.

Apprentice / Intern With a Pro Artist

Maybe a fabulous fantasy artist lives in your town and is looking for an assistant. Artist often hire assistants to help with some of their day to day needs. This can run the gambit from helping them with their house chores, to running errands, to handling business paperwork, to stretching canvases, to helping them ink backgrounds on their graphic novel, you name it.

The whole idea is that the artist is looking to unencumber themselves with some of the requirements of life, so they have more time to create.

These can be unpaid internships, paid positions, or barter arrangements where the master will give you painting lessons in exchange for your good work. This kind of arrangement can be invaluable because you get to observe a master doing what he does best, you get hands on lessons and critiques of your work, you see how one working artist lives and what is needed to succeed, you shoot the shit about art, you get to meet others in a network "above" your current station, etc. It can be really cool and a lot of fun.

Life Drawing Night With Local Artists

Artist or organizations in your area love to host drawing nights, often with a live model. A great place to learn, network with other artists and draw from life for a nominal fee.

BaxaArt Academy offers one on one **Portfolio Reviews and Art Critiques**. Let Tom Baxa bring all his years of experience to bear to help you streamline your portfolio for maximum effectiveness or offer you solutions to those hurdles you just can't seem to beat in your work. Constructive criticism from a professional can be extremely useful. Tom does crits online or in person. More details at the BaxaArt Academy Critique and Portfolio Review Page: www.baxaart.com/BAA/crits.htm

Art Clubs

Every town has some kind of group or club you can join. They are often comprised of great folks who do art for a hobby, or are growing their art business. There are photography clubs, painting clubs, etc. They often have a very social element that can be uplifting and fun. Some may be very serious and comprised mostly of industry professionals. They're a great place to learn and get feedback on your work. They also give you a deadline to paint – you've got to have a new painting done by each month's meeting.

Art Stores and Art Boutiques

Your local art store, large or small, may host classes or seminars. Privately owned shops or boutiques can be especially surprising. There is one in Santa Monica, California, owned by an art director for major films. She has had some big names come in and give seminars, like Patrick Tatopoulos, the famed special effects creator and director of the *Underworld* films.

Seminars

There's a wide range of seminars being offered everyday covering all kinds of topics that could help you with your art or business like: self-promotion, legal matters, copyright law, taxes for artists, etc., and of course, seminars about making art. These might be offered by your local township or art center, museums, galleries, organizations, and even big companies that you might aspire to work for like Pixar or Disney. The seminars might be a couple hours or a whole weekend.

Online Courses or Webinars

Many institutions, colleges, and artists offer art instruction classes or webinars online. You can take college classes online, some even have live classrooms where a professor gives a lesson in real time over the internet where you can interact with him and ask questions.

There are tons of webinars online as well. Some short, some long. Some pre-recorded, some live. Faster computers, streaming and greater bandwidth is making it easier for artists to host their own webinars and training courses online as well. Besides the more grand undertakings, a lot of artists have step by step tutorials, either in text and pictures or video, on their websites.

Instructional Dvds and Digital Downloads

There's a wide range of instructional dvds (and digital downloads) available online covering all kinds of art topics. The cool thing is that there are many fantasy art dvds; something that's hard to find in the large chain stores or even art stores.

I have created an instructional dvd with Gnomon Workshop, the leader in instructional videos, called ***Dynamic Fantasy Painting With Tom Baxa.*** In it you can watch me paint as I discuss all the things I'm thinking about as I plan and execute a painting including: composition, story, character design, creating drama, dynamic poses, lighting, color, form building and more! Check it out at: www.baxaart.com/BAA/videos_index.htm

BaxaArt Academy offers instructional videos covering a range of topics from simple tricks and tips, to full blown painting videos, like *Dynamic Fantasy Painting With Tom Baxa*. BaxaArt Academy will be releasing more videos soon. BaxaArt Academy Videos Page: www.baxaart.com/BAA/videos_index.htm.

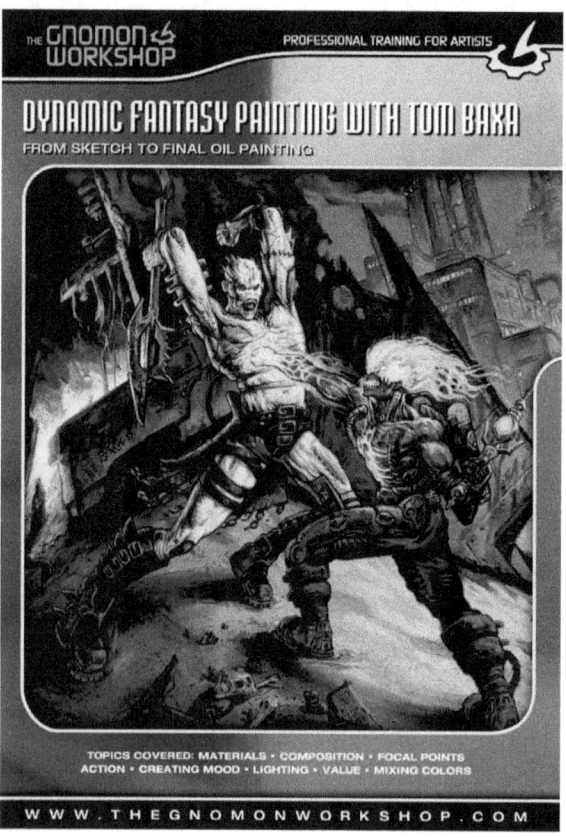

Gnomon Dvd, *Dynamic Fantasy Painting with Tom Baxa*

Books

When I was learning my craft there were very few art instruction books related to our field. Now, with the growing popularity of video games and digital art, there are a lot more, which is awesome! More and more books are being published about the concept design of films and video games like:

Avengers: The Art of Marvel's The Avengers
Elysium: The Art of Daarken
Art of Darksiders II
Art of Blizzard Entertainment

These types of books contain top notch art for your delight, show various stages of the design process, discuss techniques, working with directors, and more. They contain very valuable stuff to get you inspired and going on your own projects.

A lot of artists are publishing art books nowadays. Many of them have how-to sections that talk about their approach to painting, techniques, materials, etc.

There have always been how to books from the "fine art" disciplines as well that are quite excellent, ageless, and apply to whatever subject matter you are painting. Poke around the art section of Barnes and Nobel and your local art store to see what's out there. You'd be surprised how much you can learn from an unassuming soft-cover book about traditional portrait painting.

There are also some of the great classic anatomy, drawing, and art books from some of our century's master illustrators like: Andrew Loomis and Burne Hogarth.

There a ton of very *specialized* books covering all aspects of art like perspective drawing, color theory, wet into wet painting, pastel drawing, etc.

There are also excellent magazines on the subject of art. *Step By Step* magazine is quite good. *Imagine FX magazine*, which focuses on fantasy, horror, film and video game art, also has instructional articles and artist spotlights for you to soak up.

Besides art books, you could also benefit greatly from books about the business side of being an artist. If you choose to freelance, you will have to learn some aspects of running a small service business.

You can certainly take on a partner to handle that stuff, but it doesn't hurt to get up on some things like contract language, marketing yourself, copyright law, taxes, etc.

Jpegs

Just as with books, you can learn a lot from looking at other artists' finished works in digital form. There's no limit to the amount of art you can find online. But don't get sucked into hours of surfing for jpegs. Get sucked into hours at the drawing board! There is no need to have gigs of files if there is so much you can't even look at it all. Make sure you don't use surfing for reference or art samples as an excuse for not painting. Here are a couple of awesome portfolio sites that have very inspiring artists:

www.CGHub.com
www.DeviantArt.com
www.ConceptArt.org

Scrap

This is more often done digitally these days, but tearing photos, art images, reference, or other inspiration out of magazines (scrap) can also be inspiring. And the cool thing is that you can pin them up on the wall all around your workspace for mega inspiration all the time. Magazines hire top gun photographers who come up with stunning images of the amazing things in our universe. Pull from that. I especially like fashion magazines as inspiration for costume design. Buy magazines, ask your friends for their discards, or look for stacks of them at garage sales or flea markets.

Copy a Painting by the Masters or Pros as a Learning Experience

A powerful learning tool is to try to mimic a painting by one of the Masters, old or contemporary, to figure out how they achieve certain effects, color combinations, compositional tools, etc. Looking at a work is one thing, but when you actually try to paint the same way, things can get tough in a hurry. It's a great learning experience. You can copy a whole painting or just sections that intrigue you.

Of course, I'm not saying you should work in another artist's style. We've seen our share of mimics out there. It's one thing to admire Frazetta and pick up techniques from him; it's another thing to pass yourself off as an artist by painting just like him and trying to build your rep on the backs of others. Just don't do it.

Quick Note about Copyrights

[Disclaimer: I am not a copyright expert and do not claim to know the laws verbatim. The advice herein is only to be used as a guideline. I suggest you do your own research at www.copyright.gov and/or consult a copyright attorney.]

Before we continue, I want to give you a little heads up on copyrights. Generally speaking, if someone creates an image, they own it, period, until they sell or grant ownership rights to another. This includes artwork, photographs, sculpture, fabric designs, logos, website designs, graphic design, etc. So everything you see out there is owned by someone and you don't have the right to use lock stock and barrel it in your work. But you can use it as inspiration, or as reference, etc.

You can copy an image like a photo directly if you ONLY show your work of art as part of your portfolio, but never to profit from it. For example, you can do a *Predator* painting and put it in your portfolio to get work, but if you make prints of the painting and sell them, you're infringing on another's rights and could get in big trouble. But ultimately, it's best to be original. An art director is not going to get too excited by a portfolio full of copied photographs of someone else's characters.

Paint Over Photos or Master Works as a Learning Experience

Glue a photo or printout down to a board, or scan it into your favorite painting program and paint directly over it (hence the name: "paint over"). Remember, photos are copyrighted as well, so just do this as an exercise to get better at your craft.

Instead of spending time trying to get the proportions right and drawing out the photo, you can just "trace" over it as an exercise so you can focus on other aspects of image making. For instance, you can try painting over the photo in five different color palettes; you can break down the light and dark forms into flat shapes as an exercise in pattern making; you can practice emphasizing certain compositional elements with color, etc.

One cool thing is to take a photo of a statue or unpainted model kit and paint over the photo, bringing the character to life.

Draw and Paint Your Butt Off and Love Every Minute of It!
You learn the most by doing. So go paint!

Learning the Fundamentals

Why all this talk about school and seminars and paint-overs? Well, to get work as an illustrator, you do have to have *some* level of skill when it comes to painting representationally.

Now, I would never tell you what kind of artist to be. That is up to you. If you want to burn sticks and draw spirals on rocks in the moonlight naked – go for it! It might be hard to get a job as a fantasy illustrator though. But seriously, if you like working with strong graphic shapes in bright colors, you might also find it hard to get work.

There is a place out there for all forms of artistic expression. I mean it. If you love working a certain way – do it! – and find a way to get it out there. This book is about helping you get paid as a working fantasy illustrator. That comes with a certain set of expectations and limitations.

Painting Representationally

Your avant garde style, that is outside the norm of what's currently being done in the industry, *may* catch an AD's eye and you *may* get hired, but it's going to be a very tough road, and the amount of jobs available are going to be limited.

Your best chance of getting steady work is to work in a style that fits what is the norm in the industry that you are interested in pursuing. For fantasy illustration, that means painting in a realistic or representational manner.

Painting **representationally** means to render with enough detail so that objects are portrayed realistically, in a way that closely resembles elements in the real world. So when you paint a suit of armor, it looks like a suit of armor might in real life instead of being stylized in a wacky fashion.

The terms **representational**, **naturalism**, and **realism** are interchangeable, and all allude to a realistic style. Of course there is a lot of leeway within the confines of realism, leaving you room to play and express yourself artistically, both in style and content.

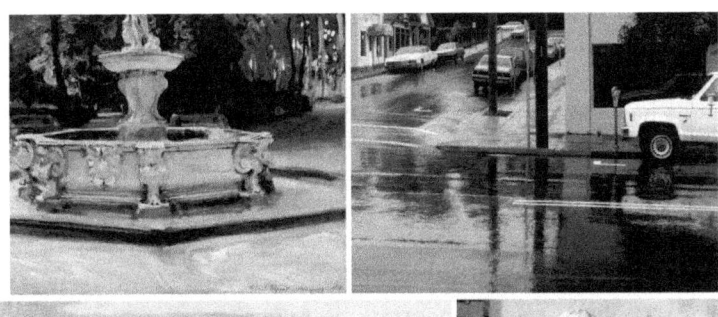
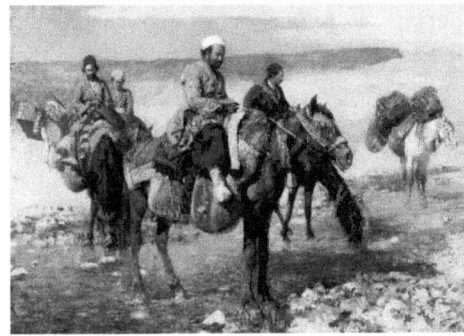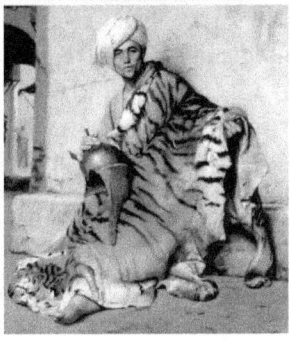

Some varied examples of realism, some have a more loose approach, some have a tighter rendering style. From top left to bottom right:
Marble Fountain At Aranjuez Spain by John Singer Sargent
Robert Bechtle (photo realism movement)
Horses At The Ford-Persia (detail) by Edwin Lord Weeks
30 Pelt Merchant of Cairo (detail) by Jean Leon Gerome

Photorealism is a term generally used to describe a painting that is rendered with such detail that it is virtually indistinguishable from a photograph. The original Photorealism Movement in the late 1960's was not really about trying to paint with technical prowess as you might think. The philosophy behind the movement was to remove the artist's decision making from the artistic process. Artist would often randomly choose a photo that they had no connection with, and copy it verbatim. It was an important idea in the art world at the time.

Illustrating today in a photo realistic style, for me, lacks artistry. (See the *Is Technique a Dirty Word?* section below). And remember, you're working a job, so those extra hours you take rendering the crap out of something is money lost and time away from your family. You also have to keep in mind that detail like that is gorgeous to look at in person when you're taking in a well lit painting in a gallery, but you're creating illos for print or the web. Detail tends to get lost when a work is photographed, reduced and printed, so all that extra detail is wasted because no one will ever see it.

You don't have to be perfectly anatomically correct and research every muscle and vein to make something feel realistic. Some artists love that and work tirelessly to make something hyper-realistic. I know an artist who's into hardware, and it really bugs him when an artist fakes a gun, so when he draws guns, he makes sure they look like they could actually fire a bullet and are correct for the time period being portrayed. I know another artist that loves rendering in hyper detail, so leather looks textured and cracked, and fabric has fibers, and skin has pores.

I, personally, don't go to that extent. What I do is build in enough believability, detail, and accuracy into my paintings as to create a level of naturalism that allows for the **suspension of disbelief**.

Suspension of Disbelief

Why do you have to paint representationally? Well, like it or not, that's what's primarily being used in the world of fantasy illustration currently; so if you want to get work, it's best you focus your energies in that direction. You can certainly have your own flair, style and artistic approach and still paint naturalistically.

The reason this is the norm is that a realistically rendered painting helps with the suspension of disbelief. You may have heard this term applied to film, or other art forms. Well it definitely applies to illustration.

The term **"suspension of disbelief"** is the idea that when a viewer takes in a work of fiction (in this case, a painting), the work is infused with enough basis in reality, that the tendency to disbelieve the made up elements is set aside by the viewer so that he can immerse himself in the fictional world.

In other words, when you paint in a realistic style, and you have naturalistically rendered people in an unreal environment like an alien space ship, the *viewer is more apt to also believe the unreal elements* and take them as real for the sake of the story, because the people, something he knows be real, are portrayed in a believable way.

This is one argument for painting in a realistic fashion: it helps suspend disbelief. It's another argument for doing your homework and getting good reference. If you're going to paint a dragon, you'd better figure out how scales pattern across the skin, how bat wings and their underlying skeletal structure works, what muscle groups look like on a quadruped, etc. Making the dragon look like his body could actually move and exist in the real world by giving it elements of creatures that we already understand, ones that currently roam this earth, help make them feel more believable and pull the viewer into the story.

How many times have you looked at a painting and said, "That creature's arm couldn't bend that way?" If you have, that means the artist failed to make a fantastical creature seem believable. He did not nurture the suspension of disbelief.

As an illustrator, your job is to tell a story with all the tools at your disposal; the main one being, painting representationally. For you to get good at rendering in a naturalistic way, you need to get good at manipulating your art tools. It's time to learn good technique.

Technique

As creative people, we have tons of cool ideas floating around in our heads that we want to put down on canvas. But if you don't develop the skills or techniques to accurately represent what you're seeing in your mind, it doesn't do you much good, does it? Your painting isn't going to come out the way that you envisioned it, and you may not be able to meet the objectives your client has set out for you.

Techniques are the specialized artistic methods or procedures you apply to achieve certain desired results. For example: *Scumbling* is a technique where you put a very small amount of paint on a dry brush and lightly drag it across the painting surface to produce a broken, gritty stroke. *Stippling* is tapping downward with the tip of your brush bristles to create different type of broken, uncontrolled mark with an aggressive feel.

Techniques aren't about ideas or story or characters. They are the tools used to create images. Alone, these techniques are just little tricks or approaches to applying paint, but when combined with your creativity, they are the components that conjure up the magic of art!

Techniques can certainly be learned on your own. The minute you pick up a brush you are applying all kinds of techniques that you may not know the name of, but you're doing them. And who cares, really, if you know their names, it's more about learning tools that can better aid you in expressing your ideas.

Scumbling, stippling, and spatter techniques.

It is to your benefit to learn a wide variety of techniques at the beginning, and throughout, your artistic life. Why reinvent the wheel? Trying to figure out techniques on your own is kinda like starting a home improvement project and saying "I want to build this chest, now if I only had something that could pound some kind of sharp thing through the wood to hold it together." Wouldn't it be silly not to learn what a hammer and nails are, and how to use them effectively to achieve your result of building a chest? Well, it's the same thing with art – it's best to learn some of the time honored tools of the trade and how to apply them.

Is Technique a Dirty Word?

No. However, technique is often considered a dirty word, especially in fine art circles, because it implies that a work of art that focuses on technical prowess is shallow or devoid of content. If that is all that an artist offers in his work, we can admire the skill and be amazed at his ability, but that's where our experience of his work usually ends. There's not much else to enjoy and no deeper meaning to ponder.

That leaves me a little flat. Just like when you see a big action movie and drool over the special effects, but leave the theater not giving the film another thought because there was no story or thematic content.

Don't get me wrong, I love admiring artwork for all kinds of reasons, including purely for the technique. There are some amazing things being done. I mostly get excited about techniques I see because I want to learn from them, try them in my own work, and add them to my arsenal of art weaponry.

The problem with art that is purely technical in nature, like a photo realistically rendered painting of a knight on a horse, is that copying photos takes NO imagination. Where's the idea? Where's the inventiveness? Where's the artist's personal touch, his voice? What is he trying to communicate?

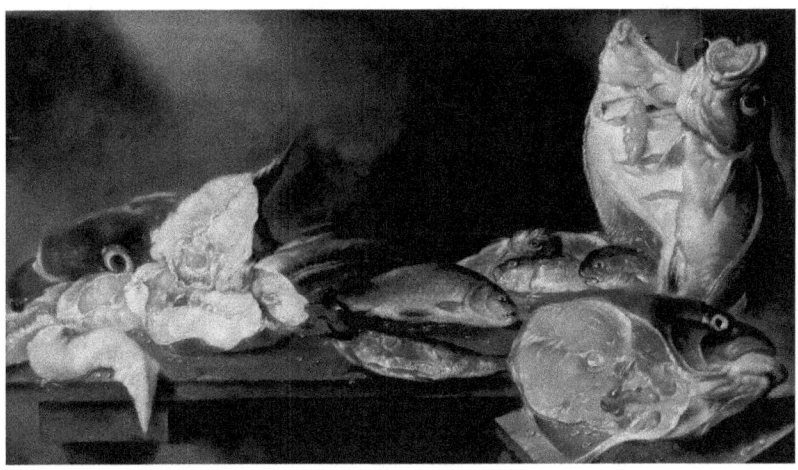

Still Life With Fish by Alexander Adriaenssen. Even thought this is a static image of a still life, it illustrates my point that a purely technically proficient painting can be devoid of life.

For the most part, anyone can render a photo competently with enough practice, so it lacks artistic vision and originality. Now there's no doubt that there are some guys are just virtuosos and no one can touch them, and that's astounding, but it's mostly a skill, devoid of emotional content or a personal statement. Again, kinda boring.

But the skill of being able to paint photo realistically can be a valuable commodity in some commercial art applications. If you can paint that way, and love it, keep it up and find work in the areas that appreciate that style, like advertising, movie posters, portraiture, medical illustration, etc.

The key is to *combine* strong technique with other artistic elements and thought provoking content in your work to push it over the top with a richness and power seldom seen in illustration.

Let me give you some idea of what I mean. In the painting I did for the Gnomon dvd **Dynamic Fantasy Painting With Tom Baxa** entitled *Toxic War* (see below), there are many planned elements that enriched the work beyond simple technique.

The first thing to do is create evocative characters that are original, have cool design elements to their bodies, clothing, and weapons, and that convey emotion in their expressions and poses.

Secondly, you want to consider compositional elements that can add to the impact of your design. I tilted the axis to create an unstable feeling in the viewer. I put the camera low facing upward and used a slight three point perspective to create movement. The triangular metal shard behind the figures enhances the upward thrust of the zombie's arms and is used to frame them and focus your attention on them.

There are story elements added in the background as support material like a raging fire indicating disaster and mayhem; a gritty industrial landscape with a factory that spews caustic smoke into the air, etc. There's lighting, color use, pose, and more…AND there's good technique.

As you can see, a lot goes into a painting in order to raise it to a level beyond just strong technique. Don't freak out – a lot of these things come very naturally to you when you sit down to create a painting.

I discuss these and other elements of creating a dramatic painting in the dvd.

I want you to learn good technique so you have the tools you need to create your masterpieces, but keep in mind that there is more to be explored in a painting, especially if you want to stand out from your competition.

In *Book 2: Breaking In and Staying In* I go into great detail about other aspects of your artwork that will help you build an exceptional portfolio, including how to tailor your work to grab the attention of art directors and art buyers.

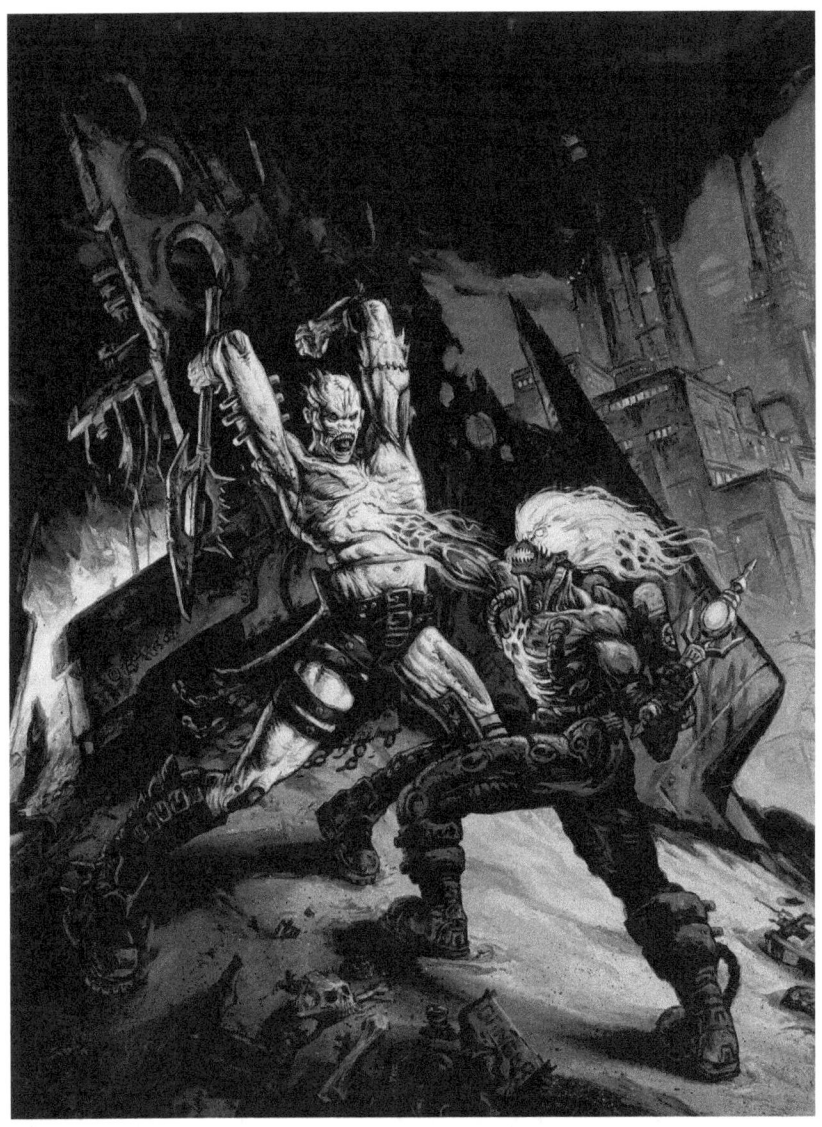

Toxic War © Thomas M. Baxa 2007

Speed

Techniques, tricks and tips from other artists can really improve your growth as an image maker. Not only that, they will help you get faster. But, speed is not everything. I often hear artists brag that they can do a painting in X amount of time. That doesn't mean much to me unless the work is strong.

But, let's face it, when you get paid a flat rate for doing a job, the faster you can get it done, the more money you make. And the more jobs you can do per week, the higher your income.

Speed can also be a valuable asset in certain art jobs, like concept design. Being able to work quickly and generate a lot of ideas in a short amount of time is a desirable skill in the eyes of your prospective employers. If you can
texture map a model in 6 hours, you're going to be more in demand than the guy who takes 2 days. But, again, only if your final product is strong.

But don't worry about working fast right now. Focus on learning strong technique along with strong storytelling and creativity. You'll start to get faster, the more you work and the more you trust in the artistic process.

Speed Paintings

I'm sure you've seen a lot of what's being called "speed paintings" on YouTube or artists' sites. Don't be fooled, speed paintings are not about being able to do finished illustrations in a short amount of time. Speed paintings are really just sketches.

The idea behind speed painting is to push yourself to work quickly and for a short amount of time to help you stay loose and focus on what's absolutely essential to getting your idea across. It's an *exercise* to help prevent you from noodling on too much detail and get you to view the image as a whole. It's also a way to practice one small aspect of art in a short drawing or painting session, instead of worrying about the problems associated with larger works and more complex compositions.

Some speed painting videos are really just time-lapse paintings. The painting may have taken 15 hours, but the video is sped up with software to create a short video and then labeled a speed painting because you can watch it materialize very quickly. Speed painting videos are great fun to watch, but not some kind of clock to aspire to for doing your work.

There are Rules, Sort Of

I know, I know, you're an artiste – you won't be restricted -- you won't compromise your art. Well, I'm afraid life is a series of compromises. As I said earlier, if you want a successful career as a working fantasy illustrator, you may have to make some adjustments in your artistic approach and work within the parameters of what is considered the norm for your chosen field.

So again, having a certain level of technical knowledge is important.

I'm sure you've heard the phrase, "It is important to know the rules before you can break them," right? What the heck does that mean? Well, the idea is that having a strong foundation of tools and techniques is critical.

If you want to be experimental and do some really strange stuff, it's best to understand the elements of art (the rules) before you try to do something that goes contrary to them. This way you know what you're doing and why.

It's about **being *conscious* about your choices** in your art. You may have an instinct for dynamic compositions, and when you do a layout, it works most of the time. But that one time that it's not working, because you haven't learned the fundamentals, you'll have no idea what's wrong or how to fix it. And your deadline is looming.

With a strong understanding of the rules, or proven approaches that yield certain results, you will be able to analyze your own work and fix what's not working. And that's a great skill to have when you're trying to create an awesome illustration and make your client happy.

You'll also be better equipped to create the images in your head that you're excited about. You'll spend more time having fun painting your ideas, rather than trying to figure out how the heck to render metal.

Translation

Our world is three dimensional. Paintings are not. They're flat, and the best they can do is allude to the feeling of depth. It's your job as an artist to observe the real world, translate what you see, filtered through you own personal artistic vision, and apply various learned techniques to convey the illusion of 3D form on a two dimensional surface.

The word **translate** is the key. You are interpreting what you see, and coming up with inventive ways to convey those things in paint.

All art is a translation. Think about how a form rounds away from you. You can't actually do that in a painting because the canvas is flat, it's two dimensional. But you can *imply* the roundness, *imply* three dimensions. This is where some of the techniques you've learned can be applied to give your images the illusion of depth, mass, and form.

Obviously, it's very hard to discuss these things in words. That's why you need to watch art being made, learn some techniques, and try it yourself. Watching tutorials at BaxaArtAcademy.com can help.

Photos are another falsehood. They're a 2D representation of the real world, just like a painting. But our brains have become so accustomed to seeing photos and accepting them as valid and "true" representations of the real world. That's why a painting looks more real if it's painted like a photograph; using the inherent flaws produced when the 3D world is translated to a 2D photo, like lens flares, hard shadows from a flash, and depth of field focus issues. This can be used to your advantage to represent certain special effects, and attempt to heighten the reality factor in your work.

My point is that as an artist you are merely trying to represent life, not *replicate* it. It's your job to convey a sense of life in an inanimate painting, and come up with inventive ways to give the illusion of scale, motion, depth, mass, form and light.

Seeing: Drawing from Life

A very important part of your education as an artist is to develop your ability to *see*. I know you have the ability of sight. What you need to develop is the way you look at the world around you; sharpen your powers of observation and covert what you see into art on the page.

The key to drawing representationally is being able to observe the characteristics of objects in the real world, the things that are unique to them, so that you can *represent* them on the page. How does a rubber ball look compared to a metal ball? What is it about them that makes your brain instantly identify and distinguish between them? And how can you convey those differences in paint?

You need to be able to *see* these differences in order to *paint* them. That's what being a representational artist is all about.

When working on a video game property, artists are given renders of low polygon in-game computer models as reference. This is often problematic because it's difficult to tell what materials objects are made of because they are painted in a similar manner in a texture map. Is the armor made of metal or bone or wood or leather or cloth? Something gets lost in the translation from the way a texture map artist sees the item in the real world and how he chooses to interpret it in a 2D skin.

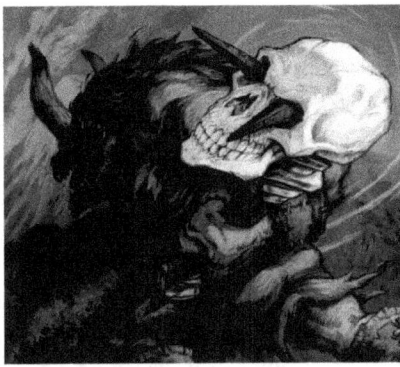
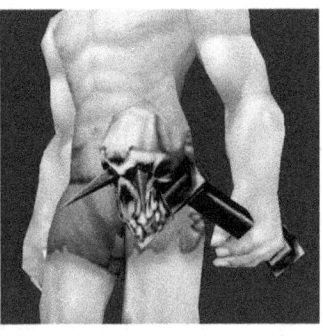

In the case of this Warcraft tcg card of the *Hungering Bone Cudgel* (Images used by permission © 2013 Blizzard Entertainment Inc.) I wasn't sure if the skull in the supplied reference (right) was supposed to be metal or bone until I emailed the AD for the answer

An excellent way to develop your "eye," your powers of observation, is to **draw from life**. That means sit down with an actual object, still life, landscape or live model and draw as you observe them in three dimensions.

Drawing from life has so many advantages. More than anything, drawing from life helps you to vastly improve your ability to translate what we as people are used to seeing with our eyes into a convincing and interesting interpretation in your artistic medium of choice. In other words, foster the suspension of disbelief.

Let's use life drawing as an example. One huge advantage of drawing from a live model, as opposed to drawing from a photograph, is that you can walk around the model and take in all kinds of information that helps you better represent life when you finally stop, choose a singular vantage point, and create a 2D image.

Knowing what something looks like from the side or behind helps you better understand the form as a whole and make better informed decisions when it comes to how you want to present that object.

Part of your job as an artist is to choose characteristics that are quintessential or most representative of the thing you are painting. Drawing from life can help you identify those quintessential qualities.

With this in mind, let's say you are painting a lawful good wizard with a dog familiar. From the front, a rat terrier and a doxen have similar builds and faces, but if you were drawing from life and were able to gather information about your subject in three dimensions, you would see that doxens have an elongated body. Armed with that information, you would choose to emphasize this unique quality by doing a three-quarters angle and exaggerating the length just a bit.

Drawing from Life Gives You Insight Into:	
• Three dimensional view • Depth, mass and form • How things work / mechanics • Movement • Surface detail / identification • Differentiate materials • Quintessential markers • Structure	• Block out in geometric shapes • Wire frame skeleton • Reducing what you see to the essentials • Nuances lost in photos or video • Lighting, bouncing light and color • Color nuances • Perspective

Working from a photo can be tricky because, even though you can copy the shapes you see in the photo, if you don't understand the object in 3D, you may make mistakes because you can't reconcile what those shapes represent. A viewer who *does* understand that object is going to see that you fell short.

Another critical advantage to drawing from life is that it helps you understand how things work, their underlying mechanics, and how they move through space. This can be extremely helpful when painting action scenes. But even for static poses, especially of people, having an understanding of the way the body moves, how the muscles work and connect to the skeletal frame, and how the skeleton moves can vastly improve the way you represent the figure. Obviously, an anatomy class would serve you well, but observing body mechanics on the surface in a life drawing setting can catapult your degree of realism to a new level as well.

Drawing from life also helps you appreciate the *nuances* of form and materials in a heightened way, to help you get a genuine sense of their nature, which in turn helps you represent them better in paint.

What happens for you as an artist when you observe things and especially when you draw them, is that you begin to fill your brain with data about how things look and how you can represent them artistically. You create a reference file in your neural net that you can pull from at anytime in the future.

Ideas for Drawing from Life:
• Take a trip to the zoo and draw animals
• Go to the dog park, horse stables, or a farm to draw animals
• Sit in the park and draw people in everyday situations
• Sketch interactions of people in groups
• Draw beautiful architecture
• Draw nature, grand or minute

Plein Air Painting
Plein air is a French term meaning "in the open air". Plein air painting means going outside with an easel and some paint, and painting what you see in natural light. The term is most often applied to landscape or scenic painting, but you can bring models or still lifes and paint anything you like. This is a wonderful way to enjoy the out-of-doors and paint from life. Make a day of it with some artist friends and a picnic basket.

My friend and artist and art director extrodinaire, Rohb Ruppel, being the ingenious guy that he is, actually takes his laptop on location and does plein air painting digitally! He concocted a foam core shadowbox around the laptop to shield the screen from the sun so he can see it better and it works like a charm.

Drawing from video can be a good second choice, especially over photos, because you can see the subject from different angles, get a sense of spatial relationships, and how it moves. But there are a lot of limitations to video as well, so choose to draw from life whenever possible.

Stretch Your Horizons

As illustrators we think mostly in terms of subject matter and images to tell a story and represent life. But remember my fine art professor, John F. McCarthy who wouldn't let me do narrative art in his classes? Well guess what, he taught me some fundamentals about Art, with a capital "A", that aren't usually talked about in illustration class.

There are many devices you can employ, alternative ways of expressing ideas, with the medium instead of the subject matter. I'll save a lengthy discussion for a video demo, but for now here are a couple of things to think about:

Color

Color choices alone can create a lot of content and emotion and lend a hand in conveying the "reality" of a moment in your work. For example: by using a red field of color next to a character you can allude to blood, danger, emergency, internal organs, fire, etc. Paining your entire painting in a limited palette can also work wonders. Painting a lizard in predominantly cool blue colors can allude to night, sadness, depression, water, etc.

Mark Making

Let the way you make a mark or stroke with your brush as you apply paint offer some content. Using aggressive gouge-like strokes alludes to anger, aggression, deconstruction, and shattering. Using smooth, buttery strokes alludes to calm, softness, invitation, and intimacy.

Compositional Elements

Using a tilted axis or exaggerated perspective can make a scene feel unbalanced, unsettling, dangerous, abnormal, other-worldly.

Miles of Canvas Before You Sleep

You can see how many elements come together to make a good illustration beyond just technique or strong rendering skills. When the person viewing your work has an experience or emotional reaction to it, that reaction can heighten the reality factor and make a 2D image more engaging, evocative, and thought provoking. And that's good illustration!

It takes time to develop these skills and learn how to get them working together. Don't freak out, you don't have to be a genius right out of the gate. No one is. And you can't possibly learn and apply all this stuff overnight. Ease into; focus on different aspects with each new piece you do and it'll come.

Start with the fundamentals and learn good technique. Draw from life as much as you can. Keep growing by staying open to new ways of expression and craving knowledge throughout your entire artistic life.
Painting is fun, not a chore. It's one of the things you love most, so do it whenever you can! Draw, paint, experiment, learn and do it all over again tomorrow!

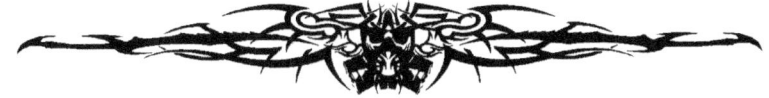

SECTION 2: Portfolio Reviews

Critiques – Don't Be Scared

As I'm sure you know, a **critique** (also called a portfolio review) is when you show your artwork to someone in order to get some feedback on it. The critiquer is usually someone that has more experience than you, like a pro artist, an art director, or editor; but you can also ask friends and non-artists to look at your work to get a general reaction or impression.

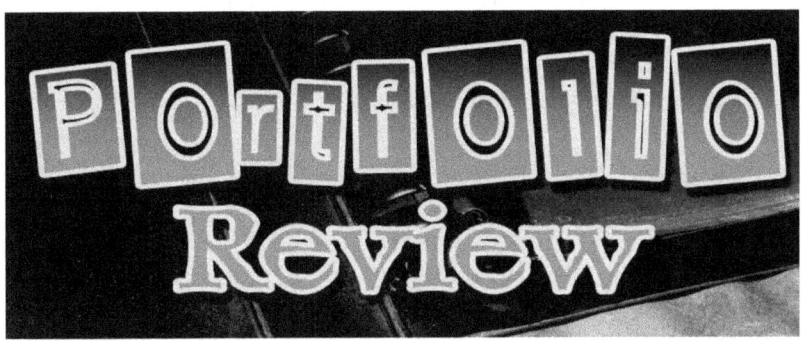

The kind of feedback you receive can vary from a review of your artistic ability and technique, to the success of your storytelling, to the immediate impact your work has, to how it fits into the marketplace, and more. It depends on who you are soliciting to give you feedback. But generally, what you hear in a critique can be anything that can help you improve so that you can achieve your goals.

> **Definition: Portfolio Review** is a term commonly used for critiques by companies that have artists or art directors reviewing portfolios at conventions, job fairs or trade shows looking for prospective hires.

We've all heard the horror stories about teachers ripping someone's art apart in a critique and sending them out of the room crying. Sadly, it does happen. And it happens for all kinds of reasons. Guess what? Many of them don't have anything to do with you.

Despite the occasional brow beating, critiques are nothing to be afraid of. The truth is that most critiques you receive with be given with a genuine interest in helping you become a better artist. Most people you show your work to have been exactly where you are: feeling a bit vulnerable and not sure what to expect. For that reason, they will be kind and generous with their time and offer you some valuable pearls of wisdom.

Adopt an Attitude of Learning and Gratitude

Critiques are a marvelous tool that you should seek out whenever you can, because they offer you an opportunity to get some outside feedback on your work and learn from someone else's wisdom and experience.

You want to be a better artist, don't you? Well there is no better way than to get direct feedback on your work. It's one-on-one hardcore training to help you grow. Want it! Crave it! Seek it out!

Unfortunately, not everyone you show your work to is going to have the tact, consideration, or skills to give you constructive criticism in a calm and professional manner. But that's ok. You can handle it if you keep in mind the things that I'm about to tell you.

> **Definition: Constructive Criticism** is a form of feedback that is intended to help you improve. Criticism implies that the feedback is negative, and a critique does often focus on what's not working with a piece of art, but because the criticism is offered as well meaning information given with your best interests in mind, it's ultimately a positive thing. The word "constructive" also implies that the comments are made with some level of expertise particular to your chosen craft, not just off the cuff observations.

You have to look at critiques as an opportunity for you to grow as an artist. In a major way! Critiques will show you what is working and what is not working in your artwork, and both are valuable. Keep in mind that a good critiquer will point out both, but on the whole it is usually assumed that you are asking for help with what is not working well, and that is mostly what you will hear. And that's ok.

Your leading thought every single time you unzip your portfolio to show someone should be "What can I learn from this?"

Period. No matter what is said to you, no matter how good or bad the delivery is, or how much it might hurt to hear.

It can be a bit nerve-racking the first time you get a critique, so try starting small – do a practice critique with a good friend. They care about you, and only have your best interests in mind, so ask them to be gentle, and ask them for their opinion of your work. Then ask more folks to get you used to hearing positive and negative comments about your art. It's good for you, believe me. Then ramp it up a notch and seek out critiques from teachers, other artists, and pros. By the time you're showing your portfolio to an art director, you'll have much more confidence and be used to taking criticism.

It's helpful if you approach people who are open and willing to help you with some constructive feedback. Teachers are one of the best resources. Critiques are a major part of their everyday teaching life and they are usually very good at recognizing strengths and weaknesses in your work and are skilled at delivering the news in a constructive way.

The key is to stay cool, objective, and don't take it personally. It's not a personal attack on your self-worth. I know your art is important to you, and you love each of your babies, but please remember that although art is a part of your being, it is not the only thing that defines you. And when you're educating yourself, you are not saying, "Do you think I'm a good person, based on whether or not my art is good?" you're saying, "I'm trying to get better as an artist and I value your opinion. Thanks for helping me grow."

Gratitude
Be grateful that the person you are showing your portfolio is taking the time to help you learn. Just like you, he'd rather be home painting or working on his goals, but he's there helping you out. I'd say that's very gracious, and I'm always genuinely grateful whenever someone takes time out of their schedule to give me some feedback on my work.

The cool thing is that they understand where you're at. They've been there too. They get how hard it is to walk up to someone you admire or aspire to be and show them your work, even when you know it might get ripped to shreds. They get it, and they want to help by hopefully making the experience as painless and as informative as possible.

Be grateful that they are open to sharing their experience, insights, and knowledge as an industry pro with you. Lead with an attitude of learning *and* gratitude!

What You Stand to Gain:
I know it can be intimidating, but it is crucial that you show your work and get feedback. There is so much to be gained from critiques. Here are a few things to consider:

- You had the balls to show your art, and that's empowering
- You got out of your basement where it's safe and you're a genius in your own mind
- A fresh set of eyes can find mistakes or shortcomings that you just can't see because you're too close to it. You don't have the experience yet to spot these things, but they do
- Learn what the pros do
- Learn specific things you need to do to work in any given industry
- You avoid mistakes by learning from theirs
- You can learn more about human nature; how it's not all about you, and how to be objective about your art and not take it personally
- You learn about yourself, your insecurities around your art and how to grow past them
- You develop the proverbial "thick skin" so you can grow faster
- You mix with other artists and pros
- You'll never get work if you sit in your studio and draw without showing it to someone
- You'll learn the things that ARE working well in your art, what you're succeeding at
- You'll get some positive feedback – and that's always nice
- You might make an impression on an AD and make a great connection
- An artist might like your work and hire you to do backgrounds, or talk you up to their AD, or give you overflow work, or talk you up and share your work on FB or their blog
- You might make a contact in an area you never even thought of
- You may get hired on the spot

Don't Take It Personally

You cannot take what is said personally. I'll tell you why – and listen up, because this is one of the most important lessons you will learn as an artist and a human being.

There are so many reasons that a person might say negative things to you in a crit THAT HAVE NOTHING TO DO WITH YOU OR YOUR ART.

Their opinion is only one viewpoint. And it's skewed by their personal preferences, experiences, prejudices, artistic slant, professional needs, etc. All people's comments are influenced by how they see the world through their own individual filter. And that has nothing to do with you.

Your job as a person receiving a critique is to listen quietly, not get defensive, and try to absorb everything that's said. As soon as I'm done with a critique, I like to find a quite spot and take a few notes about things that stuck out for me so I can think about them more later.

Sort

Some of the things that are said in a crit may not be relevant to you. That's just the way it goes.

Remember the *What Do You Want to Do With Your Life* section earlier in the book where I suggested you take some time to figure out your goals, and you blew if off because you thought it was silly because you know that you want to be an artist? Well if you did take the time to get more specific with your artistic and professional goals, you would see how that could be useful here.

If you have some direction, some idea of where you want to take your art career, then you are better equipped to sort through the information you get in a critique. And that's what you really want to do. If you're lucky, everything the critiquer says to you will be pure gold! But that's seldom the case – because of *their* filter. Your job is to SORT through the information you received for the things that apply to you and your personal goals.

For example, a critiquer might say to you, "You have a very whimsical style to your characters; you would be perfect for children's animation." Ok, start with your attitude of learning. This is something you may have never considered and is very intriguing to you; you may even want to develop that tendency some more. Or you currently have no interest in cartoons - you want to work on books.

But salt all comments away in your noggin, because since you're always evolving as an artist, and your goals or interests might expand at a future date. See how *every* comment can be a learning experience in one way or another.

What the comment did not say was, "You're not suited for print work, go into something else." It was not a personal attack. If you're taking it that way, then you need to look at the reasons why you are hearing legitimate and helpful suggestions about your art only as derogatory statements about your worth as an artist or a person.

Don't you see, it's all about how you "hear" the comments made in a critique? Lead with an attitude of learning and gratitude! Any other way will likely upset you, and that just defeats the purpose of showing your work and doesn't serve you.

Emotions Are Part of Life

If you do get a little hot during a crit and have an emotional reaction in the moment, don't worry, it happens. But curtail the need to lash out at the person critiquing you, even if they are being an asshole. Take the position of the better person, thank them for their time, and reflect later on what was said and see if there was anything of value to you in it. The fact that you did react so strongly is a lesson in itself. Maybe you've learned that certain topics push your buttons and it's something you have to look at closer. Maybe you got upset because the critique was spot on, and it was a hard pill to swallow. See what I mean, you can learn something from every critique, even the brutal ones.

The idea here is not to dismiss the critiquer as a jerk and stomp away angrily saying, "He doesn't know what he's talking about!" Better to say to yourself, "It's too bad he wasn't nicer, but did he say anything that I can apply to my art that will help me in the future?" If you dismiss him, you're the one who might be missing out.

Despite a bad delivery, what is said may have a great deal of value to you. I remember getting a critique from an editor that was a really quirky guy with poor social skills, bad hygiene, and even worse breath. He was agitated, harsh, and very abrupt. But I made a real effort to look past those things so I could grab a few gems of wisdom from this seasoned veteran, and it was worth it.

It's nothing personal. Maybe the person reviewing your portfolio is having a bad day and is a little short or flat with his comments. Ok, that sucks, but listen to what is offered and take what you can learn from and throw away the rest. Don't get your panties in a bunch because he didn't get super excited.

Even if the person is trying to personally attack you, you have the know-how to recognize it as such; know that they are spouting off at you because of their own insecurities and issues. You can see that they have nothing to contribute to your artistic growth and simply walk away unaffected.

Possible Reasons for a Nasty Critique That Have Nothing to do with Your Art
• He's having a bad day (because his boss just chewed him out, his dad just died, he lost a promotion, or for any number of legitimate personal upsets)
• He's frustrated because he's already looked at 75 crappy portfolios before yours
• He feels uncomfortable giving advice because he doesn't feel qualified
• He doesn't have good communication skills
• He has to work the con when he doesn't want to
• He wants to be home making art instead of working
• He wants to be a working artist instead of whatever job he has, and he's taking it out on you
• He may be your favorite artist, but he's just an asshole
• Brainstorm a few of your own – it will make you feel better

If you get all pissed off when you get some negative feedback, you're doing yourself a real disservice. You'll be saying in your head "this guy's an ass," and you'll be missing an opportunity to listen. If you can stay cool and objective, you'll hear a lot of things that will help you grow as and artist.

Why expend energy on being angry, when you can channel that energy into something you enjoy, like making art? Just don't go there. It deflects your focus from what is really important: becoming a better artist and getting work.

My Precious
One thing that might help you be more objective about your work is to think of each painting as a transition to your next phase as an artist. In other words, each piece you do is merely an exercise, a stepping stone to the next piece.

The act of creating is very powerful and can feel quite personal. And it is. It's supposed to be, that's one of the things that makes it so pleasurable. And that can make our work feel very precious. It is, and it isn't.

As you are getting better, you will most likely see you older work in a new light. It's no longer that sacred gem that deserves your undying love. It has withered into an amateurish piece of crap! And that's actually a good thing, because it means you've grown.

That piece is still precious in the sense that it has special meaning to you because it represents your struggle and a milestone met in your artistic growth, but it's no longer your crowning achievement.

So when you're having a crit, remember that even though you really like your latest piece, you might hate it in the very near future, and totally get why the critiquer is breaking it down.

Test Your Mettle

Here's a little exercise you can try: Do a drawing then tear it up. It might sting at first, but it will be freeing – trust me. If you can't do it, grab an old drawing that you don't like anymore and tear it up. And it will help you not hold your art so preciously. Give thanks for having gone through that stage, because it brought you to where you are now – then tear it up, burn it in effigy, give praise to the art gods, and move on to your next challenge

---

You Are the Source

Sometimes a critiquer may have very little of value to contribute. And that's ok too. Thank them for their time and move on. Trust me, it was still helpful. You got a little braver about showing your book. You got better at listening to grumpy comments and not getting upset. You recognized that some people just aren't very good at giving feedback. You learned not to ask for a crit when the guy is eating lunch. See what I mean?

Hopefully, the majority of your crits will be very pleasant experiences. In fact, more times than not, they're exciting and motivating! I get stoked when I learn something new that I never heard before – I usually want to rush home and try it out in my next painting.

You will hear good things about your work in crtis too. And that feels good. Everyone likes affirmation that their hard work is starting to pay off. One thing to remember though is that YOU are the source of your own power. No one else. Others cannot validate you. You have to know that your creativity is important and your artistic pursuits have meaning for you, no matter what anyone says, good or bad.

Don't Defend, Just Listen

This is huge. It's always our first instinct to defend what we believe in or what we think is right. But remember, there is always another way, one that might be better. That's what learning is all about. You're getting a critique to see if there are some things that you don't know yet that can help you on your quest.

If you only defend your current position, your current knowledge base, then you'll stay stuck where you are and never get better (and probably never get work). That's pretty silly isn't it?

I took a creative writing class once, and **I learned one of the most valuable lessons I have ever learned**, and it had nothing to do with writing. The class was run following a process spelled out in a book called *Writing without Teachers* by Peter Elbow. Basically, you read your short story aloud in a group, then you are *not allowed to speak*, only listen, as they give you feedback. Then it's on to the next writer. The same approach can be applied to an art critique.

What this teaches you to do is not expend energy or fill up your short crit time with you yacking away defending your work. Even if the critiquer is way off the mark, you still don't need to waste time trying to change his mind. You're there to listen and soak up every bit of knowledge that you can. Listen and sort later.

One of the main ideas behind this process is that *all reactions to your work are valid*. How viewers react is how they react. If 20 people feel your children's book illo is too gruesome for tots, then it probably is. Even if 20 people comment about something seemingly irrelevant to what you were trying to achieve, that can tell you something about how your painting is being received and that you might want to address that element.

Even if someone is coming at you pretty hard, take a breath and remember not to take it personally. **Getting defensive just shows that you're not confident**. You come off as argumentative and wounded. Even if you are feeling attacked or unconfident about where you are with your art, you can still stand confident knowing that you are immersed in a *process* of learning and growth – you are confident that you can stay open to feedback for your own good!

You certainly don't have to stand there mute during a crit, but let the "teacher" do most of the talking and resist the temptation to defend your work. It is helpful to engage the person – show them your passion. Be courteous, be professional, answer questions and thank them for their time and mean it. You just learned something!

If you find that you're not in an open and accepting state of mind when someone is offering you advice, it's also *totally acceptable* to say, "I appreciate that you're trying to help me, but I'm not up for any feedback right now. Can I hit you up later for some advice?"

Ask Questions

It's perfectly acceptable to ask questions during a crit. As always, be courteous and don't interrupt and don't defend. And don't geek out on the guy, even if you are a huge fan. Remember why you're standing there. When the moment is right, usually towards the end of a crit, ask some questions that you've been wondering about, or ask for clarification on something he said earlier.

You may want to prepare yourself with some questions before you go into a portfolio review situation. What are some things you'd like to know about your work? Have you been struggling with something? Ask: What can I do to improve my portfolio? What kinds of things do you look for in a portfolio? Will this get me work in your industry?

Say Thanks, Give a Sample Pack, Get Their Card

Depending on who you're talking to and what was said in the crit, there are a couple things to do as the crit wraps up. Always shake the person's hand and thank them for taking the time to review your work. Gratitude.

If you're talking to an art director, or someone that can potentially give you work, then you'll want to give the person a sample packet of your art and your business card.

> Definition: Sample Packet: A compact, usually printed, booklet with samples of your artwork; a mini-portfolio that you give to prospective clients to keep for their files. Sample packets are also referred to as *Leave behinds, Tear sheets, or mini portfolios.*

Ask the person if you can contact them in the future and ask for ***their*** business card. This is very important: you want to secure a way that *you* can contact them so you can follow up and stay on their radar in the future. Keep it short and sweet and say, "Thanks again, you've given me some great advice to think about."

Book 2: Breaking In and Staying In is chock full of advice on sample packets, portfolio reviews, and making contacts. It would benefit you greatly to check it out.

Types of Critiques

Critiques can run the range from a casual discussion with your friends, to a high pressure job opportunity with an art director. All are equally important to your growth. You'd be surprised what kinds of insights you can gain by showing your work to non-artists.

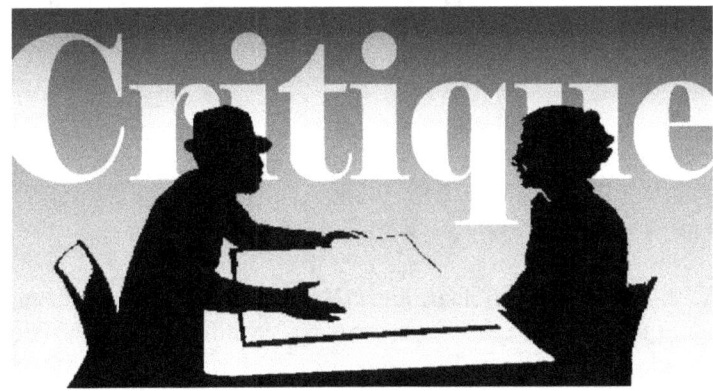

When you first start showing your portfolio, you may want to start small to get used to hearing comments about your work. If you're finding it difficult, there's nothing wrong with telling your critiquer what *type* of feedback you are looking for: "I'm a little sensitive about my work, can you please be gentle," or "I'd like to know only if the colors are working well," etc. This is actually helpful even as a pro. I like to ask artist friends for feedback on very specific areas of a painting that I have questions about.

With professionals, always ASK if they'd be willing to critique your work, then whip out your book with confidence and let them take the lead. A crit is organic like a conversation and will flow naturally. If the pro has done crits before, he will guide the process and give you some good advice.

Crits can be very casual, like two old friends sitting around talking about things they think are successful in a piece of art. Or they can have a much more formal tone, especially when you are showing your work to a very busy art director. Whenever you are speaking to a pro, you want to carry yourself with confidence and professionalism, and the crit will go fine.

Where to Get Critiqued

School

Critiques will be an integral part of your curriculum in any art program. That's one reason going to some kind of classes is so valuable. Not only will you benefit from crits from the instructor, you'll also likely hear from all your peers as well, because in a classroom setting it is most common for everyone's finished assignments to be hung on the wall so that all the students have a chance to look at them, comment on them, and benefit from critiques of everyone's work.

This can be tough sometimes, because you're not just showing your work to one person who might say negative things about your work, there's a whole room full of people who might say negative things about your work! Or worse yet, *hear* your work being broken down.

Lead with an attitude of learning. You're all in the same boat, and you're all there to help each other grow by learning from each other. All the same ideas I've been talking about for crits with pros or ADs applies in every situation, so be brave and pin your work up on that wall with pride.

Artist friends

One of the most excellent ways to get feedback on your work is to ask one of your artist friends, or any of your peers, no matter where you are in your art career. If you're a student, ask one of your classmates what they think. If you're a pro, reach out to other pros working on the same project that you are.

Artist friends fully understand where you are and what you're going through, so they are perfect people to get a critique from.

Pro Artists and ADs at Conventions

Professional artists are a really great resource for critiques, because they know exactly what you're going through, because they've been there themselves. They've had an opportunity to grow from other people's generosity in giving them critiques, so they like to pay it forward by helping aspiring artist out. A lot of art directors do as well.

Conventions related to your field of interest are a fantastic place to show your portfolio around, not only to get feedback on your art, but also to make contacts or even find work. The shows have tons of professionals showing their work so you can see what's being done out in the marketplace to help tailor your portfolio to the niche you want to pursue.

Many companies send their art directors, editors, and other art buyers to conventions to do portfolio reviews. They are there to help young artist to get feedback, but the main reason they are there is to find new talent to hire. This is an invaluable opportunity, so polish up your portfolio and take advantage of it.

Portfolio Reviews take place in different areas at a show. Sometimes there are dedicated areas where a bunch of companies set up, sometimes they are held at individual companies' booths. Do you homework before the show.

In addition to conventions there is a wide range of events where you can show your portfolio for feedback or to drum up work such as job fairs, professional conferences and trade shows. These types of events usually have a more pointed purpose than a convention. Conventions are open to the public and have a mix of professionals, fans, retailers, and companies showing their wares. Job Fairs, for example have no retailers, only companies looking for talent in a specific niche. But each of these events offers a great opportunity to meet face to face with art buyers.

Workshops
Workshops are usually designed to be a hands-on learning experience with a teacher of some sort. As with any learning experience, workshops often include critiques and are therefore a great environment to get your work reviewed. There are even workshops that revolve primarily on critiquing your work and strengthening your portfolio. It's another chance to get one on one feedback from a pro and input from your peers.

Online
As digital data delivery gets faster and faster, the internet continues to be an invaluable resource for learning via video. Virtual classrooms and workshops abound, giving you the opportunity to learn in the comfort of your own studio. The internet gives you live access to pros you may never have opportunity to meet in person. Critiques are the very best way to learn, hands down, and this is one more way to get them.

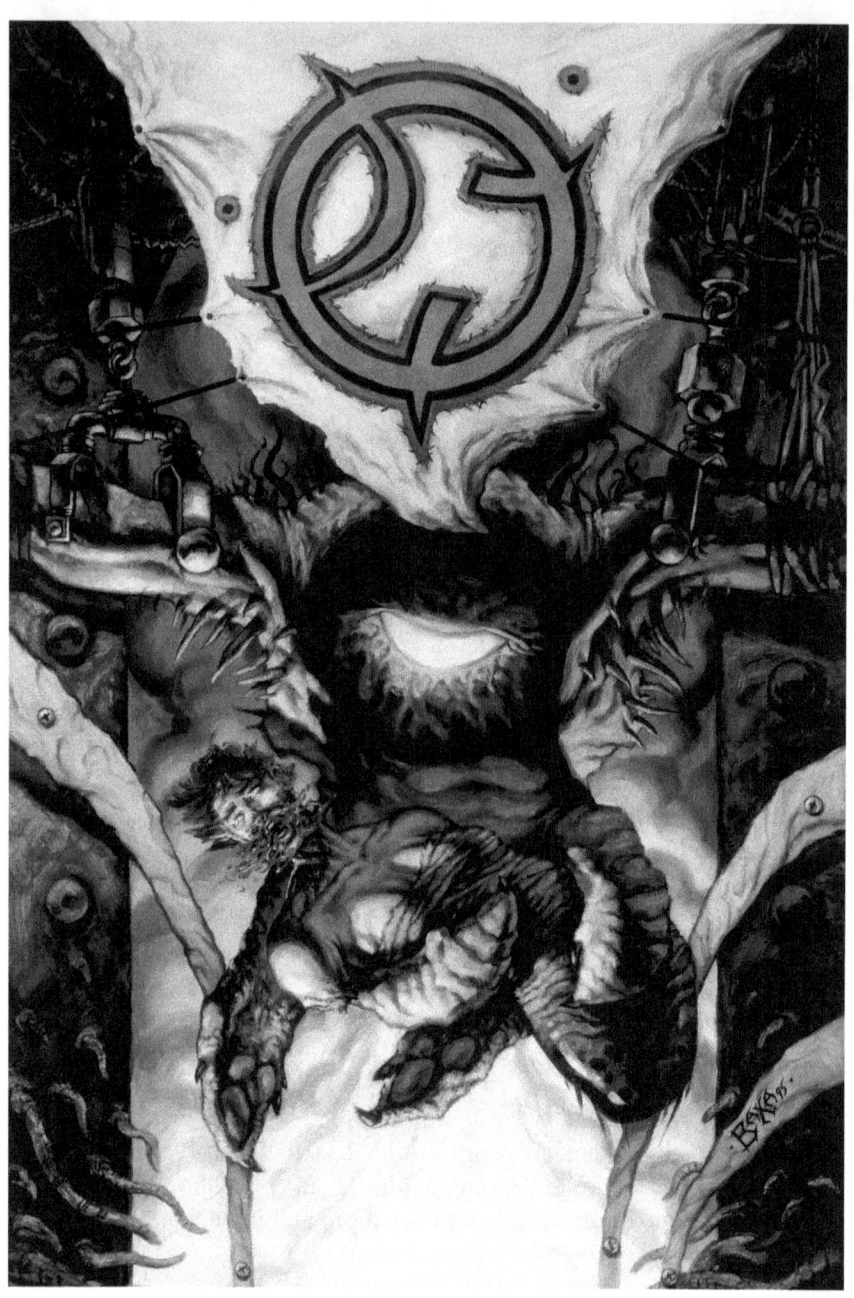

Book of Hunts © 1995 Thomas M. Baxa

<u>**REMEMBER**</u>

<u>**REMEMBER**</u>

- Always lead with an attitude of Learning and Gratitude.
- Don't take it personally.
- Set your goals and sort through the feedback you get and apply what is relevant to you.

BAXA·A**RT** *A*cademy

Let Tom Baxa review your work and give you well intentioned and extremely helpful constructive criticism. More details at the BaxaArt Academy Critique and Portfolio Review Page .

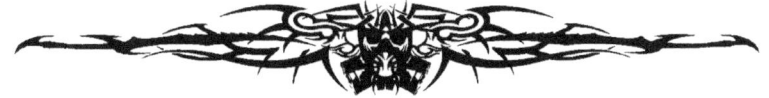

Get Work as a Fantasy Artist:

Book 02
Breaking in and
Staying in

By
Tom Baxa

INTRO

You're on Your Way to Success:

First off, let me commend you on taking action and buying this book. Congratulations! You're one step closer to being a working fantasy illustrator!

You have in your hands a valuable tool, loaded with real world insights, information, insider tips and little known strategies for getting work that I still use today to thrive as an illustrator.

By buying and reading this book, you will have a leg up over the competition, and that edge could make all the difference in the world. Of course, nothing takes the place of hard work and dedication. I know you have the passion for art, now it's time for you to kick it into high gear and follow your dream of making art for a living. And I'm here to help.

Art is Art – No Matter What Your Medium

I'm traditionally trained and still prefer pushing paint to pushing pixels. But I also enjoy painting digitally, doing photo montage, and playing with graphic design. I tend to speak mainly about painting, but all of the ideas I'm putting forth to you in this book are universal and apply to you whether you're an oil painter, color pencil artist, watercolorist, or if you've never picked up a brush and your tool of choice is a Wacom stylist and pretty glowing pixels.

Remember, It's a Job

I know, I know – you're an artiste. You are not swayed by the trappings of the material world! Be that as it may, there's one thing I want you to remember as you read some of the advice in this book: your primary objective is to **make a living as a working illustrator.** That basically means having a really fun and rewarding *job*. And make no mistake, it is a job, and at times, it's best to think of it that way to further your success.

Your "boss" is the **Art Director**. The art director ("AD" for short) is the person employed by a company to oversee things related to visual art. In a large company, there may be several art directors, art managers, and a creative director that oversees the department. See *SECTION 4:Working with Art Directors* below for a look at the different types of ADs.

Depending on the industry, art directors may have different titles; and on some jobs you may be reporting to a person other than the art director like an editor, a producer, a production designer, etc. **For the purposes of this book, I will use the term "Art Director" to mean** *any* **person who is in a position to hire you to do artwork for a company.**

This book focuses on being a freelance illustrator, but *many* of the tips and strategies can apply to finding a full time position as an illustrator.

Quick note: I often use the word "painting" in this book to describe making art, but I use it as a blanket term for all forms of art-making, whether you are a traditional artist or digital artist. And, because I'm a man, I refer to most people in this book with male pronouns. Women, please do not take offence – I know full well that women are fantasy artists and in creative positions of power.

Get Excited, Not Discouraged

This book is designed to help you, and get you fired up as you arm yourself with great information. It may seem like a lot to take in right now, but these processes and tips will soon be a part of your everyday life.

It may all seem a bit overwhelming or intimidating to you at this stage, but it's only because you haven't personally experienced these things yet. But don't let that slow you down. Learn from my 25 years of experience and soar way ahead of the game.

Get stoked! And enjoy the journey!

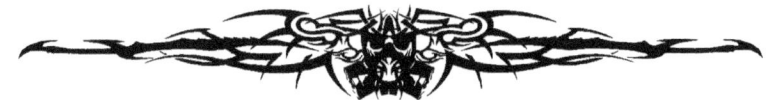

SECTION 1: Your Portfolio

Before you begin, I encourage you to first read *Getting Work as a Fantasy Artist: BOOK 1: Artistic Growth*. It contains a ton of information that is critical to your continued education as an artist, including:

- What direction do you want to take as an artist?

- Fundamentals that are crucial to being a fantasy artist

- Art Education and continuing your learning process beyond formal education. There are tons of ways to grow as an artist that you may have never considered. I cover some of the things I still do as a pro to further my skills and get inspired.

- Critiques are one of the very best ways to learn. I take you through the ins and outs of critiques, the mindset you should take with you into a critique, the value they can have for you, and why you should seek them out every chance you get.

Critiques are strongly tied to building your portfolio and to getting work, so it's important to embrace them and use them in a meaningful way. With the info from *Book 1* fresh in your mind, read on and develop your portfolio to crush it at any portfolio review or job interview.

The Almighty Portfolio

So what were you doing all that time in college? Hopefully you were honing your skills and developing a strong portfolio.

In the art field, the number one, most important factor in getting a job is the quality of your artwork. Forget about volunteer work, grades, awards, degrees, all the sleepless nights, the calluses on your hands from painting into the wee hours. It all boils down to how good your art is. That's why it's so important to keep learning and painting all the time.

Your portfolio, also referred to as your "book", is your calling card. It tells a prospective client everything he needs to know. Or at least it should.

Your portfolio defines you as an artist. It can say "Baxa has a unique voice and dynamic imagery." Or it can say, "I do dark fantasy with an edge," etc. Most importantly, your portfolio should tell a prospective client that you understand the type of art that he needs for his marketplace.

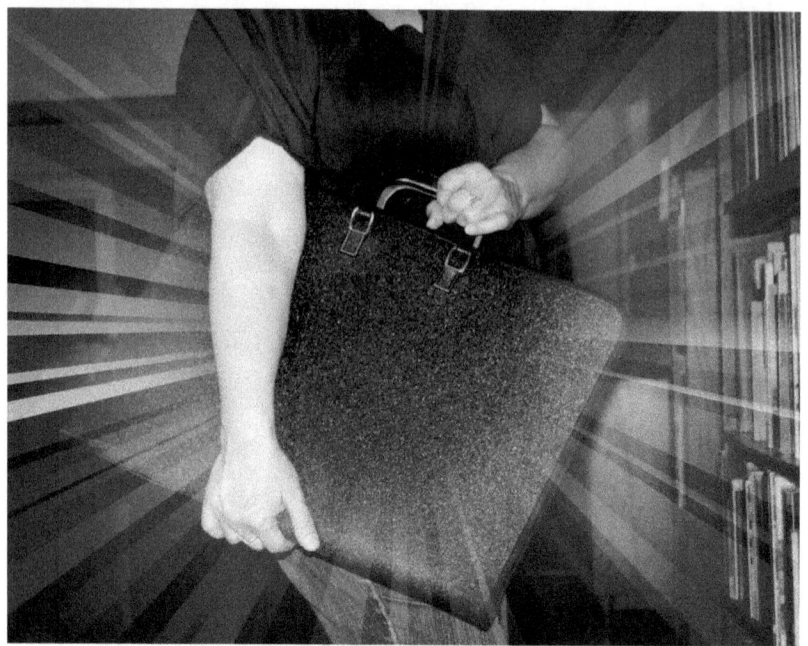

Your portfolio should have your very best work in it, even if you don't have a lot of art yet, only include your strongest pieces. **It's better to have a small portfolio of great pieces, than a large portfolio with a couple great pieces and a bunch of mediocre pieces**. The weaker pieces bring the portfolio down and make an art director unsure if you can deliver good work all the time.

Now I know this idea of having an amazing portfolio can be scary, especially for you perfectionists out there. I'm going to let you in on a little secret – and this is one of the most important things you'll ever learn: Working on your portfolio incessantly until it's perfect is nothing more than a mental block! It's holding you back and keeping you from putting yourself out there. P.s. It will *never* be perfect, so get out there.

I get that you want it to be the best it can be. And that's exactly what you should do: make it the best it can be for where you are as an artist. And, just like your artistic ability, your portfolio is an ongoing process. As you get better, you update your portfolio and make it stronger.

Even if you don't feel that you're work is as good as the pros yet, don't let that stop you from reaching out to those pros, other artists, and art directors to get feedback on your work and learn more about the industry. You'll also learn how to strengthen your portfolio.

It's true, that you don't want to show your work *too* early, because you want your first impression to be a good one. But I've seen artist come back to me several years in a row with their portfolios who have show a marked improvement each year and real dedication to their craft. In doing so, they demonstrated to me, and art directors, that they have been working hard and improving.

All the information about portfolios that follows holds true for any presentation of your work, whether it be a physical portfolio, an online digital portfolio, your sample packs, or artwork hanging on a wall. They are all representations of you as an artist and deserve your considered attention.

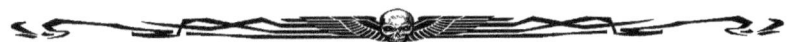

Physical and Digital Portfolios

In a minute I'm going to discuss building a physical portfolio that you can carry around with you for when you meet ADs in person, which is the very best way to make contact and get work. It is critical that you have a physical portfolio of some sort. But it's also equally important to have a digital portfolio, especially an online portfolio.

The following is a list of the main types of portfolio formats. Ideally, to market yourself fully, it would be beneficial to have all of these forms. But in the beginning you must have 1.) A physical portfolio, and 2.) An online portfolio.

Physical portfolio

This is a portfolio that you can hold in your hands, usually in the form of some type of binder with interchangeable pages that hold copies (or originals) of your artwork. An AD looks at it like he would a book. Some artists who have had an art book published use that as a portfolio or give them to ADs as sample packs.

Sample Packs
This is a small booklet or brochure that you leave with a prospective client after you've talked to them for them to keep in their files and remember you by. Your sample pack should be on the smaller side and easy to handle with about ten pages or so, and include your contact information. See *Your Sample Packet* below for more on this topic.

Digital portfolio
A digital portfolio, as you know, is a portfolio of your work comprised of files like jpegs or tiffs that can be delivered in a digital format like over the web or email. There are several venues for a digital portfolio:

Online Portfolio
In today's digital age, this is a must. You should have at least one online portfolio that you can point clients to. This is very useful if you are not meeting an AD in person. If your initial contact is over email, you can direct the AD to your online portfolio. When you have them on the phone, he can be looking at your samples on the computer. You can have the URL to your portfolio on you business card. The applications are endless.

It's best to have your own website, with your own domain name, for your main online portfolio.

If you don't have an online portfolio, you're missing out huge on opportunities to market your artistic services, and you'll be considered old school and unprofessional.

It's best to have your own website, with your own domain name, for your main online portfolio as opposed to a portfolio on a third party site like www.DeviantArt.com. Here's why. You want to be building yourself as a brand, and develop your reputation as an awesome artist. Deviant Art is great, and it doesn't hurt to have a portfolio there as well, but sites like that are full of amateur artists. You're a pro and should conduct yourself as one. As your business grows, you'll have your destination site up and can add to it by adding a bio, blog, news page, store, etc.

I also recommend a website over a blog for your main portfolio. Blogs are excellent for talking about your work, what you're working on, new releases, etc. They have an informal and conversational format that is great for engaging your audience, but they are less impressive as a professional portal to your business. Build a website, even if it has nothing other than your portfolio and contact info.

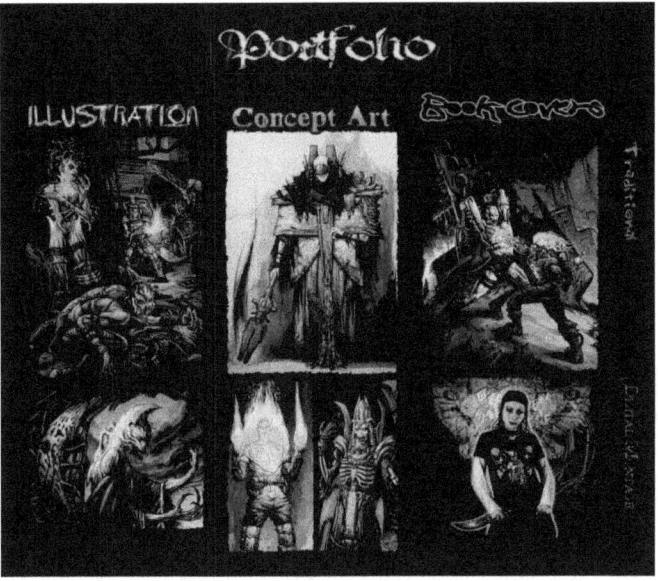

Baxa's Online Portfolio index page at Baxaart.com

On a Handheld Device
This is a good option for a digital portfolio because you can carry it around with you easily. Your iPad can hold many portfolios, one for each industry you're interested in. You can also have video and audio/music with your presentation if you like. Showing your portfolio on a smart phone is not a good idea – it's too small. Buy a tablet.

Make sure your portfolio(s) are in their *own* folders and not mixed in with personal photos or with portfolios designed for other industries.

There are some dos and don'ts for portfolios on handheld devices below in *SECTION 2: Getting Work : Pounding the Pavement: How To Talk with Art Directors and Pros at Cons: Handheld Device Portfolios.*

On a Thumb Drive or CD
You can carry your portfolio on a thumb drive or a cd. This way you can have it with you to show anyone and anytime, providing there is a computer around. This makes a descent leave behind for samples, but not my first choice for a portfolio. What if there is no computer around? You're screwed.

PDF Portfolio

It's a good idea to create a pdf file portfolio because it is one file with many images in it, it can easily be emailed to prospective clients or uploaded to a site, the quality is good, and most people are used to pdfs. It's becoming common on job sites that you can upload a resume as well as a pdf with additional info (like your artwork).

 Eye On BAA: For more info, and an upcoming book on how to market yourself as an artist, keep an eye on BaxaArtAcademy.com.

Social Media and Portfolio Sites

As I mentioned earlier, a portfolio site like DeviantArt should not be your only or primary location for your online portfolio, but it, and other sites like it, are very popular and well trafficked so they are excellent options for secondary portfolio placement. Having a portfolio available on specifically targeted sites like www.ConceptArt.org can expose you to ADs that are looking for talent on these specialized sites. You should also be using social media sites like Facebook to post samples of your work. The more sites you are on, the greater your online presence, and that's good marketing.

Art Annuals / Source books and Their Companion Sites

Art annuals or source books like Showcase, Workbook, etc. are thick catalogs of artist for hire that you pay to be included in. When you pay for pages in the book, you also get to put your work on their companion website. This is another way to get seen and have a portfolio online. Supposedly, these sites are highly searched by art buyers and art directors when they are looking for clients. Annuals are quite expensive, and their success rate at getting work, especially for a fantasy artist is debatable. But it is an option.

Slideshow, Flash Trailer, Interactive Portfolio

With your art in digital form, you can create a jazzier multimedia portfolio if you like to show on your website or handheld. You can create a video, slideshow, animated flash trailer, or clickable interactive portfolio. Have fun with it if you like, but all that effort, while pretty cool, probably won't improve your chances of getting work over a more static portfolio type.

Hanging Artwork

You can also do gallery shows or hang your artwork in other public venues as a way to show your work, but this is much less effective than direct marketing unless you are showing to a highly targeted audience like at a fantasy convention art show.

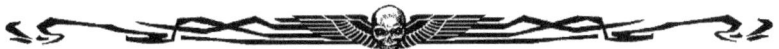

Professional Presentation

First and foremost, you want your book to be clean and crisp, with you artwork neatly attached to the pages. Nothing says, "I'm not a pro" like a ragged portfolio with random drawings on torn paper falling out all over the place. If your book is disorganized, then so are you, and ADs won't want to deal with you.

Buy a new portfolio. There are many styles out there, but they all have similar elements. Shop around and look for sales because some portfolios can be quite expensive. You want one that looks clean and professional, but don't blow your paycheck on a high-end leather portfolio. Pay more attention to the functionality (and your artwork). It's a good idea to try them in person at your local art store, instead of just ordering one on the internet. You especially want to test to see if the pages turn *easily*. Here's what to look for when shopping for portfolios:

Page Size

You want to get a portfolio that is large enough to show off your work, but not so big that it's unwieldy and difficult to whip open on a table at a convention. Remember, you want to make it easy for ADs to take a look no matter where you might run into them.

I personally use an 8.5" x 11" portfolio. It's a little on the small side, but I can carry it in my bag when I'm walking around and it's easy to hold in your hands and flip through, or to view on a table with little space. 11" x 17" is a great size because there's room for original art, and your art is shown at a size that is impressive. 16" x 20" the absolute largest I'd use, and that's a little big. Anything beyond that is overkill, and too unwieldy to be effective.

Obviously, my original paintings are larger than 8.5" x 11", so I show high quality printouts of my work in my portfolio. Whenever possible, it is nice to show some originals in your portfolio, because they pack and impressive punch; and artists and ADs love looking at actual artwork. It could help you make an impression. But in today's digital age, art buyers are used to looking at printouts and it's perfectly acceptable.

Acid Free or Archival

This is usually the standard, especially with art portfolios, but you want to make sure that the plastic pages that come with the portfolio are acid free and/or archival. In actuality, no plastics are totally acid free, but if they're marked acid free, archival, or museum quality, they are usually quite safe for your work over your lifetime.

Plastic actually gives off fumes over time (a process called "off-gassing") that can yellow your work. The more acidic the plastic, the more damaging it can be.

When shopping for portfolios, you also want to check the clarity of the plastic pages. Bring along a print of your work and insert it into a portfolio sleeve page, to make sure that the plastic or vinyl is very clear and does not obscure your art. You want the pages to have a decent weight to them. If they're too thin, they may crack over time.

Insert Backing Paper

Portfolios have plastic, top-loading sleeve pages with a piece of paper inside as a backing. I like black paper as my background color. Many people like grey. If you see a portfolio you really like, but the paper color is wrong, you can always replace the paper.

Just like the sleeve, you want the paper liner to be archival as well. I like to use charcoal paper as a liner because it has a descent weight, comes in a lot of great colors and textures, and can be acid free.

The way to present your work is to mount the artwork with double sided tape in the center of the backing paper. One or two pieces per page is best. Each page comes with one sheet of paper. You can mount art on each side of the paper, but this makes it harder to update your book. I like to have two sheets of backing paper, with art on each, back to back in one sleeve, so if I want to make changes or rearrange the order of my art, it's easier to do so.

Binding

This is one of the most important elements when buying a portfolio. Your number one goal is to make sure the pages are EASY TO

TURN. There's nothing more aggravating than pages that get stuck as you try to turn them.

Most portfolios have a multi-ringed spine, which helps keep the pages uniform. It works like a notebook – the rings snap open to allow pages to be added, then snap shut. Sometimes the rings don't shut tightly, and problematic thinner sleeve pages get caught in the cracks. Go to the store and try them out.

Popular Types of Portfolios

Most portfolios consist of an outer cover that zips open for flat display, a multi-ringed binder, and vinyl sleeve pages with liner paper. Some are more like a book with a hard cover of leather or vinyl. Take a look around for one that you like. Itoya art portfolios are inexpensive, come in a wide variety of sizes and are easy to use.

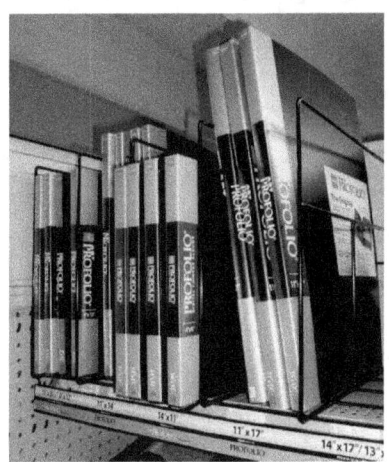

Itoya brand portfolios

A Word of Caution:

DO NOT leave your portfolio in the sun or in a hot car, the plastic pages WILL warp and crinkle up. Some pages may off-gas more and discolor your work, or even give off goo or oils. This could damage your art work. Also, protect your portfolio! It's very important to you and your career. Kindly ask people not to set their backpack on it when they visit your table, ask them not to put their drinks near it, etc. You'd be surprised what some people will do. It's your job to keep your baby safe.

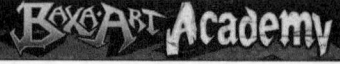

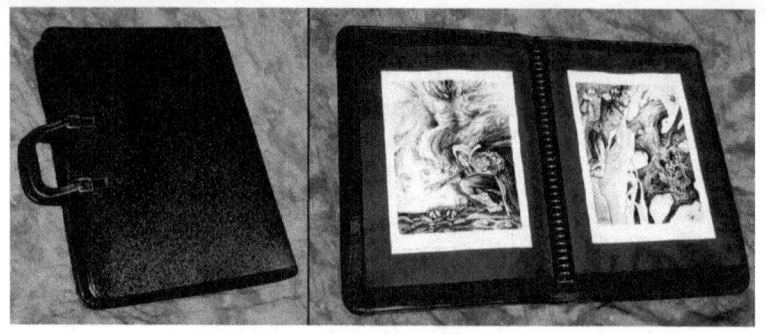

One of my earlier portfolios was a typical multi-ring art portfolio with black backing paper with original art mounted on it.

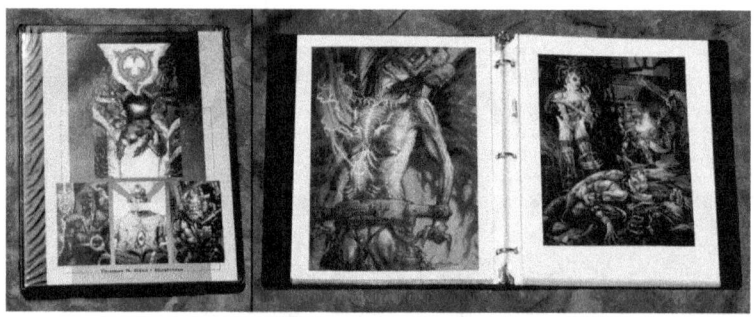

My current portfolio is an 8 1/2" x 11" three ring binder with clear sleeves holding printouts of my work. This particular binder has a clear sleeve on the front that can hold a cover image.

What to Put in Your Portfolio

This is always a struggle, even for the pros. Here are some things to think about that will help you when you're choosing pieces for your portfolio.

Keep it Lean

Every artist's first instinct is to load up his portfolio with every awesome piece he's ever done. But that's not the way to go. As I said earlier, your portfolio should have only your strongest work in it. A tight well thought out portfolio with a small amount of excellent pieces, is better that a portfolio with a few great pieces and a bunch of mediocre pieces. Here's why:

You want your portfolio to pack a punch, like a good movie trailer does. In the short time that you have with an art director, you want them to be bowled over by what they are seeing. You do that by doing good work, obviously. But if your portfolio has too many pieces in it, even if they all rock, the viewer will get overwhelmed and you will have lost the wow factor. A few pieces are plenty to show off your skills.

Obviously, your portfolio won't be perfectly targeted for every art director you meet. But you want to do your best to cover a range of your abilities and still keep your portfolio tight.

See *Creating Images that Catch an AD's* Eye below for tips on the kind of content, imagery, and ideas you should include in your artwork to convey to an art director that you understand what makes a strong illustration and that you can do the job he needs done.

Send a Clear Message

You don't want your book to send mixed messages to an art director viewing it. Remember, you may not be there to explain things when an AD looks at your samples, so make sure they speak for themselves. Fair or not, a confusing portfolio can inadvertently send a *negative* message. Here are some pitfalls you want to avoid:

A sloppy presentation
Message: This artist is disorganized, messy, and doesn't take pride in his work. He didn't even take the time to make his portfolio presentable; I doubt he will take a job or deadlines seriously. He's not a pro.
Solution: Make sure your portfolio is clean, tidy, and put together in a professional manner.

A few excellent pieces mixed with mediocre pieces
Message: This artist is inconsistent and I can't count on what level of work I'll get from him if I give him an assignment.
Solution: Only put your top work in your book, and cut the rest

Believe it or not, one of the most important things to an AD, even above the artistic ability of the artist, is his ability to consistently turn in good work on time. When an AD assigns a job, he wants to feel confident that the job will be done right without his having to check up on him or work too hard with the artist on revisions.

If you are too much trouble, miss deadlines, don't respond to his emails in a timely fashion, or turn in sub-par work that needs revision, the AD *will* drop you and work with someone else that gets the job done with little effort from him. ADs will often work with less talented artists because they know they can count on them without fail. It puts their mind at ease that they can send out an assignment and know it will be done right and on deadline.

Student work in your portfolio

Message: This guy hasn't created much artwork yet, and doesn't have much, if any, work experience. He is untested and I'm not sure what will happen if I hire him.

Solution: Put only finished illustrations in your book that incorporate the things you've learned

It's usually best not to include student work in your portfolio. Most work you do in school is designed to teach you something or help you develop your skills. *They are exercises, not illustrations.* Examples of things **not** to put in your portfolio include: life drawings, perspective drawings, sketches, warm up drawings, color swatch exercises, rendering exercises, etc. These things just tell an AD that you took some classes, and not much else.

It may be true that you are right out of school, and that's ok, but your portfolio shouldn't broadcast it. You want to seem like a pro, even if you aren't one yet. Show the AD that you understand what it takes to be a working pro.

Don't worry, even if you are new to the game, if you present yourself well and your work is strong, ADs will hire you. In fact, many ADs pride themselves on giving new artists their first shot!

If your portfolio is a bit heavy on student work, take it all out and spend some time doing one or two really great illustrations that incorporate the things you have learned. For example, do one illustration with scantily clad barbarians (figure drawing) in a dynamic pose (drama) fighting a giant lizard (rendering skills) from a worm's eye view in a cathedral (perspective + architecture). See what I mean, in one finished illustration, you can show an AD a lot of things.

Exception: If the industry you're trying to break into likes to see certain preliminary stages of artwork, then you *should* include that work in your book. For example, animation ADs actually want to see life drawing pieces in your portfolio to see if you have a good understanding of human and animal forms. Concept art positions require quick idea development, so a page of sketches is ok to put in your book.

Unfinished work in your portfolio

Message: Why didn't he take the time to finish this illo? Does this artist have trouble bringing things to conclusion? Will he be late on his deadlines? Does he have trouble coming up with interesting compositional solutions? Is he a quitter? He's not a pro.

Solution: Include only finished illustrations

There is no reason to put unfinished work in your portfolio. No AD wants to hear a list of excuses as to why you couldn't get it done. Just finish it! Or leave it out. There are times when you want to do demos or show your process, but save that for your blog, not your portfolio – unless it is an integral part of the job you are applying for.

How can an AD determine your skills and give you a constructive critique if the work he's looking at isn't finished. All it does is make him wonder about you and your professionalism.

Too wide of a range of subject matter or styles

Message: He's all over the map – I don't know who he is as an artist or what style I'll get. I can give him some direction, but it might be more trouble than it's worth.

Solution: Focus on what kind of work you want to do, and emphasize that in your portfolio. Or have several portfolios (or divide it in sections) for different industries.

There's a difference between showing a range of what you can do, and sending mixed messages. This is a fine line, and a tough thing to figure out. You want to show that you can do a wide range of things so that an AD will feel confident that you can handle anything he throws at you, and to maximize your chances of getting jobs. On the other hand, if there is too much variety, it might appear that you lack focus or don't understand the needs of the position you are applying for.

It's best to start by seeing what's being done in the industry that you're interested in getting into, then doing some illustrations that cover some of the iconic elements of the genre and requirements of the job.

See *Creating Images that Catch an AD's* Eye below for more on this topic.

Too little range

Message: He only paints dragons, I don't know if he can do other stuff.

Solution: Get familiar with your genre, industry, or company that you want to work for and have enough range in your book to give them a good idea of what you can do.

You want to paint what interests you, but if you focus is too narrow it will be harder to get work. And, unfortunately for a lot of ADs, if they don't see it in your book, they think you can't do it. You might also get pigeon-holed as the "dragon guy" and only get dragons to illustrate. I know you're thinking, "Great, I love dragons," but believe me, it will get old. And you'll continue to add new pieces of the same thing to an already narrow portfolio.

No Business Card or Sample Pack:

Message: How am I going to keep track of this guy? He's ill prepared, and not interested in marketing himself. He's not a pro.

Solution: Always have at least a business card or samples of your work to give to an AD.

Don't ask an Art Director if he has a piece of paper to write down your contact info. Without a business card, a postcard, or sample packet with your contact info on it you make it very hard for the AD to remember who you are and get a hold of you months down the line when a job comes up. He's going to worry that you might be a flaky artist that doesn't take business matters into account and that you're unprofessionalism will carry over into your dealings with him on an assignment.

You want it to be *very easy* for them to remember you and contact you. See *Your Sample Packet* below.

Have a Plan to Make It Great

You have to use your best judgment when it comes to your portfolio to determine how to present yourself as an artist. Your first impulse will be to put in your favorite paintings that you love! And that's great. You can start off by putting exactly what you want in your book, but this can be a hard road. You may miss a lot of opportunities if your personal style or interests don't quite align with industry standards.

There are two courses of action here. One is to be exactly the artist you want to be and put that work in your portfolio and try to find that small niche or quirky AD that will support it. There's nothing wrong with that, and ultimately it will likely be much more rewarding. But it might be very hard to get enough work to make a living as an illustrator. And that is the goal of this book.

For example: Let's say you do fantastic art on the surrealistic side focusing primarily on realistically rendered female forms constricted by sinewy intestinal matter combined with dragon-like suggestive imagery. Sounds wicked cool, right? Well, even though this type of art can be considered fantastic in nature and is rendered naturalistically, it doesn't really fit the mold of traditional fantasy art. Most fantasy game companies would consider this way too edgy and not appropriate for their audience or product lines; which means no job for you.

A more direct course of action that will be an easier road to getting work, which I recommend, is to see what's being done in the industry you want to break into and tailor your portfolio accordingly. This can be equally rewarding, especially if your artistic aesthetic matches industry standards. You can always put in a personal piece or two in your portfolio and see if you get any response to them as well.

It's best to have a plan when you build (or rebuild) your portfolio. Even as early as your senior year in college when you begin to do finished pieces to build a portfolio, you should be doing so with on eye on where you want to go.

Keep It Fresh
As artists we are constantly driven to create, and as we grow, each piece we do gets better. It's prudent to update your portfolio with new work as you do it for several reasons, the most obvious reason being that you always want to have your very best work in your portfolio.

In addition to that, it's important to keep your portfolio current. By that I mean always have some new work in your portfolio as well as some of your best older pieces. Having some "classics" in your book help art directors remember you. A particularly powerful piece will stay with them and they will remember that they've met you before when they see it in your portfolio at a subsequent meeting.

But new pieces show an AD that you're constantly working to improve your craft, that you're passionate about making art, and that you're excited to do more! And the need for new work forces you to keep painting, no matter how established you are. There's always room to improve.

But remember, just because a piece is new, doesn't mean it's better; or best suited for inclusion in your portfolio. It's assumed that each time you do a new work you are applying improved skills and new ideas that will make that piece better than your last. However, that is not always the case because each time at the canvas is a time to experiment and explore unfamiliar territory. Which means that you may learn something new, but not be very successful at it yet, or not prepared to pull it all together in a successful illustration. And that's cool – learn, play, experiment! But don't put it in your book unless it's up to snuff.

Remember, your portfolio has a goal attached to. You can have any goal you want, but in this book, the goal of your portfolio is to get you work. So it's best to only put in work that will help you on the path towards this goal.

Think of your portfolio as a living thing – it needs to be fed. And as your skills improve, as you do new kick-ass art, or your goals shift, you need to adjust your portfolio accordingly.

You also don't want your portfolio to feel dated. If you have concept drawings from a film that released 8 years ago, it doesn't look that good – it seems like you haven't worked on a film for 8 years. I often leave the date off reproductions of my work (on my website, or in my portfolio) to keep the images timeless.

Do Art That is Specific to the Industry You're Trying to Get Into
Each time you feel like doing a new piece for your portfolio, whether you're building one for the first time or updating one, remember that your goal is to get more work in your chosen industry. So an excellent strategy to consider before you sit down to sketch out your next masterpiece is to first determine 1.) What industry would you like to work in? and 2.) What are the key elements that define the type of art being done in that industry?

Why is this important? Because when an AD is looking at your book, he is thinking one thought: is this an artist I can use to get my jobs done? So you have to show him that you understand what he needs and that you have what it takes.

Each industry or area of the art market has different requirements, ways of working, "looks", and tasks to be accomplished. If you know what market you want to pursue, and understand what is required of you in that market, you can put that kind of work in your portfolio, and greatly increase your chances of getting hired.

There is some crossover between industries, and a well thought out illustration can tell a lot to a variety of ADs, but a laser target portfolio will serve you better than one that is more generalized.

See *SECTION 2: Getting Work: Get to Know the Market You're Interested In* below for more portfolio strategies and expanded information on this topic.

Published Work
If you've had some illustration jobs and your work has been published, you may be inclined to put that work in your portfolio. This can be an effective strategy, but it's not necessary.

On the plus side, it can instantly show an AD that you are working, can meet deadlines, etc. Other ADs have taken a chance on you and tested you out. If you worked for a big client or on a very high profile property (like Star Wars, Spiderman, etc.) this could give you some clout and impress an AD with the caliber of work you've done. Sometimes published work, even on high profile properties, can date your portfolio, so be careful.

But just because your work is published, doesn't necessarily mean that it is your best work or appropriate for the industry you are approaching at this time. Don't include it *just* because it's published. Only include it if it's good. Also, just because you're published doesn't mean an AD will assume all went well with the process, so he will not automatically hire you just because you've been published before.

My portfolio is just art, and doesn't indicate who the clients were. In many cases, you'll be standing in front of the AD as he looks at your book and you can tell him about your clients. Or you can include a list of clients in your resume and attach it to your sample packet. If you like you can include the logo of the client at the bottom of your sample along with a copyright notice.

Include Copyright Notices
You are required to indicate ownership of copyright on any reproduction of a work in order to be protected by law or as a stipulation of showing

work you did not create and do not own. So make sure you include a copyright notice in the form of © 2012 Wizards of the Coast [you can spell out copyright or use the © symbol, then the date the work was published, and the Copyright owner's name whether it be a person or a company].

You must attach a copyright notice to every image you reproduce whether it is a jpeg on your website, a posting on Facebook, or a print out in your portfolio. You can put it below the image, but I recommend you place it on the actual image so it's harder to crop out if someone intends on lifting the image, especially with digital copies.

BaxaArt Academy offers an excellent book on copyrights called *Copyright Basics for Artists* at www.baxaart.com/BAA/books_index.htm It covers all the important topics regarding copyrights in a language that's easy to understand.

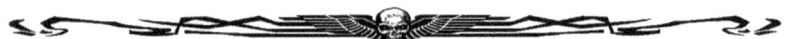

Creating Images That Catch an AD's Eye

Besides the quality of your work, there are other factors that can help make a good impression on an art buyer: professional presentation, understanding of what the industry needs, painting for print, high impact compositions, and more. In this section I'll be giving you some ideas about what ADs are looking for in a portfolio.

Put It in the Illo

Your portfolio is all about communicating what you can do to art directors. Sometimes you'll be meeting ADs face to face, but most of the time you won't, so the best way you can show him you are qualified is by putting "information" into your artwork. What I mean by that is conveying certain ideas through the choices you make when you create an illustration. I'm not talking about story ideas here. That's important too, as I'll discuss in a minute. I'm talking about ideas that show a prospective client that you have what it takes to give him what he needs.

> *The key is to incorporate the ideas you want to convey in an actual finished illustration.*

I know this sounds complicated and abstract, but it's not really. Let's say that you want to show an AD that you understand perspective, can tell a dramatic story, you have a grasp of anatomy, and that you can render well.

The wrong way is to include anatomy drawings, perceptive exercises and standing figure paintings in your portfolio.

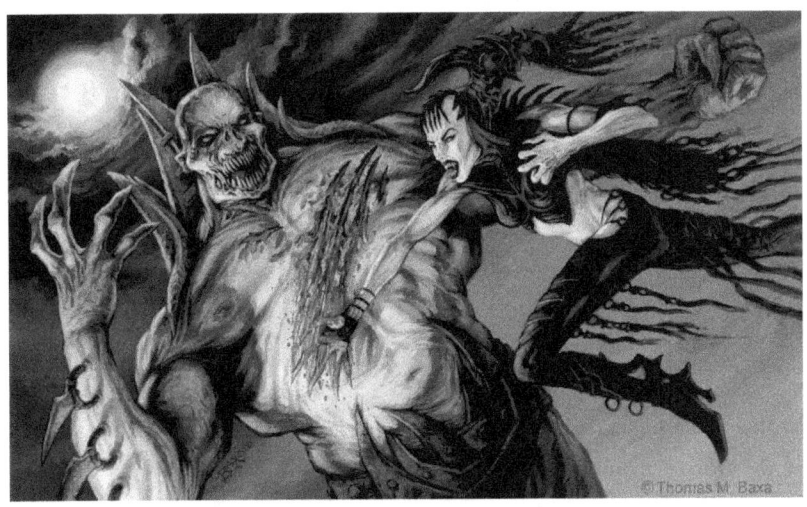

Nosferatu vs ZombieLord © Thomas M. Baxa 2012.

The right way to achieve this goal is to include all those aspects in ONE painting. It makes your portfolio strong and lean while communicating that you understand a range of ideas and can pull them together in a single image. So you can do a horizontal painting with the proportions of a Magic card illo of a female vampire in leather armor, leaping through the air to strike (action, drama, tension, movement, costume design), attacking a scantily clad humanoid zombie creature (anatomy, rendering skills, creature design) at dusk (moody color and lighting). Show the scene from a low camera angle and a tilted axis (interesting camera angles, drama) emphasizing the thrust of mass and an off-balance defender (weight, movement, tension). And there's even more going on in this painting than that.

Look at all those things you told an art director with one painting. This is how you should be thinking when you sit down to compose a new piece. What do I want to show the AD? Believe me, even with all this "thinking" there is plenty of room for going nuts and having a blast painting what you love!

You likely already do much of this intuitively and automatically. But with a little applied forethought, you can make every piece a winner, build a striking portfolio, and most importantly, get lotsa jobs!

Guess what, this is the same thought process you should apply to doing an illustration for hire as well. Bowl your new client over with a powerfully, well thought out composition every time. They can't help but be impressed and want to give you more work.

Ideas You Want to Convey

Here's a list of some of the things you want to convey to an AD in an illustration. Of course this varies depending on the needs of the position/job you are applying for. It is critical that you get to know what is expected of you, so review *SECTION 2: Getting Work: Get to Know the Market You're Interested In* below.

ARTISTIC IDEAS:
Your illustration style
For fantasy art, you should work in a fairly naturalistic style, but there is lotsa room to make it your own. What mediums do you like to work in? What is unique about the way you make images?

Strong art skills
Demonstrate your technical prowess, composition, lighting, form, anatomy, and color skills.

What you like to Illustrate
What gets you excited? Show ADs what you want to paint by putting that subject matter in your samples. If you don't really like painting elves, and you fill your portfolio with elf paintings because you think that will get you work, guess what, art directors are going to think you love painting elves and assign you elves. And then you're stuck. If you suck at drawing vehicles it will show, so don't put them in your portfolio.

NARRATIVE IDEAS:
Storytelling
Illustrations are all about telling a story, so do that. A knight just standing there doesn't say much, but a knight on the edge of a fiery precipice staving off flying demons says a lot.

Elicit an Emotional Response

Along with story, you want to imbue your illustrations with imagery and situations that make the viewer *feel* something. This can be done in an in-your-face kind of way, or very subtly.

Suspension of Disbelief

It's important to have some degree of representational rendering to the real world elements in your work, so that the fantasy elements you join with them are believable.

I discuss these art related topics in *BOOK 1: Artistic Growth: SECTION 1: Your Growth as an Artist: Learning the Fundementals*

NEEDS OF A SPECIFIC INDUSTRY:

Industry specific needs addressed

You want to have pieces in your portfolio that speak specifically to the types of jobs you want to get. If you want to do movie poster paintings you better show likenesses of actors; if you want to do children's fantasy books leave out the sexy outfits, etc.

Genre you want to work in

Choose the kind of genre you want to work in. If you have multiple interests, you can combine them in one illo, like having Predator fighting a medieval knight, or you can have multiple portfolios. Show subject matter appropriate to your genre and industry. As always, don't limit yourself too much, and don't be all over the place either.

Tell a Story

Illustration by definition is all about conveying a story with a single image. So show ADs that you can do that. That's why they're commissioning illustrations.

Before you set out to do a piece, think a little about the story around what's happening to your characters. Think of your illustration as a scene in a movie. Who is your hero? What is his background? What is his motivation? What is he wearing and what is he doing? What is the conflict he's facing? What moment in time best conveys these things?

Many of these questions get answered quickly and effortlessly because as illustrators we are used to thinking terms of story. But if you're illos are falling a little flat, you might want to give some deliberate attention to storytelling. This is a huge topic and can't be adequately explored here. You may want to analyze some scenes in your favorite movies to see what's happening, or read some good books on writing and story building.

All illustrations incorporate story, even less elaborate types of illustration like concept art. A simple concept drawing of a single standing figure can offer a lot of back-story about the character, which is a big part of good concept design.

You can imbue your concept drawings (and illos) with story by how you approach the following elements:

TELL A STORY
Costume
Level of decay, time period, rich or poor, elements available for armor, culture, intelligent or primitive, society, etc.

Stance
Is he a lover or a fighter? Aggressive or passive, friendly or threatening?

Emotion
In the pose of the body and hands, facial expression, and color choices

Background elements
Even a few simple indications go a long way to establish setting

Artistic elements
Use composition, light, form, color, line, etc. to create mood and back-story. For instance, Darksun characters should be rendered in harsh sunlight with hard shadows and warm light, whereas vampires would never be shown in this kind of lighting scheme because they can't live in the daylight.

Take a look at the illustration called *Pyros* below. What are some story ideas being expressed in this concept painting?

You can read the short story entitled *Pyros* that I wrote about this character on your mobile device or computer by going here www.amazon.com/Tom-Baxa/e/B0030NBSLY.

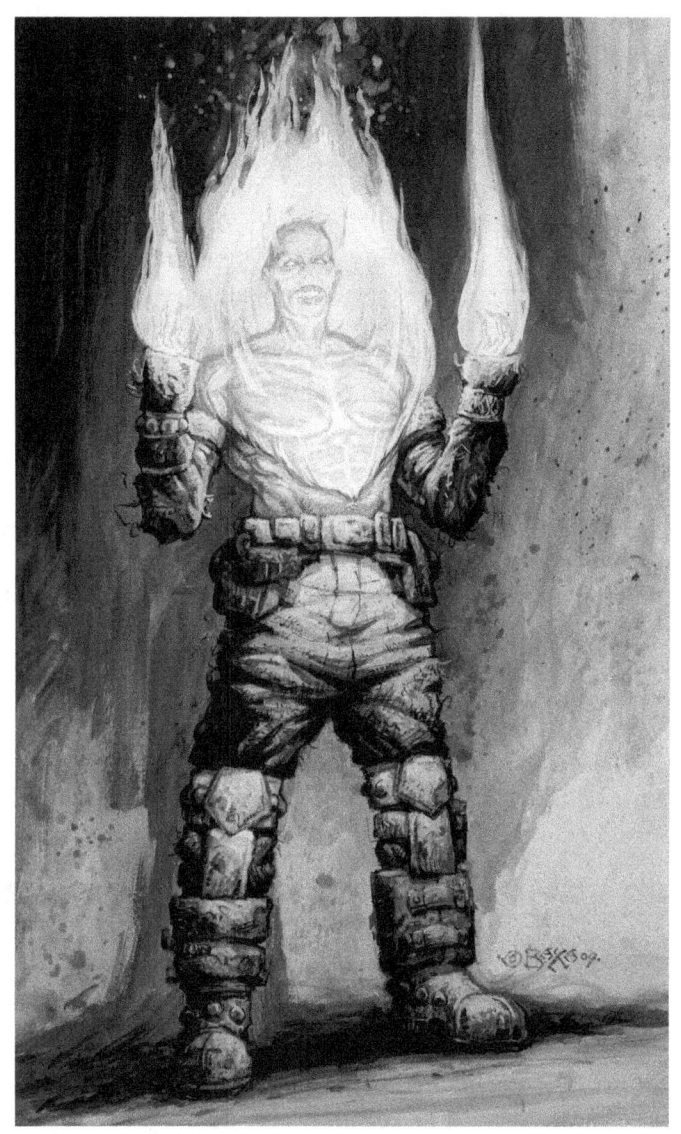

Pyros © Thomas M. Baxa 1996 + 2009.

Sit down with some of your favorite illustrations and make a quick list of all the story ideas that are put into them. Not a story that you spin from your imagination, but the story elements that the artist is trying to convey to you. You'll be surprised how many there are, and it's a good exercise that will help you think in terms of story.

Genre

Most of you reading this are obviously into the Fantasy genre. Duh. But "fantasy" can be a pretty broad term encompassing a lot of things. When you're building your portfolio, you may want to consider focusing a bit. Some of the sub-genres of fantasy are High Fantasy, Dark Fantasy, Cyberpunk, Steampunk, Historical Fantasy, Urban Fantasy, etc. You get the point. Genres can be quite varied and each have characteristics that make them unique.

The key to developing images anchored in a particular genre is to understand the conventions of that genre, the common elements used in the genre that give it its distinctive character. You want to identify those elements and include them in your illos, so an AD sees that you understand his genre and market audience.

Most fantasy art today contains elements from various genres combined together. You can have a lot of fun with this and a clever combination can turn an art director's head. Choose a main framework genre then add elements from other genres to it.

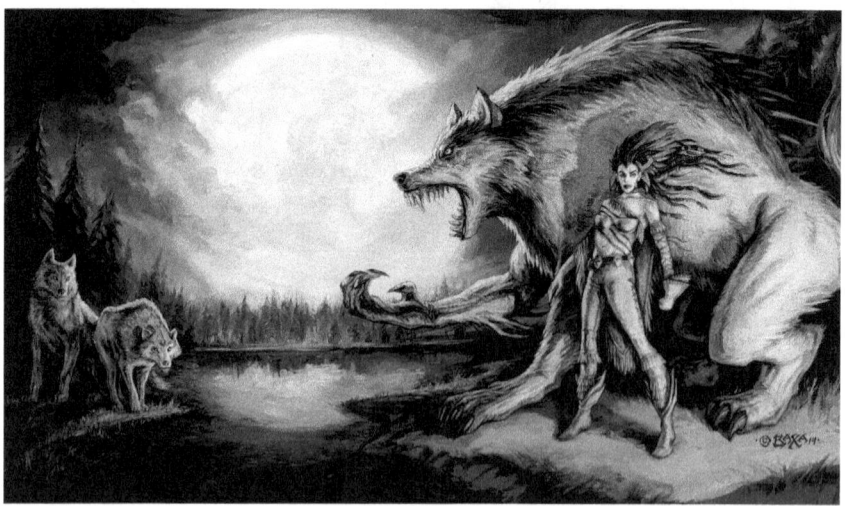

TimberWerewolf © Thomas M. Baxa 2014

Create Dynamic Imagery

You want your illustrations to jump off the page and have punch. One of the ways to do that is to create dynamic imagery, putting all your compositional tools to work for you. You can create a lot of drama, a sense of urgency, danger, and action with your choices. Just like a good movie trailer gets you excited about a film, a well thought out and dramatic illustration can make an AD stand up and shout.

Check out some of the elements in my painting *Skull Summoning* below that make this painting dynamic:

Tilted Axis
By tilting the north-south axis on an angle, the whole scene feels unsteady and in peril

Movement
A strong sense of movement creates action.

Weight and Mass
This painting has a massive thrust from right to left. This is emphasized by the tilted axis, the creature's leaping forward pose, and the sorceress's falling back pose. The creature is large and muscular, and its close proximity to the girl makes the whole scene feel cramped and gives the illusion that he's too heavy to fly.

Composition
Having the creature gating in through a dimensional door right above the sorceress creates an imminent threat and makes you think, "Look out!"

Imaginative Design
Original imagery, a cool costume, and a scary monster design add to a sense of other-worldliness, imagination, dread and creepiness, putting the viewer on edge.

Mark Making
The actual application of paint can add to a sense of motion, fluidity, and jaggedness.

I could go on, but you see how all these elements work together to create tension and drama and result in a dynamic painting that will catch an AD's eye.

Imagery can also be dynamic if it **evokes strong emotions** in the viewer. You can do this both subtly and more directly. I suggest a portfolio heavy on more direct, larger than life cinematic approach for the fantasy industry, which will grab ADs by the balls and get them excited about your work.

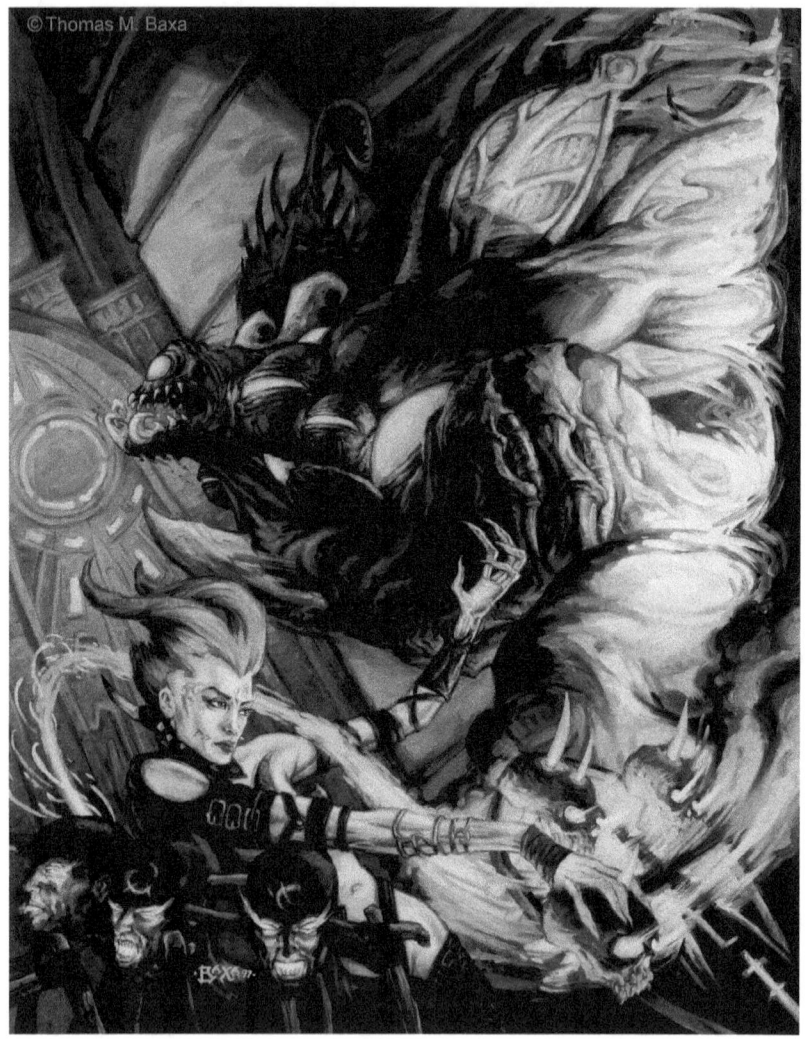

Skull Summoning © Thomas M. Baxa 1997

One of the main focuses of my Gnomon instructional dvd *Dynamic Fantasy Painting With Tom Baxa* is discussing how I created a dynamic composition and built story into the illustration with visual elements. Get the dvd at http://www.baxaart.com/gnomon_index.htm.

Mood

In line with evoking and emotional response in the viewer, you want to pay attention to the mood that the illo calls for. Dynamic paintings are often high energy and high action, but strong emotions can be brought out with other mood states. For instance, an illustration of a pensive moment for the hero before battle, or a tender moment with his queen before leaving for war can be as powerful as a battle scene. These kinds of illos focus on an intimate moment filled with emotional content.

Color, lighting, and texture can be powerful tools when trying to create mood, as well as the emotional state and pose of the characters. My *Stain of Sorrow* photo montage piece below combines the right pose with texture and color choices to emphasize mood.

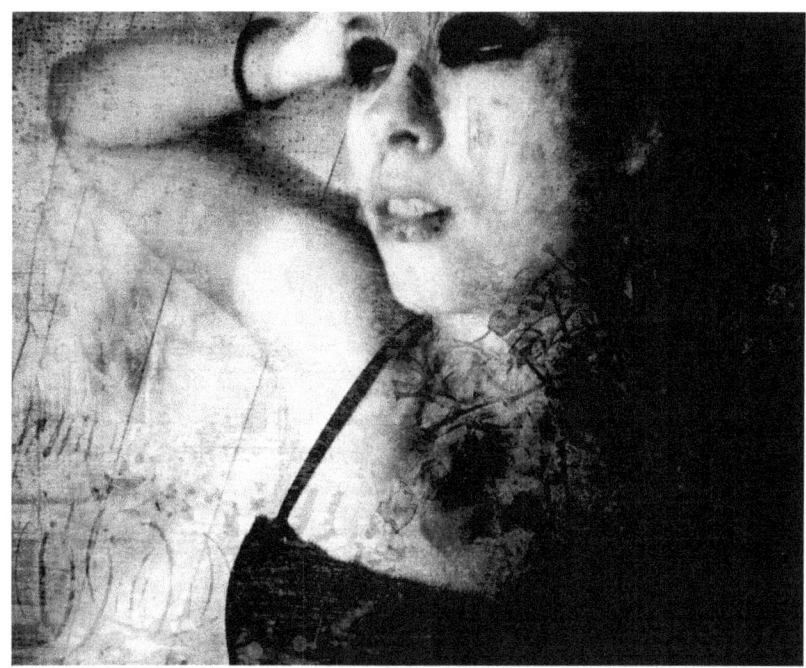

Stain Of Sorrow © Thomas M. Baxa 2011

Developing Your Illustration style

If you're anything like me, you came out of the womb with a crayon in your hand! I love making art in all forms. All people crave to be creative; it's part of the human condition. So go forth and create and have a ball!

When it comes to getting a job making art, sometimes you have to adjust your work to fit the mold of what's being done out there so ADs will hire you. That's not necessarily a bad thing; it just is what it is.

As I've said before, your main objective is to get work after showing your portfolio to an AD, so you want to do everything you can to improve your chances.

The time when begin to develop as an artist is a time of exploration and discovery. You get your hands in there and mix it up, play, create, and go nuts. Never lose that sense of wonder. But as you look towards the professional world, you may have to refine your look a bit. You can always do your personal work on the side and develop a more marketable style for your professional illustration work.

If you feel that your natural style doesn't quite fit what you're seeing in the marketplace, one thing you can try to help you shift it is to look at some of the successful artists working in the industry and borrow some elements from their work and incorporate it into your working style. I'm not saying to rip-off or mimic other artists' styles. This is just an exercise, a tool, to help you adapt your style if you're finding it difficult to do so. Soon you will feel more comfortable and your own style will flow naturally.

Stand out

At the same time you want to fit the mold of the industry, you also want to stand out. Huh? Not any easy thing to do. You want to fit the general parameters of what's being done in your industry so you can get jobs, but if you have a unique style that stands out from others, then artistic art directors will respond to that and want to work with you. Your own unique approach is what gets people fired up.

Within the fantasy genre, there's a vast variety of styles and unique voices, so there's room for yours. If you look around, you'll see how varied fantasy art can be while still conforming to industry standards.

Show Your Range

As I've said before, it's important to show a range of what you can do without being all over the map and without pigeon-holing yourself either.

You've heard the saying "jack of all trades, master of none," right? What that means is that you can do a whole bunch of things like different genres, commercial art techniques, styles, and subject matter, and you may do them well, but you are not exceptional at any one of them.

You may think that being able to do a lot of styles will give you a chance to get more work across the board. Most of the time that's not true. If you have a mish-mash of all the stuff you can do in your portfolio, an AD will just look at it and be confused. He won't know who you are as an artist and be concerned which style he will get when he gives you an assignment. So he usually won't.

The key is to focus your interests on the type of art you like to do and show some degree of range within it without going overboard, and to separate vastly different styles into separate portfolios.

A word of caution: If you don't like drawing a particular subject or in a certain style, don't put it in your portfolio. Your book speaks to ADs and if you have a lot of vehicle drawings in it, you're going to get jobs doing vehicles. Show them what you like to do and what you're good at.

But as a working illustrator you need to be flexible and be able to handle a variety of jobs, so if you fill your book with a very narrow subject, it may be hard to get jobs, especially if it's something that's not very huge in the genre. For example, if you paint nothing but dragons, you might be ok because dragons are a huge part of fantasy art, but if you fill the pages of your portfolio with nothing but illos of umber hulks, you're going to have a problem.

Plus you don't want an AD to think that all you can do is one or two things. You might get picked up to do the *Tome of Umber Hulks* which would be great, but then what? You don't want to be pigeon-holed as a one note wonder, because an AD will always think of you as the umber hulk guy and assume you can't do much else. So mix it up a bit.

So what to do? Let's start by talking about three main areas that it is helpful to show range in: 1.) Content or subject matter, 2.) Artistic style, and 3.) Disciplines you excel at.

Content

The number one thing *every* AD wants to see from an illustrator is that you can draw human beings in a naturalistic way in a variety of poses and from different angles. It also helps for you to be able to make them look attractive, heroic and regal. This is very important and should be the first focus as an illustrator and in your portfolio. They also like to see that you can show figures interacting with each other in an environment. So obviously learning to draw the figure well is paramount.

So you need to show a variety of humans, or human-like characters (like elves etc.) interacting with each other in a cool setting. This shouldn't be some stilted exercise in figure drawing. Come up with exciting ways to show off these skills. Have a scantily clad fair skinned nymph swinging a sword to ward of a muscular satyr who is trying to abscond with her in a forest glade.

Now do another illo from a worm's eye view of a barbarian leaping though the air to save a bronze skinned Mayan queen from the clutches of a celestial dragon.

See what I mean. Mix up your subject matter, characters, creatures, types of humans, camera angles and settings to covey your ability to cover a range of topics all within the fantasy genre. It's best to keep the genres related, but you can play with that as well. You can do a mash-up drawing like sci-fi characters facing off against fantasy characters.

You want to show an art director that you can handle male and females of different character classes using a variety of weapons fighting nature based creatures as well as totally imaginative creatures in believable situations and settings. If you only paint dragons, he's not going to think of you when he has an assignment for dwarves.

Style

Your artistic style is a place where you want to limit your range. Stick to one or two max. The more consistent you are, the more confident an AD will be in hiring you, because he can predict what kind of work he's going to get out of you. Remember, ADs have a job to do, and it doesn't entail giving you free reign to experiment with your style. They want to hand out an assignment and feel confident that it will come back to them in a way that they can use.

You can have different styles for different disciplines like graphic hard lines for comics, buttery oil paintings for romance covers, and a tight but painterly style for gaming art. But keep your eye on the industry you want to get into and show the right style for that marketplace.

Disciplines You Excel At

Here's where you want to show an AD the different things you're capable of. For instance, you may want to have spot illustrations, full blown cover paintings, turnarounds for 3D models, concept paintings, and other related abilities represented in your portfolio. Note the word "related." Many companies may require art in all these categories and the AD might hire you for any or all, so you want to show your range of disciplines.

You might want to divide your portfolio into sections for illustration, marketing art, and concept art, etc. to make it clear that you have multiple skills and understand the characteristics of each of them.

But if you are pushing hard to work in a particular job, let's say you've always wanted to do concept art for films, then it's best to laser focus your portfolio to just concept art and hit the production companies you want to work for.

Tips for Painting Representationally

Art directors love awesome art and often appreciate off the wall stuff, but unfortunately, they seldom have a use for it in the products they have to acquire illustrations for.

The vast majority of art being done in the fantasy field is some form of realism. So that's another thing that ADs want to see in your portfolio: Can you render naturalistically?

Painting **representationally** means to render with enough detail so that objects are portrayed realistically, in a way that closely resembles elements in the real world. So when you paint a suit of armor, it looks like a suit of armor might in real life instead of being stylized in a wacky fashion.

The terms **representational, naturalism,** and **realism** are interchangeable, and all allude to a realistic style. Of course there is a lot of leeway within the confines of realism, leaving you room to play and express yourself artistically, both in style and content. This is a broad topic and beyond the scope of this book, but here are a few tips.

Reference, Reference, Reference

I'll say it again reference, reference, reference!!! Sure there are those guys that can paint anything from their photographic memory, but for the rest of us we need a little help.

We are constantly referencing the world we live in with our eyes. Stop and soak things in, really study them, and put them into your mental reference file.

You may think you know what something looks like, but trust me, you don't. And the guy who knows more than you is going to call you on it. So get some reference to help you make what you're painting more believable.

You don't want to copy other people's fine work (like the photographers who climbed a glacier to photograph that rare flower you're about to draw). Appreciate their effort and don't rip them off – just use photos to give you more information about what you're trying to paint.

Grey is King

The world is a series of greys and browns. Don't believe me? Pull any photo from a magazine, even one that seems to have bright colors like a forest fire, and mix some oils to match the colors. You'll quickly find that the hot orange color is actually not as saturated as the cadmium orange you just squeezed out of the tube. It has some brown and white in it, as does the vibrant yellow flames that you would swear are super saturated. And they are, but not as much as you'd first think.

The more you work in color, the more you start to appreciate the subtleties of color in grey and how much color in our world is muted down, if only just a bit as in the case of the forest fire. So I tend to mute all my colors down, which helps make them feel more natural and add to the sense of realism.

I know what you're thinking, "I've seen super bright colors in nature." That's true, there are very saturated colors in nature, and they can be used in your work. But it's pretty tough to do. You have to be a sophisticated colorist to make them work. And one of the biggest problems is that some of the more saturated colors can't be reproduced in print anyways.

Also, a sure mark of someone just starting out using color is that he tends to use colors straight out of the tube, and it shows in the work because the colors are unduly saturated.

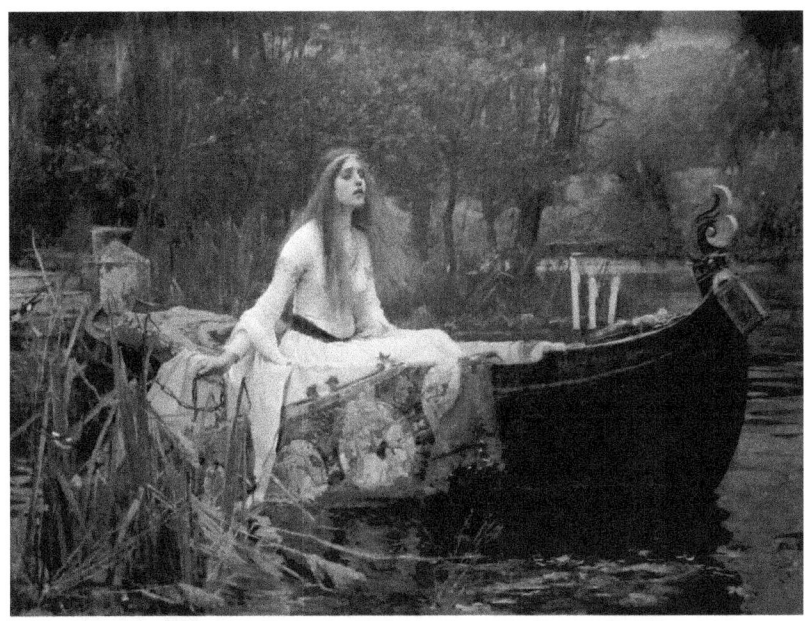

John William Waterhouse, *The Lady of Shalott.* A masterful use of muted colors.

 Eye On BAA: Color is a vast and complex topic. Look for upcoming instructional videos from www.BaxaArtAcademy.com on color theory.

Variety of Strokes
Use a variety of brushes, tools and marks to add variety to your paintings, whether they're digital or traditional. Choosing a type of stroke for water and another for rock helps capture the characteristic of the item you are rendering, and makes for a richer painting.

Level of Detail
The human eye can see a lot of detail. When you bring a heightened level of detail to your work, in form and in texture, it adds to a sense of realism. Fantasy art is marked by high detail, so it's something ADs, and especially fans, love to see. I'm not saying you have to be a hyper

realist. Just bring some detail to the main focal areas of your work to elevate the realism.

Make it Your Own
You have to be happy as an artist, so don't feel like you have to be super realistic to get work. Actually, the tighter you try to paint, the more you look like other tight painters and start to lose your individuality. There's a broad range of styles in realism, so have fun with it and find your own way of working in a representational manner.

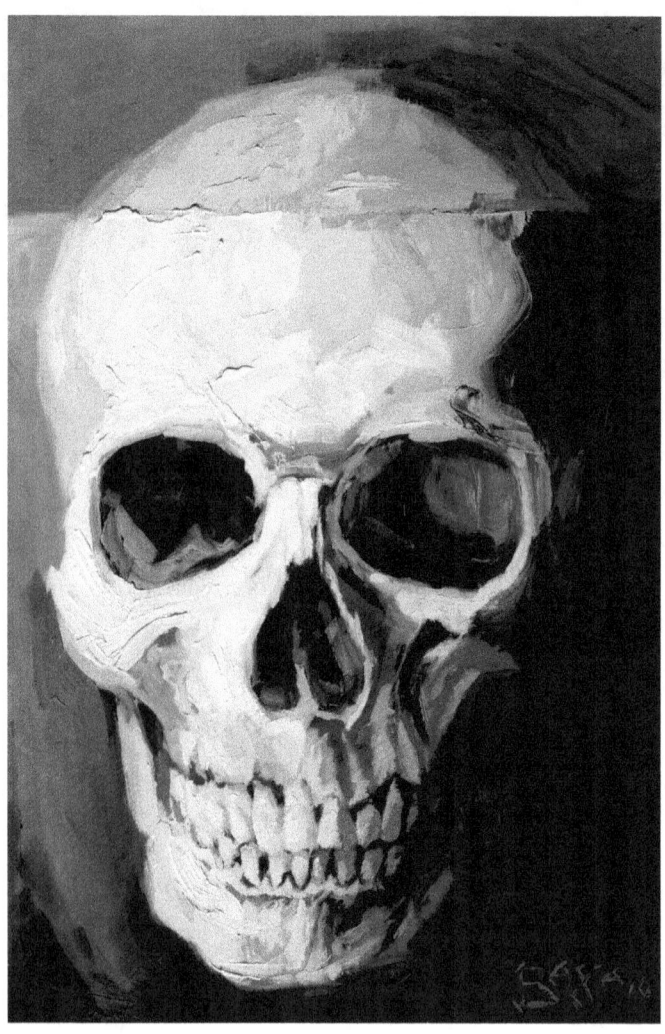

Skull Blue Pink Top © Thomas M. Baxa 2010. This painting of a skull is representational, but still has a lot of expressive color and paint application.

Consider the End Product

Art directors are also checking to see if you understand how to do artwork that meets their needs. So familiarize yourself with art being done for their industry and create portfolio pieces with the requirements of the industry in mind.

Not only do you have to consider subject matter, styles, and techniques used in the industry, you should also consider what *size* **and** *format* **the final product is being published in**. Is it being printed on high detail glossy stock (magazine), printed on coated card stock at 1.5 " x 2" (card games), is it for a printed poster (entertainment advertising), a billboard, online only at 72 dpi, etc. The output format can greatly impact how you approach a painting.

For example: if you're interested in doing art for collectible card games, which is a small format output, you shouldn't fill your portfolio with hyper detailed line work like comic artist Jeff Darrow. It just wouldn't translate to a small scale, and any AD worth his salt will recognize this and tell you that your work is inappropriate for his needs.

Is the final output being printed or viewed on a screen? This has a huge impact on the final result and how you should plan a piece. So these are some things you should consider as you plan your portfolio.

See *SECTION 3: Assignments and Doing Business: Final Art: Painting with an Eye on the End Product* below for more detailed data about producing art for print and screen output.

Sex, Drugs, and Rock & Roll

Be careful about overt T+A. If you're thinking that paintings of super sexy women are the way to catch an AD's attention, think again. A heterosexual male AD might enjoy a scantily clad barbarian chick, but a female or gay male AD might take offence. And remember, in bigger companies with a wide range of staff, there are always more women who will be seeing your art and may be in on the approval process. Keep it tasteful, always.

In the fantasy genre, the artists, animators, art directors, and other staff are more often males, who tend to be into skin, so you can usually get away with more. Plus, the history of fantasy art has set a precedent for it. But I'd err on the side of being a bit more suggestive, rather than overt.

And for chrissake, if you're going to give a woman big boobs, look at some *real* women for reference, not silicone enhanced porn stars! C'mon guys, save it for your special alone time – it cheapens your art, and ADs will pick up on that.

Age Appropriate

Also, make sure you take into consideration the product line and *targeted age group* of the product you are trying to get work for.

If you want to work on *Dungeons and Dragons*, some tasteful amount of sexy clothing is ok; if you are applying for work for adult comics – go crazy, but you'd better not have the same pieces in your portfolio, no matter how good they are, when you sit down to show your work to *Scholastic*, a children's book publisher.

This not only goes for sex, but also other subject matter that may be deemed too adult for youngsters or offensive in general like: violence, gore, drug use, bondage, rape, racism, etc.

Again, I would never presume to tell you what kind of artist to be. If you love depicting the female form and want to do nude pin-up art, have at it. I'm, once again, trying to help you get a career in fantasy gaming art, which on the whole is geared for a broad audience where these things have to be taken into consideration.

Your Sample Packet

Sample Packet Defined

It's important that you learn to market yourself. After all, if no one knows who you are, or they forget you five minutes after they meet you at a show, all your efforts will be for nothing. One of the most valuable things you can put together besides your portfolio is a sample packet.

> **Definition: Sample Packet:** A compact, usually printed, booklet with samples of your artwork; a mini-portfolio that you give to prospective clients to keep for their files.

You mail sample packs to prospective clients and you'll always want to have some sample packets and business cards with you whenever you are looking for work at a con or if you have a meeting with an AD. At the end of the portfolio review or meeting, shake the person's hand, thank them for taking the time to review your work, and hand them your sample pack and business card.

It's also the opportune time to ask the person if *you can contact them* in the future and ask for their business card. This is very important: you want to secure a way that *you* can contact them so you can follow up and stay on their radar in the future. Keep it short and sweet and say, "Thanks again, you've given me some great advice to think about." It's that simple.

The following terms for sample packet are slightly different, but essentially mean the same thing and are often used interchangeably:

Leave Behinds

This is a blanket term for anything that you "leave behind" with the client after you're done with your meeting. It's usually some sort of booklet of your art work. But it can be other marketing items with your contact info on it like a pen, a business card, a thumb drive with your art on it, etc.

Tear Sheets

This is an older term that refers to samples that you would "tear" out of a printed product. When you advertise in an art annual, you are often provided with loose copies of your pages that will be bound in the book that you can give out as samples. Publisher sometimes provide you with loose copies of a novel cover you painted. Same thing. This really isn't that valuable anymore with the advent of inexpensive digital printing where you have more control over what you print for your samples. But that's where the term came from.

Slicks and Flats

Same as tear sheets

Mini Portfolio

Exactly what is sounds like, a smaller printed version of your portfolio

Brochure

A printed document that is often one sheet of paper, printed on both sides, and folded in three or four for easy handling.

What to Include in Your Sample Packet

There are some things you'll want to consider when preparing your sample packets, some of which are critical. Remember your packet is not only a mini portfolio it also serves to cement you in the mind of the client with information and branding.

Format

Your sample packet should be no more than 10 pages showing your best work and the disciplines you can illustrate for. A great size and format is a 5.5" x 8.5" booklet (a piece of paper folded in half and center stapled). You want your packet to be secure with staples or some other form of binding. You don't want loose pages in an envelope, for example, because you run the risk of the pages getting lost. Don't make your portfolio any bigger than 8.5" x 11".

Contact Info and Branding

The whole point of your sample packet is to give an AD your contact info and connect it with your artwork, so he remembers who you are and that you would be a great candidate when a new job comes across his desk.

At the very least, you want to include your Name, your logo, title, phone number, email address, and online portfolio url in easy to read type. It's important to put your contact info on *every page* of your packet in case some of the pages get separated. If you have your contact info only on the last page and that gets lost, you're screwed.

I recommend you have a logo for your business and include that as well. Branding yourself is a useful tool to help people remember and recognize you. If an AD sees your logo on Facebook, on your website, and on your samples he's going to be more likely to recognize and remember you and your work.

Resume or CV

If you've had some decent experience, you may want to include your resume with a client list as the last page. Employers commonly ask for your "CV", a latin term *curriculum vitae (CV)* which is the same as a resume, but the term has broadened to include your resume, portfolio, demo reel, and other materials appropriate to highlight your experience and qualifications for a job.

Creating Your Sample Packet

Once you've set up your portfolio, creating a sample pack is pretty easy. It's really just a smaller and abbreviated version of your book with your contact information added. You do want to edit down the number of pieces you have in your packet compared to your portfolio, and you want it to be compact and easy to carry in a briefcase or pocket. I often put a couple illos on one page to reduce the page count.

Remember, a sample pack is not supposed to be a high end art book. Its only purpose is to help the AD remember who you are, provide him with a small sample of your very best work, and give him your contact information in a format that is easy to keep on file and not to lose.

Make Your Own

You want your samples to be as high quality as you can afford; starting with good scans of your work, decent paper, and a good printer. Digital printing is so excellent nowadays that you can layout and print your own samples on your home computer, which is what I do.

Good design work never hurts when laying out your pages either. It's cool and makes you look more professional.

Chances are all your artwork has already been scanned and color corrected for your portfolio, so that's done.

I recommend you have a cover for your packet with your brand logo, contact info and some high impact art. A cover makes your packet feel more like a book which adds perceived value and professionalism.

Next I create a template for each page with my logo, contact info, and art category (like book covers, concept art, etc.) at the top in Photoshop and plug in illos as I see fit. And I include my resume as the last page. I do have different sample packs just like I have different portfolios depending on the industry I'm shopping for work in.

My sample packet is 8.5" x 11", stapled together. It looks pretty impressive, so I often don't carry a portfolio around the cons. I just carry a bunch of packets, show them as my portfolio, then leave one with an AD when we're done talking. However, I don't recommend this if you're not a pro with lotsa stuff in print.

I use an Epson Stylus Photo 2200 inkjet printer, which uses 7 colors, archival inks, and prints up to 13 x19 sheets. This is an excellent quality printer, even though it is a bit older. The key to great color representation in an inkjet printer is having 6 or more ink colors. It helps reproduce a broader range of colors. Archival inks and paper are great for prints, but not critical for samples.

I use Epson Matte Presentation Paper (# S041062). It is an archival, acid free coated stock, with a brightness of 90, and it's thin like printer paper as opposed to photo paper. The print quality is superb. You get 100 sheets for under $10 at www.atlex.com, which has great prices on ink as well. I use a thicker stock photo paper Epson Ultra Premium Matte Presentation Paper (#S041341) for my cover. Incidentally, I also print my business cards, signage, postcards and prints on it as well.

One excellent advantage to printing your own sample packs is that you can print only as many as you need, and you can make changes easily. I highly recommend you only print a dozen or so to start, or as many as you need for a particular mass mailing, etc. You're always growing as an artist and you'll want to update your packet often, so don't get stuck with a ton of copies that quickly become obsolete.

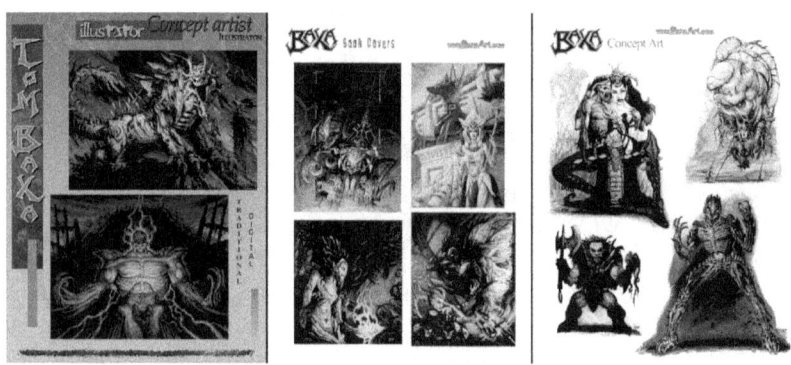

Some of my sample packet pages.

The main disadvantage to making your own sample packs is that it takes time, and quality inkjet paper and ink can be a bit costly; and it's wear and tear on your printer. You'd likely layout your own pages, being the perfectionist that you are, anyways which takes the bulk of the time, even if you have them printed elsewhere. But once the layout is done, that's it. And it's easy to update the pages if you create templates.

Use a Printer

You can create the layout files yourself, and opt to have them printed at a printer or service bureau too. Kinkos allows you to bring in a disc and will print and bind your packets for you. You can even do it online by uploading your files, have them print the job, and have it shipped to you or delivered to your local Kinkos shop for pick up. Not dirt cheap, but reasonable and pretty handy.

One of the main disadvantages to using a printer is that you usually have to do a pretty big print run, and that could leave you with too many outdated copies.

Print On Demand (POD) is a great option. Print On Demand is a printing option where you upload your layout files, usually in the form of pdfs, and print just as many copies as you need. You can always go back and print more. The main advantage is that you can print as many or as few as you need, but the per unit cost is usually a bit high and the printing quality is not always excellent for artwork. I suggest you shop around and order a copy of whatever you create to test the quality. See *Appendix A: Resources* below for some printer recommendations.

Printed Booklet or Brochure

Printed material like a booklet or brochure carries another level of prestige; it shows that you value yourself as a professional artist, and you are willing to do it up right to promote yourself. But that can be expensive, and in my opinion, it's not worth it. Let your art do the selling, not fancy expensive print runs.

A tri-fold brochure is a great option for a leave behind because the quality is high, it's compact, and you can fit a decent amount of images on them. Don't print too many because as you get better, the work you chose for the brochure will be out of date.

There are a lot of more affordable digital printers available online like www.GotPrint.com. They are excellent, have great prices, low print runs, and a variety of products you can use for leave behinds. Print On Demand may also be a good option for brochures.

Art Book

If you're lucky enough to have an art book of your work in print, you can use that as a leave behind or sample pack to solicit new clients. Just imagine how impressed an AD would be to get a copy of your book in the mail.

An art book gives you an air of credibility and professionalism that's hard to beat. It says you've been around a while and have a large body of work under your belt. Even if you self publish your own book of mostly unpublished work, it's still impressive.

Everyone loves getting a gift in the mail. They may be so grateful that they take special note of you or even contact you right away. The cool thing about a book is that the AD will keep it and keep it handy for sure! It might also go in the company's studio library for all to see. At any rate, it's an excellent tool because it will get looked at over and over and keep you in the mind of the AD when a job comes across his desk.

Here's an excellent opportunity to make use of Print On Demand. You can create your own art book and print just as many as you need to promote yourself. Again, check the print quality.

Alternative Sample Packs

Many artists choose to hand out cds or even thumb drives with their art on it as a sample pack. This has some advantages. It's compact and can hold a lot of images. You can even have a slide show, flash video, or video demo reel on a cd. This is also useful if your art is all digital and designed to be viewed in and output to a digital format.

If you do use a cd, definitely print a label with some of your art and your contact info and affix it directly to the cd, as well as on the case.

An alternative form of sample packet might help get you noticed or picked up out of the slush pile, but if it's too different, you will just get points for being clever and not much else. I don't recommend cds, dvds, or other alternative forms for your packet.

I believe that a printed sample pack is best.

Here's why. First of all, a cd can get broken or scratched in transit rendering it unreadable. There may be computer compatibility issues, although this is not really an issue much nowadays. If an AD is at a show and doesn't have a computer with a disc drive (maybe he just has a smart phone, iPad, or no computer with him), he can't review your samples until he gets back to the office, by which time he may have lost your cd. There is always the risk that he will throw your cd in the slush pile and forget to review it.

But with printed samples an AD can look at them anytime, anywhere. And the greatest advantage to printed pages is that an AD may have your packet in his briefcase or sitting on his desk, and he can glance at it by chance and *instantly* be reminded of you and your art. And boom, he's picking it up and calling you.

Same thing if he's looking through his file of "new artists I'd like to use". Your printed samples will be seen before samples on a cd.

Heck, he might even tear out a page and pin it to his cubical wall.

Bookmarked Sites and Computer Files

ADs certainly bookmark sites and keep jpegs on file on their computer of artists they'd like to use. You do too. How often do you look at them? Probably not very often.

Hopefully ADs do review their bookmarked sites when they are looking for artists, but if they have a hard copy of your packet around their workspace it gives you an extra advantage. Plus, ADs are artists and love art books and the printed matter. They love fingering through paper submission files as well. So paper submissions feel like art to them and they will subconsciously favor them.

Compact Leave Behinds

When meeting ADs at conventions or other quickie meeting opps, having a small leave behind can be a real bonus. Remember ADs might meet a hundred artists in a con trip. That's a lot of packets to lug home on an airplane. Most welcome it, some don't.

As I said 5.5" x 8.5" is good size for a sample packet booklet, and a brochure is an excellent choice as well. But it's good to also carry something even smaller that's easy to slip into a pocket like a postcard, sticker, magnet business card, etc.

Any compact leave behind should always have your contact info, your logo, and at least one piece of your artwork on it.

Compact Leave behind

After speaking to an art director in at a con, I try to give them my 8.5" x 11" sample pack. Most take it, especially those who think ahead and have something to collect and carry all the stuff they'll be handed.

On occasion, an AD will tell me that they have too much stuff to carry, or that if I hand them something they'll just lose it, and they'd rather I send them the packet next week when they're back in the office and can have a proper look and file it away. In that case, get *their* contact info.

You never know who you're talking to, so it's best to be prepared. Some ADs might be total scatterbrains. If they don't want to take your packet, that's fine.

Offer them something small like your business card or a postcard with your artwork on it. They can stick that in their pocket and go. Then do your due diligence and send them your packet as the asked.

Business Cards

Always have one, always carry them, and always hand them out, even if you are also giving out a sample pack.

They are easy to collect and carry, and many ADs either use a business card scanner or a phone app to scan them in and put you in their data base, or have a way of storing them in their office.

Just like other leave behinds, you want to include at least one memorable piece of your art on your business card. It makes it easier for an art director to remember you.

Make sure the text on your business card is legible and easy to read. Remember that the purpose of a card it to give them your contact information; design should come secondary to that objective.

Your sample pack and other leave behinds is just the start of your marketing efforts. In fact they are the bare minimum needed.

You are a service business and you have to advertise your business to let people know you are available for work. Marketing is very imprtant.

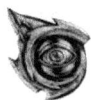 **Eye On BAA:** I'll be covering a wide variety of marketing strategies in an upcoming book. Stay
tuned to www.BaxaArtAcademy.com .

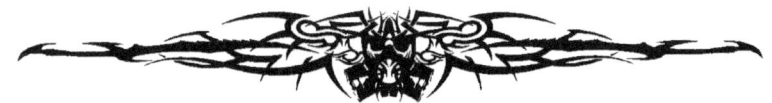

SECTION 2: Getting Work

Alright! Here's what you've been waiting for – some solid advice about how to land some freelance illustration jobs! I'll be outlining some of the **strategies I use to this day** to find jobs, track down art directors, and get my samples in their hands.

Unfortunately, nothing is guaranteed. It's up to you to hustle and put yourself out there. You can be the most awesome artist on the planet, but if you don't get out of your studio and make yourself known, you'll never get any work. It's just a fact of life. So it's a good thing you've taken your career into your own hands and bought this book!

There are a lot of factors that come together in order for you to get work. One of the main things is persistence. Never give up and keep planting seeds out there; they will eventually turn into jobs. You have to keep going out into the marketplace to find art directors that are looking for artists, or position yourself in the places they are looking.

It's not always easy to do, but this section will help tremendously. As always, it has to start with good solid artwork, so keep working on your skills and building up your portfolio.

Get to Know the Market You're Interested In

Right off the bat, let me say that the terms **industry, market, marketplace, field** and **niche** are used in this book interchangeably to mean an area of interest defined by the products that are produced and sold by them (for example: the video game industry, the CCG industry, etc.).

As a working illustrator, you are seeking out art directors of companies that are producing products in various areas of commerce (industries) that might be in need of your services.

So before you can go after work in a particular industry, you have to familiarize yourself with the kind of artwork being done in it. You have to get out there and do some research to 1.) Discover industries that you may have never thought of for work possibilities, and 2.) Get to understand the industry and how to get work in it.

Chances are you're already familiar with many of the industries that use fantasy art, because you are a fan or consumer in those industries. The following list is by no means exhaustive, but it's a pretty good list of industries you could be looking at for fantasy work:

Art Markets That Use Fantasy Art	
Gaming	Concept design
Paper and pencil	Video games (PC,
RPG games	casual, handhelds)
CCGs	Miniatures
Board games	Films
Table top	Animation
miniatures games	Toy Design
Book Covers and	Toy packaging art
interior illustrations	Merchandise
Magazines	T-Shirts
Textbooks	Stickers
Children's books	Advertising
Novels	Storyboards and Key
Non-Fiction books	frames
Key art	Graphic art
Dvd covers	Web design
Movie posters	Private Commissions
Comics and Graphic	Corporate art
Novels	And more!
Penciling, Inking,	
Coloring, Fully	
Painted	

There's lotsa room for illustrators in these markets and their sub-markets. But it's important to keep your eyes open and always be on the lookout for other areas to do work in. Often the major industries get over saturated with artists, or the trends in illustration don't suit the way you work, etc., so you need to get creative in your thinking and seek out alternative markets when you can.

As a freelancer, it's good to diversify and find work in a lot of different areas. Often smaller markets can be great because you'll be a big fish in a little pond and stand out above the crowd.

How Do I Figure Out What's Being Done in an Industry?

The same way you research anything you're interested in, whether it's schools, jobs, games you want to buy, movies you want to see, creative inspiration, etc. You're young, you know your way around the internet, so go to Google and start poking around. You'll quickly find what you need in most cases. Also, go out into the world of commerce (the stores) and see firsthand what's being released in your industry.

I go into great detail about tracking down information in the *Finding Leads* section below.

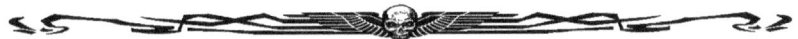

Tailor Your Portfolio to the Visual Needs of the Industry

This seems kind of obvious, but you'd be surprised how easy it is to lose sight of this important factor. Not to mention, that it's one of the top reasons that an art director won't hire you. Even if your work is awesome, if an AD's not seeing the type of work he needs for the types of projects he does in your portfolio, you're not going to get too far with him.

Let's say your book is full of beautiful full page book cover oil paintings, but the AD you're showing your book to produces iOS games and only wants digital artists. Maybe your portfolio is full of loose Photoshop character concepts, and he's looking for tight turnarounds for miniature sculptors in China.

See how a mismatch can mean the difference between a job and no job? Don't despair, some ADs will take a chance on an artist that he sees potential in. Maybe he'll ask you to do a sample for him to see if you can work in the way that he needs.

When you're thinking about building your portfolio, consider the two things I mentioned earlier when you sit down to design a piece

1.) What industry would you like to work in?
2.) What are the key elements that define the type of art being done in that industry?

What Should You be Zeroing In On?

You need to determine the key artistic elements of the industry you are looking to break into. Don't try to cover the entire industry right off the bat, you'll likely get overwhelmed and scare yourself out of making art. Start with one of the leaders in the industry and examine their product lines.

First, take a look at the common elements of ALL the product lines by any one company. Are they similar? Or are they vastly different from division to division or product to product? Then look more closely at one product line and take note of the common elements of all the images in that product line. Later you can broaden your research to other companies.

The following paragraphs cover some of the elements you should be looking at.

Tasks Required

Take into consideration the duties you'll be asked to perform in the industry jobs you're interested in. What does an AD need to see to show them that you understand the position and would be good at it?

Examples: Quick sketches, finished paintings, digital montage comps, turn-arounds, exploded views, schematics, precise renderings, etc.

Subject Matter

What type of subject matter is being drawn? This can cover a lot of ground in some industries, so you can always find something you like to draw. But some industries focus on smaller sub-genres or handle subject matter differently depending on the consumer groups they are targeting. And brands may also focus on a core audience like teens, urban kids, senior citizens, etc. and the subject matter might reflect that. Scope it out.

Genre Conventions

Consider Genre iconic elements. For example, some genre icons for the fantasy genre might be dragons, knights in armor, wizards, fairies, elves, dwarves, etc. Genre icons for sci-fi might be huge intricate mother ships, spry attack fighters, alien creatures, cool space suits, laser rifles, etc.
But be careful, ADs have seen a million dragons. Cover the standards, but do a fresh spin on them.

Art Style

What kind of art style or techniques are being used? Many industries have certain "looks" or trends in the visual style of products. It's important to be aware of these. Some industries are very strict about the style, some are not. You may need to mold your approach a bit to help you get work. You definitely don't want to be working in a style that is out dated or doesn't fit at all.

You can decide if you want to mimic current styles to fit in, do your own thing, or walk a line between the two. But always wow them with original ideas, dramatic scenes, interesting characters, cool lighting, etc.

Examples: Brushy oil painting, tight airbrushy digital, loose expressive digital, photo realistic rendering, Image Comics style inking, etc.

Dimensions

Be aware of standards in orientation (horizontal or vertical illos) and proportions. This is not always critical, but helpful.

Examples: Movie key frame art has a 16:9 aspect ratio, Magic cards are always horizontal, book covers are almost always vertical with room for a large masthead, etc.

Demographics and Target Audience

Traditionally demographics are statistics based on a section of the population according to factors like age, race, gender, ect. In commerce and advertising, the term has broadened to mean any group of people that you want to target to sell your product to. It's important to at least have a general idea what demographic a product is geared towards so you can tailor your portfolio accordingly with appropriate subject matter.

Examples: Age groups like pre-teens, teens, gen-x, millennials, thirty-somethings, baby boomers, senior citizens, dead people, newly risen, etc. Gamers, gamblers, college grads, professionals, executives, ravers, punks, metal-heads, smokers, movie goers, online communities, Barbie doll collectors. You name a group, and it's been targeted to sell to.

Make sure you understand what is required to make you a viable candidate for work with the company or industry you are showing your book to. Then show the ADs what they need to see to determine that you have what it takes to do the job. Create new pieces for your portfolio with a plan in mind based on your market research.

Let's say you want to work on Magic: the Gathering. What are some common elements of most Magic cards? Well, Magic art is a horizontal format, with a couple figures max, it reads well at a small size, figures are well lit and rendered naturalistically, there are five colors in the game and a card from that color has a lot of that color in the illustration, etc. Create a new piece the feels like a Magic card.

Look at what some of the often used artists are doing in the field and emulate their approach. Don't rip them off, study their approach and integrate it into your own style. At the very least, modeling an illustration after what the pros are doing in the industry can only make you a better artist.

Pay Attention to Trends

Pay attention to trends in illustration styles in the industry you're interested in, and adjust your portfolio if you feel it's warranted.

Now, you can't chase every new look that's being done, but if things look like they're going to stay a certain way for a while, and you keep doing art in an older style, your art will be seen as out-dated or old school, and you might not get work.

And you also don't have to jump on every new approach either. Some concept design is being done in 3D programs like Zbrush and Maya, and we're seeing more of it in the field, but it hasn't become the standard yet (and maybe never will), so it would be foolish for you to chase that trend because *it's not what's expected from industry art buyers*.

Some trends I've seen:

- Interior book illustration used to be all black and white line work, because it was too expensive to print color book interiors. But with the growth of the personal computer and digital printing, most interior art is full color and highly detailed.

- Concept art has also made a shift from traditional mediums like marker renderings and quick paintings to highly rendered mini-paintings. And more recently, with more robust digital painting tools, the trend the market has moved towards more reliance on custom brushes and photo textures.

- Movie posters, dvd covers, and cd covers almost never use paintings anymore. Get into photo montage if you want to work on these products.

Trends hang around for a while, then phase into something else. Below are some strong illustrations, that were primo at the height of their trends, and still make beautiful pieces of art, but if you were working in one of these styles today, your work would feel dated and you'd have a very hard time getting work.

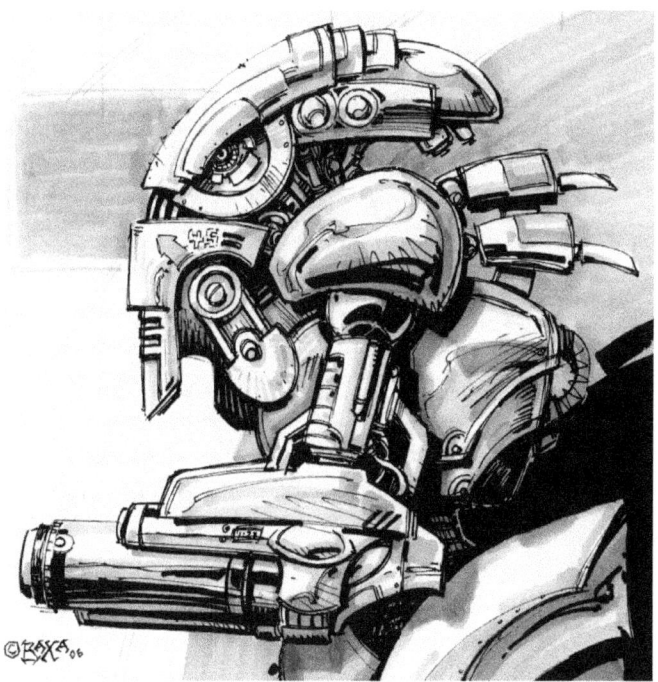

Robot 02 © Thomas M. Baxa 2006. Despite the competency of this drawing, it feels dated because marker renderings are not used much anymore for concept design.

Some Common Elements of Various Industries:

CCGs like Magic:The Gathering

Full color, digital or traditional (photo montage generally not accepted), horizontal format, iconic composition that reads well at a small size, a couple figures max, figures are dramatically lit and rendered naturalistically, there are five colors in the game and a card from that color has a lot of that color in the illustration, modern fantasy subject matter with edge.

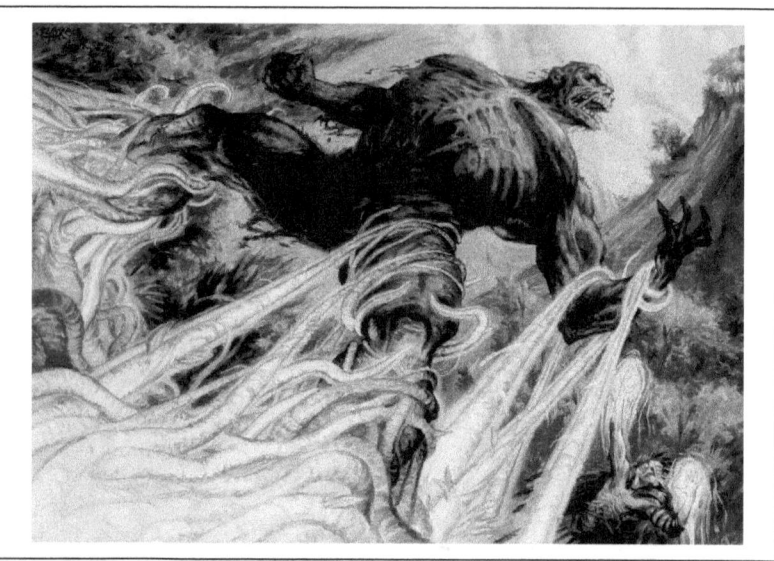

Entangled Vines © Wizards of the Coast 2008.

RPG Game Book interiors

Full color, digital or traditional, full page, horizontal, or 2 column page format vertical illos, vignette or bordered, highly detailed, naturalistic rendering, representation of the universe in characters and environment, good sense of storytelling, characters interacting with each other and the environment, traditional to modern fantasy subject matter.

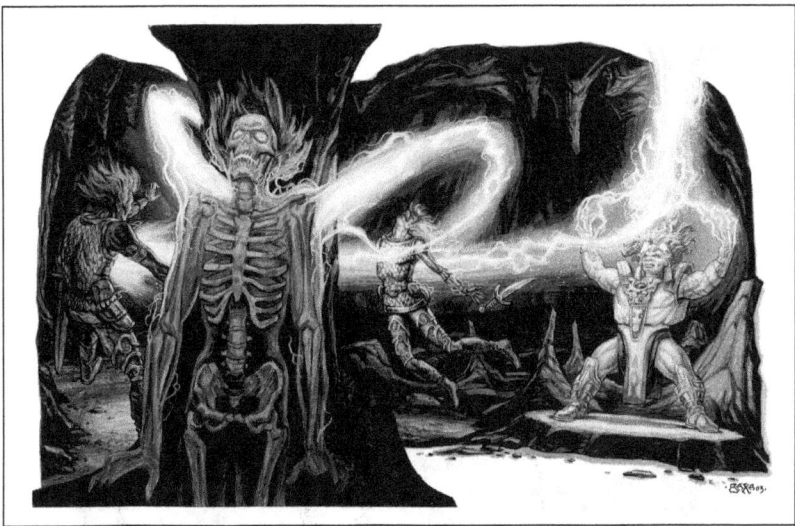

Heavenly Lighting Spell © Wizards of the Coast 2003.

Book Covers

Dependant on demographics as to type of art used. Full color, digital or traditional, usually a vertical format based on book proportions, highly detailed, naturalistic rendering (although some more experimental imagery appears on occasion), representation of the novel's characters and universe, good sense of storytelling, characters interacting with each other and the environment, broad spectrum of subject matter. Many book covers are photo montage, usually one or two figures with simple design elements. Cover designs require lots of room at the top for a masthead.

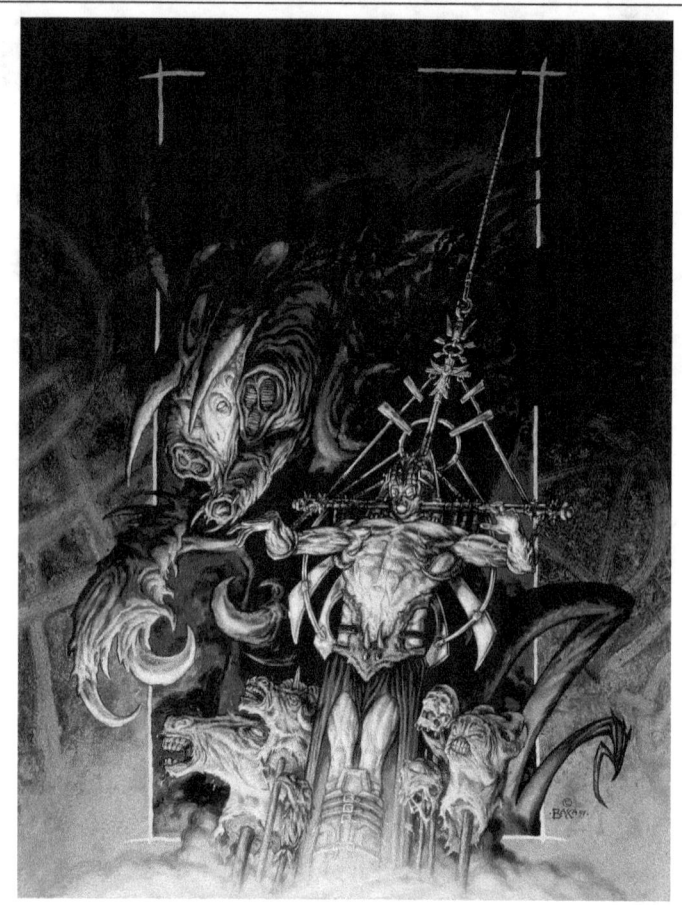

Mortal Magic © Thomas M. Baxa 1997.

Concept Art

A concept job requires someone who can generate a bunch of imaginative designs quickly, usually in full color, and often in a digital medium either painted or photo (3D renderings used as well), highly detailed, naturalistic rendering, ranging from single character designs to turn-arounds to full scenes, gear, vehicles, weapons, etc. Environmental design is needed much more than character design.

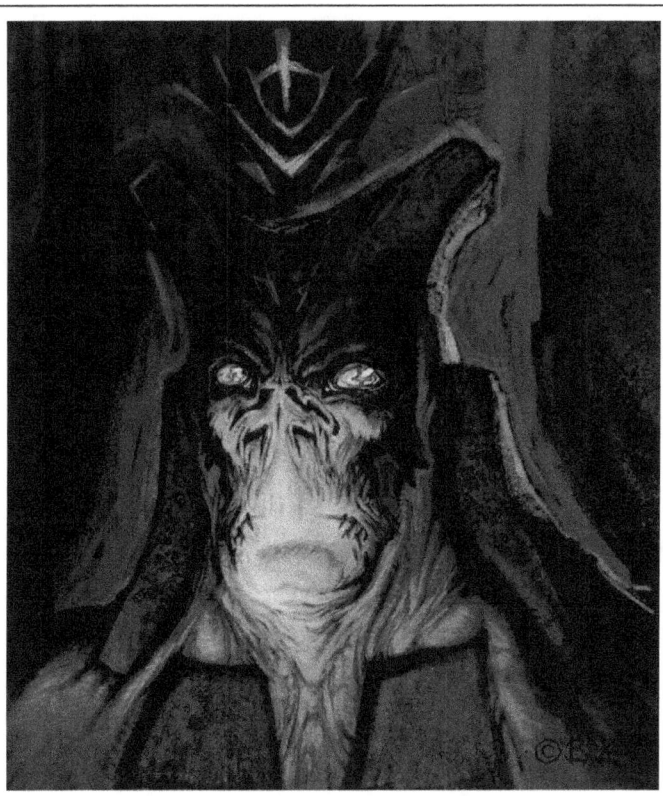

Iron Demon © Thomas M. Baxa 2010.

Miniatures Concepts

Usually requires turn-arounds with front side and rear views, b+w or color, digital or traditional, detailed enough for sculptors to have all the info they need, especially about the pose. Must take molding limitations into consideration when designing the pose and details.

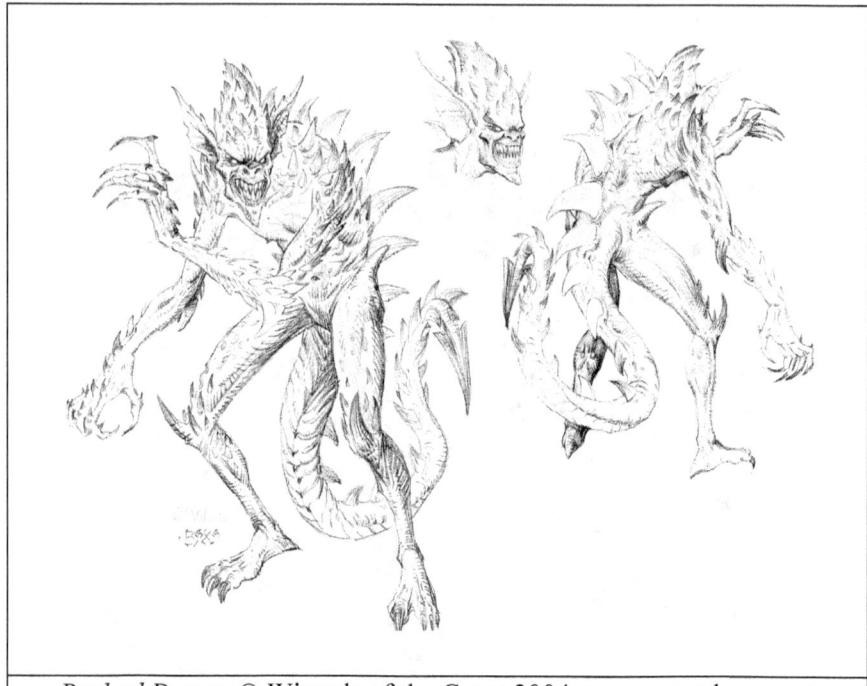

Barbed Demon © Wizards of the Coast 2004, turn-around concept drawing.

Several Portfolios

If you're looking for work in related, but different fields, an excellent solution is to have a separate portfolio for each of the fields. For example, if you're making a trip out to a comic convention, bring your portfolio of cover illustrations and sequential art. If you're going to Siggraph, bring your concept art portfolio.

Another equally successful strategy is to divide up your portfolio into sections for each of your different disciplines. Lead with your strongest and most comprehensive pieces, then put a dividing title page introducing each new specialized section (book covers, packaging art, concept design, etc.). Make it easy for AD to know what you're showing him.

What are Art Directors Looking for in Your Portfolio?

They Have a Job to Do

Art directors are looking for artist that can deliver the kind of art they need for their products. Period. They're not looking to discover the next great artist, they don't want to boost your career, they don't want to represent you, and they don't want to give you art training.

On occasion, art directors will generously give of their time to help young artist by giving portfolio review sessions or seminars. But when they are on the clock working (which includes being sent to conventions on the company dime), they are looking for artists to fill their needs.

Art directors are good at their job and are prepared when they are in a position to meet new artists. They're quite familiar with the product lines of their company and what they need to fulfill them, and they may have a current agenda for new products coming up.

They may also have directives they have to follow from upper management, rational or not, like only use digital artists, only use hip young artists, use only comic book style line art for this product, bring in only old school oil painters, etc. (Case in point: The recent ad campaign for the *John Carter of Mars* film captured the classic novel cover flavor, and that AD was looking for a specific kind of artist when he hired out for the work.)

Art Skills

Some **art skills** they will likely look to see if you are proficient at are: human and animal anatomy, rendering in a naturalistic way, dramatic lighting, interesting compositions, cool concept designs, and visual story telling.

Remember, ADs work with a lot of artists, and they won't say it, but they're usually trying to decide if you can do the job better than the artists they are currently working with. So be creative in your work and wow them!

If They Don't See It, They Think You Can't Do It

Oddly enough, sometimes ADs can be quite short sited. You can be a totally kick-ass artist, but if they don't see something specific that they are looking for in your portfolio, they may think you are incapable of doing it. Surprisingly, I hear this over and over from artists, even ones who are quite good.

It's frustrating because there are definitely elements of what they're looking for in every one of your pieces. The subject matter or your style might be slightly different than the other artists that they usually use, but you'd think they'd be able to look past that.

On the Job

John Nyberg is an excellent, well respected comic book inker. Years ago, he was on the lookout for new work opportunities, and went to one of the major comic companies with his portfolio. Now you'd think a big company AD would know better, but he asked John, a long time pro, if he would do some samples "to see if he could work well over his penciller." John replied with a kind [paraphrasing] "No, I don't do free samples - look at the last 10 years of *Nexus* to check out my inking skills." Nuff said.

I know that since you have full blown illustrations in your book, you figure that a concept AD should be able to see your strong character design in the painting. Believe it or not, they seldom do. It's a really weird phenomenon that if your art doesn't look like what they're *used to seeing* in the *same way they are used to seeing it*, they get kinda stuck and won't hire you.

But it's also understandable too, because ADs have the very hard job of trying to determine if what they see from an artist will fit their product lines and please their bosses. They're taking a big chance because they've never worked with you. There are a lot of unknown factors, and that makes them nervous. It's easier and safer to stick with the guys they can rely on and know do good work.

I can see their point to some extent. If you want a job in fantasy, and you show a portfolio of your western paintings, even if they are incredible, an AD will likely not be that excited about you.

They'll think that you're not that enthusiastic about their genre if you don't have it in your book and that you'll just take any illustration job you can get your hands on. And in their minds, if you're not into the genre, you might not do as good a job on the illo.

It doesn't matter what kind of artist you think you are or if you know you can handle an assignment, what matters is that you *show* that you can do it. You have to **demonstrate** that you have the chops, and you do that with industry targeted artwork in your portfolio

So you want to hedge your bets and create samples that are industry specific to GREATLY increase your odds of getting picked up. If you do, an AD can immediately visualize that you can do the kind of art they need, and that you understand and are passionate about their genre. Now all they have to worry about is whether you can deliver the same quality as your portfolio consistently and meet your deadlines.

Offer To Do a Sample Illo
If an AD is impressed with your art but still hesitant, offer to do a sample illo. Or better yet, ask him to give you an actually paying assignment with the caveat that they don't have to pay you if they are dissatisfied with your work. That way, even if they don't see what they want specifically in your book, but see that you have strong artistic ability, they may take a chance on you. You know you can do it, and now you have the chance to prove it because you've convinced the AD to give you some work.

If an AD sees potential in your work and asks you to do a sample, don't get on your high horse and pooh-pooh the idea. Unlike John Nyberg from the anecdote above, you haven't been a working pro for 10 years when the request came in. Even if you have had some success, you may still consider some kind of sample arrangement because you really want to work with that client, because it might lead to bigger and better things, or you really just need the work. Hey, this AD is giving you a chance at a paying job. Kindly accept and *discuss the terms* of the "sample" work.

Treat this sample work like any other job. Discuss the terms of the job and ask for a written agreement or contract.

Ask if they will be paying you to do that sample. Some guys will pay you some kind of fee for your time, as it should be. Ask if they're not paying you outright, if they will pay you if they like the work and use it. Or you can just do it for free, you have to weigh if it's worth it or not.

Inform them that you will own the rights to the piece if they decide not to pay you for it and don't use it.

> **Definition: On Spec:** Doing a free sample or an actual job for free is called doing work "**on spec.**" You are doing the work on a "speculation" basis in the hopes that it will lead to something else, usually a paying gig. There is a lot of controversy about doing work on spec and how it possibly devalues illustrators and the work they do. Decide for yourself.

There is a nasty trend out there that you should be wary of and likely avoid. Some publishers are soliciting artists to submit artwork for free for their "collections of..." books (like *World's Best Fantasy Artists, Today's Hot Digital Painters,* etc.). This is tempting, because it plays to your ego, and you figure it is good exposure and will lead to jobs. In actuality, it does very little for your career. What it does is make money for the publisher on your sweat and tears. And it leads publishers to think that they can create an art book without paying for our services. Just don't do it.

In a similar vein, some unscrupulous publishers go around asking a bunch of artists to do free samples and use the work for their own gains and never hire the artists or pay them for the work they did. So you have to be careful out there.

Finding New Leads

This is what it's all about when you're a freelancer. One of your main goals in life is to find new clients and work opportunities. A **lead** is some bit of information that may *lead* to a job, such as hearing about a new card game being assigned out, a company is looking for a new graphic designer, a lot of CCGs are being produced for iOS, etc. Anything that gives you an inkling that if you were to follow up, you might find work at the end of your search.

If you have an agent, it is his job to find leads and bring them to you, but most of the time agents or agencies don't bring you a ton of work, at least not in the beginning. So even if you do have an agent, you have to do a lot of legwork yourself as well.

Leads can come from anywhere, but here are some proactive things you can do to try and find work opportunities. Believe it or not, I still hunt down leads with these strategies, as do most of the pros I know.

Find the Art Director's Contact Info

Your main goal when tracking down leads is to find out who is in charge of hiring artists, usually an Art Director, and to get their **contact information**. You want to determine their **Name (spelled correctly), direct email address, company address, and direct phone number.** You greatly increase the odds of your envelope being opened if you address it to an actual person by name rather than to "art director", and an email address is awesome for direct contact and portfolio sending. You may also want to look for a photo of the person if you're going to try to meet them at a con.

Nowadays, email is usually the first contact. People always look at their email before they go through the slush pile. Once you've established contact, ask the AD for his number and give him a call and make a stronger connection.

See *SECTION 4: Working with Art Directors: Types of Art Directors: Different Industries Have Different Art Department Structures* below for some explanations of the different types of art directors you may be approaching.

Cyberstalking Clients: Using the Web to Find Contact Info

Obviously, I use the term "cyberstalking" in a joking way. You never want to hassle a prospective client, or any individual for that matter, on the web. What you do want to do is use the information available on the web to make contact with a company you'd like to work with.

There are all kinds of resources at your disposal like: Search engines such as Google, databases and news sites covering the industry, blogs, fan sites, Facebook, LinkedIn, company websites "about us" pages or staff listings, national news media outlets, press releases about the company or new game releases, and the list goes on.

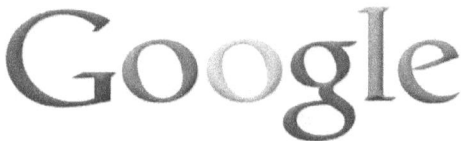

A simple Google search will likely get you what you need, but sometimes you have to get a little creative, especially when you're trying to get contact info. For example, many company websites are designed to interface with users, not pros, so the only contact info provided is for customer support for their products.

Search Process

- I hear about a product or game I might want to work on

- I Google the **product name**, looking for the company that created it

- Look at the **company's website** for their **About Us pages** which usually list owners, founding members, staff, and hopefully the art director.

- Google the **art director's name**

- Look at their **Personal Website, Blog, Linked IN, and Facebook pages** for data about them. Most guys list at least an email address on one of these pages.

If You're Having Some Trouble

Sometimes you can't find the AD's name very easily. Here are some work-arounds I try. If one of these yields results, then go back to the search process above.

Google other company principals and look at their sites. They may talk about the AD they work with.

Search for **press releases** about product releases, changes in personnel, etc. Sometimes they mention principal players.

Check for **credits** and by-lines on products or online databases like www.MobyGames.com. They often list the art director or graphic designer.

If it's a really big company like Random House, and it seems like there are too many gatekeepers or the AD is just not very accessible, find the contact info for an **assistant art director** or their **administrative assistants** and solicit through them. Sometimes you can actually reach them, or speak with them on the phone, and they will help you by finding your submission in the slush pile and looking at it and/or making sure the AD looks at it. They become your point of contact and advocate.

If all you have is a non-descript info@ email or customer service email address, write them and see if they can lead you in the right direction.

Try contacting professional organization sites or forums, or even some diehard fan sites or forums; they might have some info for you.

I'll search **Google Images,** if all I have is the game name. This brings up a bunch of images, usually in-game art and sometimes concept art for the game. First off, this gives you a look at what type of art is being done on that game/product and whether or not your style fits it. If you've used Google Images before, you know that when you click on a thumbnail it brings up a larger image and provides a button so you can visit the website that the image came from. That site might give you some clues as to the studio that produced the game.

Results can be tricky though, especially with video game companies. Often the product you are searching for is released by a large publisher that didn't actually produce the game, they just *distributed* it. You have to dig a little deeper to find the actual company that developed the game; they're the ones who would hire you.

Sometimes you'll discover that a video game or mobile game is really just a digital version of an existing card or board game, and is being "ported" to another format. Usually in that case, there is little to no opportunity for work because the artwork used in the digital game was originally produced for the card game, and then also used for the iOS card game. So you have to go back to the CCG company and find work on that level.

Go to Local Shops

This is an excellent place to find leads and it's a lot more stimulating than sitting in front of a computer. I often go to the local gaming and comic shops to peruse new products being released that might grab my interest as something to do art for. Go to the stores and poke around. It's fun and that's where the products are!

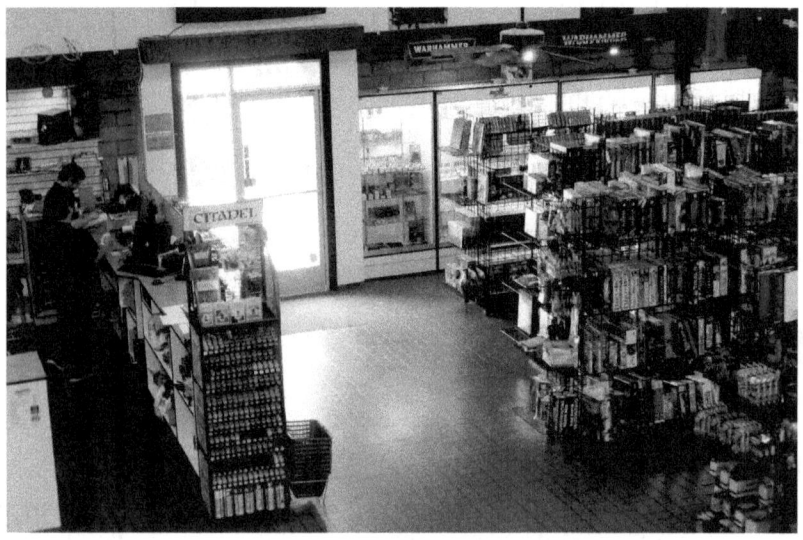

Emerald Knights game shop, Burbank, CA.

Check out any store that might carry merchandise you'd like to work on such as: Gaming shops, comic shops, video game stores, magazine stands, book stores, board game shops in malls, cd stores, head shops, skate shops, surf shops, clothing stores like Hot Topix, Halloween stores, you name it.

Try to think out of the box here a little too. Everything you see out there has some kind of imagery on it that was concepted and created by an artist. Figure out where you can insert yourself in that pipeline.

You're looking for product lines that fit your interests and your style of art. Bring a small note pad, or take notes on your handheld device when you find something interesting. When you do, scour the product for the kind of contact information you need. Every product will have the company's name, and sometimes their address or website. Books often have more information listed inside.

You might think that if a product is already on the shelves it's too late. Wrong. If a product sells well, the company will make sequels, expansions, additional products, merchandise and more to keep their profits flowing. So it doesn't hurt to send your samples to a company regarding products already available for sale.

Where to Find Contact Info:

On Product Packaging

Companies brand themselves and want people to find them, so they will always have some kind of info on the outer packaging. You can always find the company name and usually a website, and sometimes an address. All good places to start your search.

Even merchandise has some form of data on it. I once saw a patch in a store for sale and the creator's website was printed on the packaging, so I was able to research him and the licensing company that created the patch from his art.

Credits in Books

Open up the book to the credits page, usually one of the first few pages, where they list all the people who worked on the product. Art directors and graphic designers are often mentioned by name.

In Magazines

If you want to do work for an industry magazine or be featured in an article, check their credits page. Magazines also have articles about principal players in the industry and advertisements from companies in the industry that may provide leads. Try other media outlets such as newspapers, trade journals, etc.

Shop Owners and Patrons

Ask the shop owner for information. These guys are often very knowledgeable and deeply involved in games and other products they are selling. Sometimes patrons of the shop can help you out as well, and they enjoy talking about the games they love. This is your chance to meet some like minded people and do some personal networking.

Bookstores

Go to brick and mortar bookstores like Barnes and Nobel. They have tons of resources for you in a wide range of industries that may pertain to you. They sell products, they have magazines, they have reference books and directories about businesses, they have books about your favorite industries, and more.

Look for specialty bookstores as well. For instance, Los Angeles has a bookstore called Samuel French Bookstore that specializes in the film industry.

Also try ancillary products for leads like "the making of" books, video game strategy books, biography books about industry leaders, how to art mags, mags about the gaming industry, trade magazines which are filled with products you want to work on and the key players responsible for them.

The Artist's Market Book

You should click on this link and buy the *Artist's Market* immediately at Amazon http://amzn.to/1m6b7Va! It's that good. Released and *updated* yearly, this reference book has tons of places where you can send your samples and comprehensive data about what kind of art they're looking for as well as current contact information and submission policies. This book will give you lots of ideas and options for work, and it has insightful articles from industry pros on both sides.

Equally useful is the *Writer's Market*, because they list all the major and independent publishers. There are other books in the series as well including: *Novel & Short Story Writer's, Children's Writer's and Illustrator's, Photographers, Literary Agents*. Look for the deluxe versions which come with a cd of all the listings or free access to their online database, which makes searching much easier.

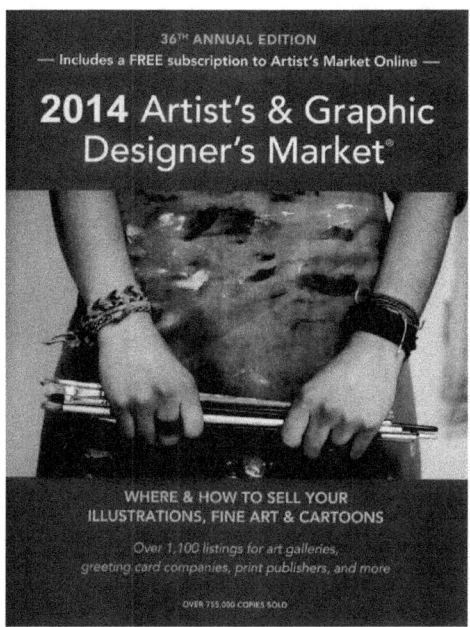

Artist's & Graphic Designer's Market

Keep Tabs on Working Artist

A good place to find leads is an artist's list of clients on their website. Often artist will, in an effort to look professional and impressive to prospective customers, have a list of the clients and companies they have done work for. Take a look at client lists, take note, and Google the companies. You can also find a list of clients on their resume if posted to their site.

Follow pro illustrators on Facebook, Twitter, or their blog. Artists love to show off their latest pieces of art. In their posts, they often mention who they did the painting for. Back to Google.

Keep Tabs on Companies

Companies are constantly marketing in one form or another. This is your opportunity to keep track of their product lines and key players. Check their websites for press releases and info about new products, new product lines, expansions, mergers, personnel changes, etc.

If you know some people at the company, you can get some inside information from your colleagues as to work opportunities.

Larger companies often have in depth articles by staff members, forums, job listings, and blogs that contain a lot of useful information for you.

Job Boards, Listings, Forums, and Sites

Company Sites

Company websites almost always list jobs they have available and submission policies. Most of these are for full time positions and short term contract work. These listings are always up to date.

Job Listing Sites/Forums

An excellent resource for finding jobs are job listing sites. These sites collect data from all kinds of industries and sources. You sign up, and indicate what types of jobs you're interested in, and you can search their site or have job listings emailed to you on a weekly basis. Start with sites that cater to the industries you are interested in, then branch out. The great thing about these services is that they are pretty all encompassing, so you don't have to go to a bunch of company websites to find job listings, you get them all from one source.

Make sure you check the date job listings were posted. Listings can stay up a while and may be out of date. Don't waste your time applying to old listings.

Industry News Sites

Industry news sites like www.Gamasutra.com and www.CGSociety.com, etc., also have job listings in your marketplace specifically. There are all kinds of job finding services out there. Try: www.ConceptArt.org, www.LinkedIn.com, and www.Freelance.com.

One of the drawbacks to these sites and services is that there's usually a lot of competition for one position, but you need to try anyways. Google around and get creative about where you look for opportunities.

Also, if you notice that a company is listing all bunch of positions, it's obvious that they are crewing up for a new game or division. So even if you don't see the specific listing you're looking for, you may still want to send them your work, or investigate further.

List Services

There is a really fantastic service out there known as a **list service**. You pay a fee and a list service sends you a list of leads in either digital form, like a Microsoft Excel file, or as pre-printed labels (that's why some list services are called "label services"). The reason they send you labels is to make it easy on you. The stickers are pre-addressed to the contact person and company you want to send your samples to; you just stick the label on your promotional material and pop it in the mail.

A list service may have many lists like 150 record companies, 220 galleries in the Northwest, greeting card companies, licensing companies, artist reps, book publishers, etc. They've done all the legwork for you and keep the lists current, so it's a good deal. They have leads that would take you months to collect the hard way.

This is such an awesome service, but as you would expect, you have to pay for the leads that the company has tracked down for you. Some lists are expensive, but some aren't. Hunt around. Part of the problem is that you may buy a list of 200 leads, but only 60 of them ever use fantasy art, so you are essentially paying for leads that will never apply to you.

The killer is the cost of printing and mailing out all those sample packs. It would behoove you to start small. You can get 1000 postcards printed fairly cheaply, and the postage is less than a letter or manila envelope. Send a postcard or brochure first and see if anyone's interested, then you can follow up with your full sample pack.

Another similar service is an **email or eblast service**. You pay for a company to send your email (eblast) to a list of leads that you pay for. The huge advantage to this is that you can send hundreds or thousands of leads out without any printing or postage costs. Not all leads are viable, but if you cast a wide net, and get a few solid new leads or clients, then it's worth it.

Langerman Lists used to be the standard, but are now defunct. But here are some art related list services you can investigate:

- www.ArtMarketing.com
- www.agencyaccess.com
- www.creativeaccess.com
- www.adbase.com

Conventions

Cons are a great place to find leads. Go to them as often as you can. See *SECTION 2: Getting Work: Pounding the Pavement: Conventions* below for a detailed look at working conventions and other types of events for leads.

Ask Your Friends and Pros for Leads

Artist Friends

We artists always chat about what we're working on. When I catch wind of a possible new client or a job from a friend that might be big enough for me to get in on, like a big card set, I'll ask my friend how he got the job and if he'd share the AD's contact information with me. Your friends want to help you, so just ask.

You and your artist friends can be a great resource for each other. You can share experiences you had with a particular AD or company: Are they paying on time? Was it a good gig? Is there more work coming?

Some illustration jobs are too big for one artist, and a company will use several or many artists to get the project done quickly. For example, CCG card sets often have 150-350 cards and use about 80+ artists to get them done. If you and your friends call each other when a set is being jobbed out, if there is overflow work, or if an artist dumped out and they need someone else, then you both benefit.

Working Pros

Go to conventions and artist signings and pick the brains of professional artists. They've all been where you are, and likely still are. We're always all looking for leads. Now they might not give you the names of their best clients, but most guys will be happy to talk with you about all kinds of art and business related topics. It's up to you to ask the right questions.

Art Directors

Ask ADs that you currently work for if they have any assignments sitting on their desk that need doing, or if any new projects are coming up that you might be right for. Bigger companies have several departments and ADs. If your AD doesn't have anything for you right now, ask him if other departments have jobs and if he'd be willing to recommend you to his colleagues.

Be careful though. Make sure you have some level of rapport with your AD before asking for favors. Also, some ADs can be very protective of their artists and not want to share, so this could possibly bother them a bit.

Take Control
Even though your friends love you, they may hold information close to the vest until they make initial contact and are assured some work before they pass leads along to you. It's understandable. We're all trying to make our nut. Your friends won't tell you that – instead they'll guise it by saying that they want to check it out and see if it's a good company and the job is worth doing, because they don't want to pass you a bad lead. Well, they're not responsible for me. I'd rather follow up on the lead and determine for myself, based on *my* criteria, if a job is right for me.

I never like to leave my fate in the hands of others. Everyone has their own way of communicating with ADs, and I don't want someone else's approach to hinder my chance of making a new contact.

For example, let's say I have an artist friend that is more ginger than I am when he tries to get work. Maybe he sends *one* email with his portfolio link, and waits. If the AD doesn't contact *him*, he drops it. Or he might wait too long to follow up, if at all, and by the time he does, the job will likely have been assigned and I've lost my chance at it because I was relying on him for a referral.

Another problem with this scenario is that if the new AD doesn't like your friend or his work for whatever reason, he will be unlikely to accept referrals from him, and you're dead in the water again. Your friend may drag his heels for any number of reasons, forget about the lead until it's too late, get sick and not send an email, etc.

It's best to get the AD's contact info yourself, so you have the opportunity to act on your own behalf in your own time in your own way.

Agents
Having an agent or agency represent you can have some great advantages. But there are some disadvantages as well (see pros and cons list below).
In general, an agent finds you jobs to work on and in exchange for his efforts takes a percentage of the fee, usually 30%. So if a job that pays

$18,000, they get $6000 of your cash. You have to decide if the jobs they are bringing you warrant their commission. If they are bringing you high paying jobs that you would have a near impossible time securing on your own, then it's totally worth it. In the example above, you still made $12,000 on one job!

One thing that agents often want from you is a percentage of all the work from clients you already have or secure on your own. The thinking there is that through their hard work, they have opened doors for you and boosted your reputation. As a result of your boosted fame, that they helped create, they are entitled to a cut of all jobs you do. Again if they are kicking ass for you, there is some merit to this claim. However, that is seldom the case.

You should fight against this kind of arrangement. You built your own reputation, and deserve to keep the full fees from the clients you've secured over the years. Weigh the options very carefully. You can also negotiate your arrangement and agree to something like: if the agent brings you $30,000 worth of work for two years then they get a percentage of new clients you secure.

Pros
- Someone else is out there helping you find work
- They can open doors that you don't have access to
- They have relationships with industry people that they've cultivated over years of hard work
- They often have experience with contract negotiation
- They act as your agent when negotiating, you don't have to be the bad guy
- They deal with the business stuff, like invoicing, collecting your money, contracts, etc.
- Can usually get you higher paying gigs
- Can sometimes negotiate better terms like more rights, royalties, etc.

Cons
- Not much work at first, if ever
- Percentage may be high, usually 30%
- Percentage of all your work vs. just leads they find
- They may require an exclusive relationship (you can't have multiple agents)
- They collect all monies from clients, take their cut, and send you your part. This can be dangerous because you don't have control over your own money.

Be Realistic About Agents
Agents are not your personal career managers. They aren't spending every minute trying to find you jobs so you can pay your rent. They're trying to keep their business going and pay *their* rent. The way they do that is to have a lot of artists in their stable. If each of their many artists

have a couple jobs, the agent makes good money and he's happy. But unfortunately, the individual artists each only have a couple jobs in a year and need to supplement their income elsewhere. That's just the way it is.

Over time, as you build a reputation, the agent will recommend you more and you will get more jobs from them per year. That's the plan anyways.

Ask for Referrals

All agents are not created equal. Check for information about their reputation online and with other artists. Also, ask for a list of referrals and call them to see if some of the artists he's representing are happy with the job he's doing.

Submission Guidelines

Now that you have the contact info of some companies you'd like to work for, what's the next move? Obviously, you want to let them know that you're an awesome artist and you're available for work.

Always start by checking each company's submission guidelines either on their website or in the *Artist's Market* book before sending samples. Some companies are very specific about how they want to receive submissions. For example, some companies don't want mailed samples and will just throw them away because they don't want to file them. They might prefer digital submissions via a web form or email, which usually has a specific set of rules about attachments, etc. Some companies, like ILM, actually require you sign a release before you send them your samples.

You want to make it easy for them, show them that you did your research, and that you can follow instructions. If you submit in a form that a company does not prefer, your work may never get seen.

Contact a Company By Mail

I like to mail a physical sample packet to prospective art directors. As I've discussed before, printed samples are the best form of submission. Since you are sending a mailer, you can include a cd of your samples as well as print-outs if you like.

You want to mail your package directly to the art director **by name**. If you just can't find his/her name, address the package to "Art Director" c/o Company XYZ.

I've mailed 9" x 12" envelopes with my sample pack, a business card, and a return self addressed self stamped envelope (SASE). A SASE makes them more inclined to send you back a feedback letter. Some companies have form letters with check boxes for the reasons they might not use you at the time. You want feedback, and you want to make it simple for them to give it to you. You might even consider including your own feedback form. No one likes to get a rejection letter, but at least you might get some feedback on your work and you'll know that your samples got seen.

Sending an envelope and large sample pack can be costly. You may want to start with just a postcard or a brochure.

The Dreaded Slush Pile

Mailing your sample packet directly to an art director is a good bet. But the biggest problem is that ADs are often so busy that when they get what looks like a submission packet, they set it aside to look at another time when they have spare time. Sadly, they almost never have free time, so your awesome art packet sits in what's referred to as **the slush pile**.

Some ADs will try really hard to find time to go through their slush pile, but at the end of the day when they are beat, it's often the last thing they want to do. A lot of times, they'll wait a couple months until a project ends, then go through it. They will go to the slush pile when they are actively looking for new artists, but usually not before.

But you have to send your samples anyways and hope they get seen. I've gotten calls or emails seemingly out of the blue on samples I sent six months to a year prior. That's why you have to keep planting seeds out there all the time until some come back to you.

Stand Out Submissions

If your work is strong, you'll get the call, but an AD has to see your work first. You want to do anything you can to get an AD to open your samples right away.

If you're sending a 9" x 12" in envelope, make sure you have a large label with some of your artwork on the front. I print my own labels with my Epson on Epson photo quality self adhesive sheets (#S041106) which has the same excellent print quality as the papers I use. This way the AD sees your art right away and may open the package. You can also use window style envelopes that show what's inside. Also try fluorescent orange envelopes or labels to stand out.

You can buy postage stamps with your own image on them. This is an excellent opportunity to brand yourself and get an AD's attention (www.Photo.Stamps.com, www.PictureItPostage.com).

You're an artist, get creative! Create some kind of unique packaging. I know a guy who sculpts toys and his "business card" is a small blister packet with two plastic mini figures with his contact info on the packaging. But if you're on a budget, this kind of flashy marketing can get expensive.

Brochures or postcards are an excellent option. They are compact and light, saving on postage. Postcards have a lower postage rate than letters and no envelope is required. And an AD can see some of your work right away and be more inclined to look at it right away. Bingo!

Use Tracking So You Know It Got There

If I really want to make contact, or there is a pending deadline for submissions, I send my samples in a way that can be tracked like USPS Priority mail, UPS letter, or FedEx letter. If you send a FedEx letter to an AD by name, it is likely that it will hit his desk and he (or his assistant) will open it right away. Obviously, this is a quite an expensive option, but it can help you reach that elusive AD.

Contact a Company By Email

Email is usually your first opportunity to contact an art director off a new lead. Mainly because email addresses are often readily available on the web and company websites.

It's easy and safe for an AD to read emails. He's not looking a person in the eye, so there is no pressure. Art directors welcome email as a primary form of contact. The problem is, ADs probably get 150 + emails a day of all kinds. It's overwhelming. Once again you have to try to get their attention any way you can.

The best time to email an AD is early Tuesday morning. If you email on Friday or the weekend, by the time they get into the office on Monday, your email will be 50 emails down the list. The AD will start going through his emails, until he has his first meeting, phone call or other business. He will try, but may not look at emails again that day. And as you know from your own experience, once emails start getting far down the list, it might take quite a while to get to them. ADs have way too many emails on Monday, and it's also the day they have a lot of department meetings and other pressing business.

Tuesday morning they are fresh, and determined to get through emails. Ping them at the start of the business day to increase your chances.

Email Submission Etiquette

Due to worry about viruses, some companies are very specific about what kind of electronic submissions they will accept via email. Some companies won't accept email submissions at all. Some won't accept attachments or embedded files. Some won't accept HTML emails. Some only want jpegs or pdfs. Check the company's submission policy either at their website or in the *Artist's Market* book before sending samples. If you don't see a policy, send what you like.

Some companies have filters or virus software that screens incoming emails. If your email violates their filters, sections will be removed (like attachments), it will go to a spam folder, or it will be deleted altogether.

You may want to send a simple email introducing yourself with your portfolio link and ask the AD if you can send an attachment.

As per usual, you want to be friendly, energetic, cordial and professional in your emails. Your very first contact should be kept on a professional level. Be direct and to the point. ADs will only quickly scan your emails and will never read a long diatribe. As you form a relationship with an AD, your emails can get more casual and personal.

Make sure you use grammatically correct English in your emails. Use a spell checker and eliminate errors. Don't use emoticons or text-speak like "lol". Save that for your personal time. ADs will think you're some kid who doesn't think he's worth the time for you to write complete sentences.

The good thing about email is that you can ping an AD periodically to try to get their attention. But you don't want to overdo it. If you email someone too often it'll just piss them off, and it's too easy to be moved to their blocked sender's list and get shut out.

What to Say in Your Email
When submitting samples for the first time, you want to BRIEFLY introduce yourself in this email cover letter. Avoid a block of text by making each paragraph only one or two sentences. First introduce yourself and make yourself sound impressive, maybe mention a big client you may have worked for. Mention what kind of work you do and in what medium or software, and any other info that might be pertinent to the position you are applying for.

The main purpose of this email is to get the AD to click over to your online portfolio or open your pdf.

My name is Tom Baxa and I'm a 25 year veteran fantasy illustrator with major clients. I work mostly on [impressive titles or companies]. I've also done some concept design for the film and video game industries.

I am an expert at traditional mediums as well as digital illustration (Photoshop, Painter)

Say how you heard about the company and say how much you'd love to work with them and in what capacity (contract, full time, part time).

I saw your listing on ConceptArt.org for a full time concept artist. I'd love to join the team at Company XYZ. It's always been my dream ...

Most email submissions allow links. But if your link is excessively long or has a lot of weird numbers in it, they might be hesitant, so have a clean URL link to your portfolio. If it is at a respected and well known portfolio site like ConceptArt.org or DeviantArt.com that's ok too.

Please take a look at my portfolio at my site: [online portfolio URL]. I've also attached my resume and some samples.

Wrap it up with your contact information.

Feel free to contact me at this email or call me at 555-555-5555 (Los Angeles).
Thanks for Your Time, Tom

Call to Action

Notice the **call to action** statements in my cover letter. They are lines that prompt the reader to do something, to take some action. I use the terms "Please take a look at my portfolio" and "Feel free to contact me" essentially telling them what to do and to go do it.

In follow up emails, you want your email to be enticing. Don't just say "I updated my website" because that's not very exciting. Give them a more intriguing reason to click over that tells them something about it like "Trolls and dragons wreak havoc in the new illos posted to my World of Warcraft gallery."

Always close your emails with a call to action to click on your link, contact you with jobs, or respond to a question you pose to them.

Stand Out Submissions Via Email

Like I said, ADs get a ton of emails, so you want to grab their attention so they read your email. Write a crazy, **catchy subject line** like "You're not going to believe this!", or "Can zombies really do that?" Mark the email as **high priority** in your email client program, which puts red flag or exclamation point or something next to the email in his inbox.

Have and **interesting email address** (but make sure you don't lose your branding). Try something like BaxaBlastsBoogiemen@gmail.com or BlackLegionBAXA@yahoo.com. Make them chuckle when they see your email address in their inbox list.

It's important to have a combination of submission formats to improve your chances of getting through. So I like to have links in the body of my email, a signature at the end, attach a pdf sample packet with my resume, and embed a jpeg of my art.

THOMAS M. BAXA

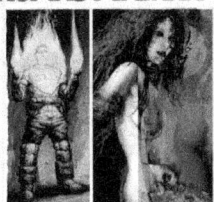 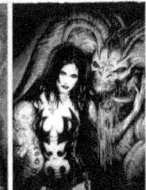 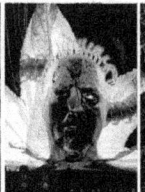 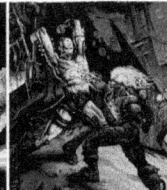 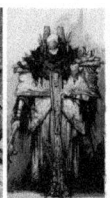

Fantasy Art   Book Covers   Traditional   Digital   www.BaxaArt.com   **ILLUSTRATOR**

Thomas M. Baxa
www.BaxaArt.com
www.facebook.com/baxaart
http://baxaart.blogspot.com/
Baxa Books on Amazon
www.cafepress.com/baxaart
http://stores.ebay.com/BaxaArt

My actual email signature. It catches the eye, shows my range with cool images, and tells the recipient where he can see more of my art, learn more about me, and buy my products.

After my succinct email text, I embed a jpeg sample of my work the "insert picture" function in Microsoft Outlook. This gives them a good sized image to see immediately to grab their attention.

Then comes my **"signature"** or contact information. Most email client programs like Microsoft Outlook have an option to add a signature to the body of your email. It is automatically added to the end of every email you send and is a great way to market yourself. A signature can include an image and text. Use both: have an image of your artwork and include your contact info and links to your portfolio sites as text. Some elements of a signature, like the image, cannot be seen if the recipient does not accept HTML emails; that's why it's important to have text as well.

You don't want to include personal information like your home phone number or address in your signature because you never know who will see your emails or who they might be forwarded to.

Html Emails
Any email with clickable links, colored fonts, inserted pictures, etc. are actually HTML emails. But HTML emails can be super awesome and look just like a website. They full of pictures, active links, even video. This can be a great way to market your wares. Again, keep it simple and quick to digest. There are services available that can help you easily format your own HTML emails with templates and tutorials.

Since some companies don't allow HTML emails to pass through, you should also include some *actual text* in the email. If you have only images or words in a jpeg image, they will get blocked and the email will appear blank after the images are removed.

Email client programs can be set to receive or not to receive HTML emails. If not, only plain text gets through. Usually anything that you have typed in, even if it was enhanced by HTML colors, fonts, etc., it will be pared down and sent through as boring old text, and links are not clickable. But your words will go through.

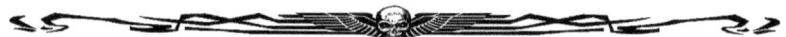

Contact By Website Submission Forms

Some companies have submission form pages on their sites. If you've been applying for full time jobs lately, you're very familiar with this format. Basically, you fill in information they request on a web form, which usually includes an opportunity for you to upload a resume or art samples in the form of a Word document, pdf, or graphic file formats.

Wizards of the Coast allows you to email samples and a portfolio link to artdrop@wizards.com.

And here are some submission guidelines for some of their products:
http://archive.wizards.com/Magic/magazine/article.aspx?x=contactinfo/artsubmission

Along with submission guidelines, some companies might also offer guidelines for an "Art Test" to see if you can follow art direction or come up with a creative solution that makes you stand out in a crowd. Here's Wizards of the Coast's Dungeons and Dragons art test page:
http://www.wizards.com/dnd/feature.aspx?x=dnd/feature/dndarttest

On occasion, art directors take their own initiative and offer a way to upload samples to them with submission forms. Keep an eye out for them. They're a direct pipeline right to the art director.

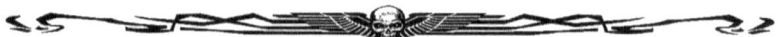

Pounding the Pavement

People Remember People

As with any venture, it's always to your advantage to deal with people one on one in person.

ADs are people, just like you, and people form lasting memories more quickly about people they actually meet and talk to, than to a jpeg sent over email. There's something about the human condition and the need for interaction and connection that makes it so. If you make an effort to talk to art directors in person it says a lot about you: you're a go-getter, you're confident about your work and your ability to do the job, you're a pro, and you're not afraid to put yourself out there.

Personal contact is ALWAYS the best way to make a lasting impression.

When you meet an AD, he has a chance to get a sense of you. Even if he doesn't know it consciously, he's sizing you up to see if you're a nice person, if you'll be professional and easy to work with, if you're confident with your skills and if you know your stuff. He'll be much more apt to take a chance on you if he gets a good read off you.

Even if you're a little shy and not that great with people, a personal meeting is still better than just an email relationship. Trust me, it will help an AD remember you and your artwork over the tons of submissions he gets in his email inbox. Even if he doesn't think you're ready, when you come back to meet him at a con next year with all new and improved samples, he will have remembered meeting you before and appreciate your determination, and growth.

Personal contact will ALWAYS give you the best chance of being hired.

Going out and meeting ADs face to face is a **major part of getting work** and should not be ignored, even if it scares you. Grow a pair and get out there! Start small and work your way up. It's not as scary as you think. You can do it! Especially if you're armed with more info from this BaxaArt Academy book!

Networking with People

Aside from just meeting art directors, it's important to hang with other artists and people in creative industries. It feeds your soul. You hear about what's happening in the industry, you learn about new leads, you see what other artists are doing to promote themselves, you see their work and get inspired, and so many more things that are healthy for you as an artist, a professional, and a human being.

When you're looking for leads, some companies simply don't have a website, or don't want to be contacted that easily. For example, I was recently trying to track down this particular illustration agency to see if they'd like to represent me, and believe it or not, I had a hell of a time finding a website for them. They don't have one. It's all but unheard of these days, but it does happen, especially with service business where personal contact is critical to the way they do business.

In this instance, you have to network with folks that are in the industry or know someone at the company so they can introduce you and give you a foot in the door. You may have to do some good old fashioned personal networking to get to them.

Some fields don't have art books or websites about them. For instance, entertainment advertising is an especially elusive profession to learn about without actually talking to people who are involved in it.

You can start by searching the web to find pros that might be talking about their experiences then email them and ask them for advice. Get to know some people, form friendships, and get involved in the industry you love.

Socializing

One of the cool things about conventions or other company events is that there are always parties, dinners, and time at the bar socializing. Just hanging out and talking art is a great way to make friends, have a ball, and cement some connections with people you'd like to stay in contact with.

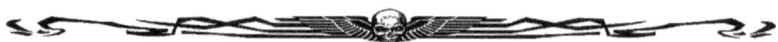

Conventions

Fortunately, the fantasy illustration industry is a pretty friendly and approachable community. One of the very best ways to try to get work doing fantasy art is to go to the conventions that are dedicated to fantasy and related products.

> **Definition: Convention:** A convention (or con) is a gathering of like minded people and fans of a particular interest organized for them to express their enthusiasm, share the thing they love with others, and meet people that work in that area of interest.

Conventions can be super geeky and focused on a very small segment of pop culture like a specific TV show or game, or it can center around very serious matters or professional endeavors like environmental pursuits, political interests, medical research, etc. Almost every hobby, TV show, and subculture or has a convention of some sort. If you're into something, it's likely there's a convention for it out there somewhere.

In order to draw a crowd and enhance the experience of attending one of their shows, organizers of conventions have vendors selling genre related items and special guests from the genre to give talks or sign autographs. There are art shows, author readings, film screenings, costume contests, gaming and more. They also invite industry pros, like artists, to show their stuff and engage the fans. Conventions have a little bit of everything and their focus is usually attendee enjoyment.

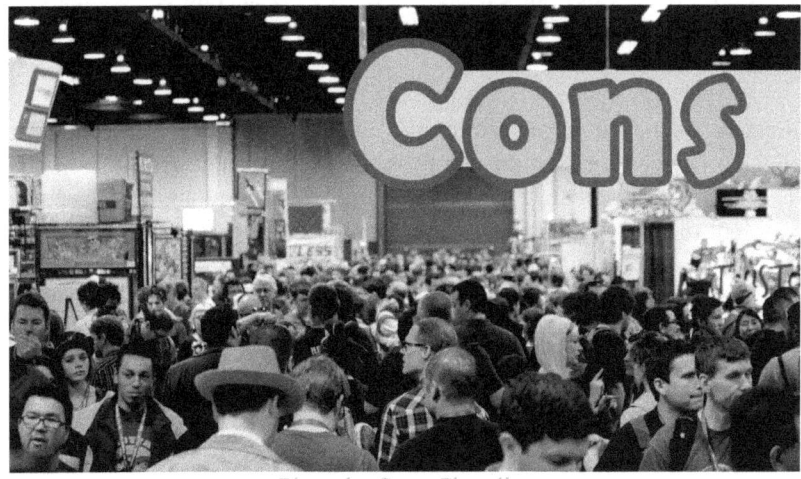

Photo by Sean Chandler

The term convention is sometimes used to also mean other types of get-togethers as well, but it's not always an accurate definition, even if the event has similarities to a con. For example, trade shows have a vibe similar to conventions, but are usually much more focused on commerce and doing business. Job fairs have lots of seminars and speakers and companies marketing themselves, but the main focus there is for attendees to speak with potential employers.

I've done a lot of fantasy conventions over the years and it's the main place I look for work. But more recently I've been exploring other industries that might have cross-over fans to fantasy. You may want to try other types of shows like comic, Goth, tattoo, horror, fairy, fetish, Renaissance fairs, street fairs, Hollywood shows, Star trek cons, etc. to find areas that you might enjoy doing art for.

 Eye On BAA: I plan to release a comprehensive guide about working the conventions, filled with strategies for getting face to face with people in charge of hiring artists. Stay tuned to www.BaxaArtAcademy.com.

Portfolio Reviews

This is the main reason you're at a convention: you want to show your portfolio to art directors to get feedback on your art and to be considered for future work. This process of showing your portfolio to art directors is called a **portfolio review**.

Companies send their art directors, editors, producers, and other art buyers to conventions to do portfolio reviews. They are there to help young artist to get feedback, but the main reason they are there is to find new talent to hire. This is an invaluable opportunity to meet ADs face to face.

Portfolio reviews take place in different areas at a show. Sometimes there are dedicated areas where a bunch of companies set up to do reviews. Sometimes they are held at individual companies' booths. Sometimes the procedure is very strictly formatted, and sometimes portfolio reviews are quite impromptu.

It's a good idea to do your homework before the show. Check the con's website to see if there are scheduled times and places for portfolio reviews. Also check the websites of some of the major companies you want to talk to, to see if they will be hosting portfolio reviews at an upcoming show.

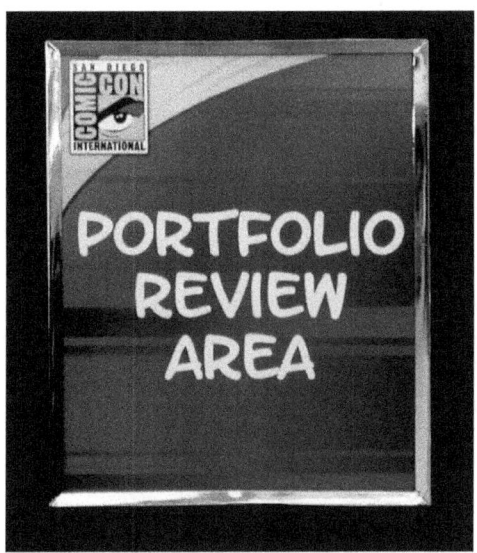

For instance, San Diego Comiccon (SDCC) has a complete listing of what companies are going to be at the show reviewing portfolios. It's a good idea to check their website before you go to the show and see who you want to talk to.

One of the bad things about this great opportunity at SDCC is that because the show is so huge and there are so many attendees, there can be very long lines for each portfolio review. We're talking an hour or more wait, so it's best to figure out who you want to talk to first and get in line early. If you have time, you can see some of your secondary choices.

If you're trying to see Pixar or Blizzard, you're going to be there a long time, but some of the smaller companies might have much shorter lines. And the waits are much, much shorter at smaller cons.

In addition to scheduled portfolio reviews, you may want to contact a company AD that you know is coming to the con ahead of time and set up your own private meeting.

How It Works

You *can't* make appointments in advance, not even at the show; it's **first come, first served**. But some portfolio review sessions have a time limit and do FILL UP, so you may be required to get on a **sign-up sheet** in advance of the portfolio review start time. In fact, this is usually the case, so check the guidelines on the con website or con booklet, and check out the portfolio review area *as soon as you get to the con* to see if you have to sign up.

Some of the big companies have tricky guidelines that may not be well publicized, so make sure you check with them or you may miss out. If I recall, Marvel and DC had sign-up sheets at their respective retail booths in the main hall at SDCC and they filled up fast.

Before the show, you would have already checked the con's website for portfolio review times, locations, and requirements, so once you're signed up you show up at the review location and get in line. I recommend you show up *ahead of the scheduled time* and get in line early, especially at a big show or for a highly sought after company.

If you're seen early, you have more time to get in another line and talk to another AD. Another advantage to being seen early is that the AD is fresher and in a good mood, and more apt to give you a solid critique. Plus, you might get more time with him in the beginning of the day than the end where they tend to speed up in an effort to get to everyone.

Regardless, you're not going to get too much time with this sought after AD, so make the most of it. When it's your turn, you meet the AD, open your portfolio, and work your magic. When you're done thank him for his time and input and give him your leave behinds.

Talking to Art Directors, Artists, and Other Pros

That's the basics of how a scheduled portfolio review goes. Obviously, there is much more involved when you are actually standing there with your book open. This next section is going to give you some tips on talking to ADs and other professionals at a con, whether you have a planned appointment or if you're walking up to them cold.

You must take full advantage of any scheduled portfolio reviews. But another big part of working a convention is walking around looking for opportunities to show your work to ADs, talking to other artist for feedback and insights, and networking with industry professionals.

Unfortunately, it can be pretty tough to find ADs at a show, especially a big one. Your best bet is to go to a company's booth and ask if the art director is around. Ask for him by name if you know it. If not, ask the person who you're talking to what the AD's name is, if he is at the show, and when might be a good time to catch him at the booth. You might even find out that he has scheduled portfolio review times. Make note of what you learn and come back later to meet the AD.

You'll also want to talk to professional artists at the con that work in the industry you'd like to break into. Most shows have an **artist alley**, which is basically a section of the con devoted to working artists and pros sitting at tables showing and selling their work.

This is a primo opportunity for you to ask pros questions about breaking into the business, look through their portfolios to see how they present themselves, get a sense of the kind of work that is currently being done in the industry, and ask them to give you some feedback on your artwork.

Working illustrators totally understand how tough it is to put yourself out there. They've been there. They're still there, so they're usually open to talking to aspiring artists. After all, guys who've come before them helped them out with some advice, so why not pay it forward.

The convention guide book is a good resource for finding out if a person you'd like to talk to is going to be a the show, whether or not his company is there, if he has a booth or artist alley table, if he's doing signings, etc.

First Contact
It's time to approach that AD or pro and chat them up. The first thing you have to remember is that they're at the show to do whatever business is in their best interest, which may or may not include talking to young artists (although most will be happy to accommodate you). However, they may seem preoccupied or a little distracted, especially if you catch them off guard or when they're not sitting down, calm, and ready to receive visitors.

Don't take that personally, and don't let it slow you down. You have an agenda too: to do your best to get in front of some art directors so they know that you're an up-and-comer with great art skills and a good working attitude.

The key is to be humble, kind and professional. But also be confident, and show your work with pride.

Unless you're in a scheduled portfolio review, you want to **ASK** if the person would be willing to take a look at your portfolio and give you some feedback. This is not only common courtesy, it's also strategic. If you catch someone off guard, they're not going to be in the right frame of mind to give you well-meaning and constructive feedback. So give them an opportunity to say yes or tell you when would be a good time to come back.

First Contact Don'ts:
- Don't ask them when they're busy with customers/clients
- Don't ask while they're eating lunch
- Don't ask them for a crit in the 2 minutes they have before they have a meeting
- Don't interrupt them if they're talking with someone
- Don't follow them into the toilet

Everyone working the convention is there to do some kind of business, usually selling or promoting their products or services. You don't want to interfere with that.

If you walk up to an artist at a con, and he's busy trying to talk to potential clients at his booth, he'll likely not be very receptive to looking at your portfolio right then. Hang for a minute to see if there's a break in the conversation, but if it looks like he's deep into something, go on to someone else or circle around when he's freed up.

If this is your ONLY opportunity with this person, take it, even if it's only for a minute. It's not ideal, but sometimes, especially with more famous people, you might not get another chance to talk with them, so seize the moment. At least you'll get a chance to meet them, hand them your sample pack, and make some personal contact.

Face to Face
You've been working hard at your art, I know you have! And hopefully you've combed through *SECTION 1: Your Portfolio*, followed my advice, and the artwork in your portfolio is blowing away the AD who's looking at it!

When you get your portfolio reviewed by an AD, sometimes he just looks and tells you if he can use you or not. But most often he offers you a critique. So I urge you to refer to the critiques section in *BOOK 1: Artistic Growth: SECTION 1: Your Growth as an Artist: Critiques – Don't Be Scared.* There is a lot of good info on how to go into crits, how to listen, and how get the most out of them.

While the AD is looking at your work, you can tell him a little bit about yourself, some experience you may have had, discuss your work, or tell him how much you'd love to work with him and his company. A little enthusiasm goes a long way. But you don't want to talk his ear off. Give him a chance to soak up your work.

And don't forget to LISTEN. You're standing there to get advice from this pro, so don't blow that. Take in what he's saying to you and respond to any questions he may ask you. When it feels right ask *him* some questions.

Some Things to Ask About
- Listen carefully to the feedback on your work, and ask questions related to your artistic growth
- Portfolio questions like: Do I have enough pieces? Do the pieces I chose say that I can do the job? What's missing?
- How do I break into the XYZ business?
- Who should I show my portfolio to?
- How do you find new leads?
- How do you find ADs at a big show like this?
- Would you hire me based on what you see?
- What can I improve on to get hired?

A portfolio review is an opportunity to have a **conversation** with someone who can give you work. Talk to him like any person you're courting. Sell yourself on why you'd be a great candidate for the job. Tell him that you're a hard worker, a fast conceptualizer, you love creating stories with your images, you believe in his product, you understand that it's your job to give the client what he needs. Anything that will convince him to take a chance on you.

A Note About Handheld Device Portfolios
It is becoming more and more acceptable to show your work to an AD on a handheld device. If that's all that you happen to have with you when you bump into an AD, then by all means show them your work on your handheld device.

But remember, ADs are art lovers. They like looking at, holding, and touching art. So showing a physical portfolio is still your best option. It gives ADs an opportunity to have a tactile relationship with the work that puts them in a subconscious pleasure zone. And they relate that pleasurable feeling with you and your work.

It's also easier to hold and view sometimes mainly because you can take in illustrations in their totality. Everyone can turn a page, not every AD, especially older pros, are fluent using handhelds. You want to make it easy for them to flip through your book. If they are fumbling with it, they may feel stupid and now you've alienated them.

Don't ever sit there and flip the "pages" for them. That will definitely make them feel stupid, out of touch, and you'll have to get close to them and invade their personal space – another no-no.

If you do choose to show your work on handheld devices, choose a descent size tablet like the iPad, not a small smart phone. You want to show your work as large as possible to make a strong impact. Zooming in and out to explore a piece on a smart phone is not the way to represent your art.

And for god's sake have your portfolio in its folder, separate from your personal photos, cued up and ready to go immediately. Nothing is more infuriating than waiting for you to fumble through thousands of pictures until you finally find your artwork. It's unprofessional.

When is it best to show your work on a handheld device? When the company's products exist only in a digital environment, like an iOS game for the iPad. Showing ADs your work on the device that they are developing for can have its benefits. They get to see your work exactly how it will appear if they publish it, and they get to enjoy your work glowing off a backlit screen which is always pretty.

Make Contact
As the crit is winding down, you want to do three things: 1.) Sincerely thank them, 2.) Give them your leave behinds, and 3.) Get their contact information. This holds true for any meeting you might have, be it at a con, or elsewhere.

Be genuinely grateful that this person has taken the time to look at your artwork and give you some constructive criticism, words of wisdom, and valuable insights. I continue to be grateful for the help my mentors, peers, art directors, and artists have given me over the years.

As I discussed above in *SECTION 1: Your Portfolio: Your Sample Pack* you want to give them your sample pack, business card and other leave behinds so they have a way of remembering you and contacting you in the future if they want to work with you.

Art directors or other people in power positions are sometimes reticent to give out there contact information. If at all possible, DO NOT leave a meeting without securing some form of contact information from your prospective employer so YOU can contact HIM in the future.

Ask for the AD's business card. He'll often give one up if you just ask, especially if he works for a company. Make sure it has an email address and hopefully a phone number as well. Ask him if it's ok if you can follow up with him a couple weeks. If he is local to where you live, ask if you can come and see the shop/company/studio some time.

More Info to Prepare Yourself
You'll want to read *SECTION 4: Working with Art Directors* below for more insights into how ADs think and how to talk with them. Here's a list of some major conventions worth checking out:

CONVENTIONS
    Comics and Pop Culture
- **San Diego Comiccon, WonderCon, APE** www.comic-con.org
- **Wizard World Comiccons** www.wizardworld.com
- **New York Comiccon** www.newyorkcomiccon.com
- **Comikaze** www.comikazeexpo.com
- **Star Wars Celebration** www.starwarscelebration.eu
- **Creation Conventions** (Star Trek, Twilight, Xena, more) www.creationent.com

    Fantasy Art
- **Illuxcon** www.illuxcon.com
- **Spectrum Live** http://spectrumfantasticartlive.com

    Gaming
- **Gencon** www.gencon.com
- **Origins Game Fair** www.originsgamefair.com
- **DragonCon** www.dragoncon.com
- **SPIEL/Essen Game Fair** www.internationalespieltage.de

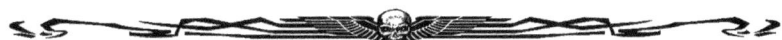

Other Places To Meet ADs
Job Fairs, Professional Conferences and Trade Shows

Conventions are often open to the public and designed for fan fun, even though a tremendous amount of business is going on at them. They are a healthy mix of professionals, fans, retailers, shoppers, artists, guest speakers, stars, pop culture, and companies showing their wares.

Some of the other large events you might want to pursue are often more specific in their purpose, and are not always open to the general public. They can be excellent places to pursue leads.

Many trade events have high entry fees, but some allow professionals to attend the show for free. A great way to avoid high fees is to volunteer. As a volunteer you might be required to do just a few hours of work each day in exchange for a free pass to the event. Check an event's site for attendance guidelines.

Job Fairs

Job Fairs, Job Expos, and Career Expos are large events where employers send recruiters to collect resumes for prospective hires. The expos have booths or tables of companies, schools, and organizations that can help you with career planning, etc. Many career expos also have speakers and seminars for your further education, and they almost never have retail vendors. Some cover all kinds of jobs, and some are more industry specific.

The people you encounter at the tables are recruiters from the human resources department. Their main function is to gather up resumes and give you some basics about the company or the positions available. I recommend you ask questions and try to get any info you can about the company structure and the name of the art director you'd be following up with. You'll seldom meet an art director or other creative manager at job fairs. But they may be hiring for art jobs, so just turn in your sample packet, resume, CV, or reel and say thanks.

Some large companies will host an open call job event. It's an opportunity for their human resources department to handle a large amount of applications on neutral ground. Sometimes the event is just for their company, or it's part of a larger job fair type show. For example:

"Walt Disney Animation Studios is hiring and we are headed to Vancouver. If you are interested hearing about our upcoming job opportunities, join us at Hotel XYZ Ballroom A. No appointments needed - drop by anytime between 10:00 - 7:00 p. m. where we will be accepting reels, resumes, and portfolios."

Professional Conferences

A **professional conference** is an event or expo where professionals from a certain industry gather together to share topics related to their field, explore new advances, educate each other, network, etc. They can be local or national, small or big.

These events have lots of seminars, lectures, and training, and focus on the profession rather than actually selling of goods or services. However, large expos will often include other perks, activities, or vendors for the attendees to partake of. Many of the companies that sell to the profession, like computer companies, will have booths to inform the attendees about new products or even be there selling products.

The terms *conference*, *trade show*, and *expo* are often used interchangeably, so you have to do a little research into the specific show to see what kind it is, what it has to offer, and whether or not it's right for your goals.

Some Pro Conferences
- **Siggraph** http://s2013.siggraph.org Has speaker panels, an art show you can submit to, animation screenings, and major companies collecting resumes like a job fair.
- **GDC** (Game Developer's Conference) www.gdconf.com. Video game industry pro conference where new games are being debuted, industry pros share tools, technology, knowledge, and news.
- **E3** www.e3expo.com Video game industry, similar to GDC
- **Gama** www.gamatradeshow.com Focused on RPG, CCG, minis, and other board games

Professional conferences can be an opportunity to show your book around and network with industry pros at all levels. They usually don't have portfolio reviews, but if you ask around you may find art directors, editors, designers, producers, etc. that would be willing to talk with you and may have information about jobs and freelance work.

Some conferences have speakers or even a panel of pros who were brought to the show specifically to look at portfolios. A private company might set up a conference because they love fantasy art. They'll bring in top talent to speak and also give you an opportunity to show your portfolio to a panel of professional ADs, and art buyers in different markets.

On the Job

Looking for leads, I attended IMATS (International Make-Up Artist Trade Show) a trade show dedicated to make-up artists and special effects make-up for films, with my portfolio in hand.

I found out that one of the greats of special effects make-up, Greg Cannom, was at the show so I tracked him down and showed him my work. As luck would have it, his studio was working on a big monster movie and needed some concept work done. It was a blast going to the creature shop to work each day!

Trade Shows
A **trade show or trade expo** is a large event where companies in a specific industry showcase their latest products and try to get them sold to wholesalers, retailers and distributors. Trade shows are seldom open to the public and you may need certain credentials like a reseller's license or proof of your business to attend or exhibit there. They can only be attended by company reps, professionals in the industry, and the press. Some trade shows have a couple "trade only" days and a couple days open to the public.

Some Trade Shows
- **New York International Gift Fair** (or The Gift Show) www.nyigf.com Largest licensing and gift show
- **MAGIC Market Week** www.magiconline.com Huge Las Vegas licensing and gift show focused on apparel
- **Book Expo America** (BEA) www.bookexpoamerica.com huge book expo

If you have a product to sell, this is the place to be. There are buyers from all walks of consumerism shopping the hall to fill their stores, catalogs, and distribution warehouses. This can be a place to find licensing leads or opportunities to offer your artistic services.
The shows usually cost upwards of $300 to attend and $2500+ for a booth. Do some research to see if this is a viable option for you at this point in your career.

Art Shows, Craft Bazaars, etc

In addition to conventions, you might try going to other types of events where artists are showing their work. You can pick up a lot of information by talking with them and seeing how they shop their wares and find new leads.

Gallery openings, art shows, art street fairs, holiday craft shows, art events like museum to-dos, art lectures, etc. Check your local newspaper and nightlife listings for art events in your area.

Portfolio Drop-offs

Portfolio drop-offs are something that is commonly done in the publishing and advertising industries. It's basically what it sounds like, you make an appointment to drop off your portfolio to have it reviewed by an art director at the company, and come back and pick it up later.

Some firms have strict guidelines for this, and some don't. Check their website submission policy sections before heading out. Publishers commonly have open drop off times on Mondays. I've known artist to take trips to New York and over the course of a couple days drop off their books at various publishers to get seen.

As always, I'd recommend having some sort of leave behind. A good idea is to put a "literature holder" type pocket on the inside front cover of your portfolio binder with a little sticker that says "please take one."

The way it usually works is that you speak with the receptionist or other gate keeper and she will assure you that she will deliver it to the right person and tell you what time you can come back and pick it up. I would kindly ask her some questions like:

"What is the name and position of the person who will be reviewing my portfolio?" (get his contact info so you can follow up later)

"Will I be meeting with him/her at the end of the review?"

"Can I come back in the future and show some new samples?"
"Do you have several art directors? Who else would it be good to show my portfolio to?"

You may or may not ever get to speak to an art director or get any feedback other than what the AD tells the receptionist to tell you; which might be a polite "they don't have anything for you now," or "your work isn't up to our standards yet."

If your work is strong and it catches their eye, an AD might come out to speak with you for an immediate assignment or to make contact for future work.

You might get lucky and have an AD or junior AD actually sit down with you right away and look at your book with you, very quickly of course. Take advantage of the opportunity and chat him up.

One artist wrote on his blog that he walked cold into the offices of Tor books, asked the receptionist if they were accepting portfolio drop offs, and she sent him directly to Irene Gallo's office! What an opportunity!

Visit Businesses

In your lead searches you will undoubtedly find businesses and studios that are close to where you live, or clustered in an area you might like to visit. You can try calling to set up an appointment, but this is not always effective.

On the Job

I was trying to get some work as a creature concept artist in the special effects makeup world a few years back, and I was feeling gusty and popped in on a few studios.

One of which was Steve Johnson's XFX, a leader in the industry. I walked into the studio doors with my portfolio in hand and the receptionist told me Steve Johnson was at lunch, but that I could wait if I wanted to.

So I waited for about 30 minutes and in he strolled. He was rude, turned his back to me, and joked with his co-workers as to how much they hate when guy pops in. But, I didn't care, because in the end this big name in the industry sat down with me personally and looked at my portfolio.

You may have to get bold and pop in on one of these studios and ask if you could show your portfolio to an art director or principal. Make sure you know the name of the person you want to talk to.

You'll likely speak to the receptionist first. He/she will call the AD and see if he has the time to look at your book now. She may ask you to wait or come back later. No problem, you can wait, or leave your business card and go to the next studio until you see someone that day.

You have to have a thick skin for this one. It's tough because the AD is not expecting this interruption in his work day and may or may not be too receptive to it. He might even act put out or aggravated. You won't get much time, but it doesn't take much time for your artwork to wow him! But if you're courteous, professional, and confident you might get far.

Chamber of Commerce, BNI, and MeetUp Meetings

Every town has a **Chamber of Commerce** organization, which is a small network of local business owners. They have regular meetings to discuss the prosperity of business in their community. Local Chamber of Commerces have monthly meet and greet type gatherings that are pretty informal and a great opportunity to network with like minded people and other business owners (like yourself).

BNI (www.bni.com) is a worldwide organization that has local chapters with scheduled meetings to help its members increase their business and get more customers by networking with other professionals. They have guest speakers, resources, training, and meet and greets.

MeetUps (www.meetup.com) are a new social phenomenon website. MeetUp.com is a site for people to put on and attend all kinds of social events. But it's also used for meetups revolving around business and professional networking. Meetups are informal and fun and a great place to meet people that are into the same stuff you are. You can even start a meetup group of your own.

These kinds of meetings are great for meeting other professionals that you could learn from, collaborate with, or who might be in need of your artistic talents. There's usually little formal organization to these get-togethers, so it's up to you to talk with folks and swap business cards.
Each meeting might have one or two presenters giving a Power Point talk about their services, or an informal talk, and then it's socializing over

nosh. You may consider giving a presentation of your own. You'll likely walk away with a lot of people interested in your services.

The cool thing is that *there is no competition for what you do* in the room, and you'll be a rock star. Remember, these are business people. They don't have much need for fantasy art (unless you're in an entertainment industry meeting), so you may want to bring a more broad portfolio to one of these. But they desperately need artists, because you have a skill that they don't and they will pay well for it. Or they will refer you to their friends and associates who need art to help their business.

Book Signings, Personal Appearances, Autograph Signings

Famous people, industry leaders, and movers and shakers, are hard to meet face to face for any industry. Many just don't go to shows or are in industries that don't have conventions where they go and do portfolio reviews. So you have to get creative and try to meet these folks any way you can. I'm not saying you should follow them home and climb over their fence when their in the pool! I'm saying try to meet them at some sort of public appearance.

Target people you'd like to work with whether that person is an art director, editor, writer, filmmaker, producer, or what have you. Then look to see if they are making any public appearances that you can go to and have an opportunity to speak with them, even if it's briefly.

The big wigs do often give seminars or presentations at professional conferences, and are usually available afterwards to talk to, or other representatives from their organization might be there fielding questions. Plus if you're a fan, you get a chance to meet them in person and shake their hand and say thanks.

Try art openings, book signings, book launch parties, art seminars, signings with artists, actors, directors, and other famous people at cons, bookstores, or other events. You'd be surprised the access you might have if you take a chance.

On the Job

Here's how I met Clive Barker! Ok, so it's not that hard to meet him after you stand in line for an hour at a signing at Meltdown Comics in Los Angeles, but you have to give me props for ingenuity.

I heard Clive was doing a signing and though it would be a great chance to get in front of him. I bought something for him to sign to support the store and him.

When it was my turn, I told him that I was a big fan and introduced myself as an artist. I told him how much I'd like to work with him and handed him my sample pack/portfolio. He kindly looked it over, was impressed, gave me a business card and told me to contact his producer. Which lead to a meeting with his producer at their Beverly Hills home office.

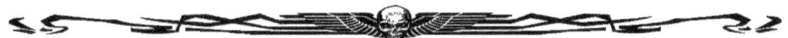

Be Where Art Directors Search For Artists

Companies send their art directors and other art buyers to various events, expos, happenings, etc. to scout for talent. Or they take it upon themselves as part of their job to find new and interesting artists to work with.

So an excellent way to get your work seen is to be where art directors are searching for artists, either physically like at a con, or digitally on the web like at popular art sites.

The strategy is just like the market saturation concept in marketing. If an AD starts to see your work everywhere he goes, he will take note of you, and perceive you as a big deal, a hard working illustrator, who's involved in the industry, and someone he just has to work with.

Convention Table or Booth

Art directors definitely go to the larger fantasy, comic, and pop culture conventions. Some go and do scheduled portfolio reviews, and others just walk the show looking at art and talking to artists.

Aside from people with actual positions in companies, there are all kinds of people walking around looking for artists to work on their own projects, pitches they are preparing, personal commissions, start-up companies, you name it.

People that you would never expect will approach you to help them with their projects: directors, producers, licensing agents, actors looking for artists for a pitch, haunted house producers, theme park designers, t-shirt companies, skateboard manufactures, and the list is endless. They don't have booths at the show where you can find them. They're just walking around scouting for talent.

One of the best ways to maximize your visibility at a show is to have a table or booth in the "artist alley" area, because art directors always go through artist alley and look at art.

Working a convention is a big undertaking and there are a lot of things I've learned over the years that can help you tremendously. I'll be covering all kinds of convention strategies in an upcoming book.

Only a small portion of art buyers are readily available to you at a con. The rest are lurking. They don't want to be found. They just want to walk the show and look for artists on their terms. Which makes them nearly impossible to find. **So let them find you in artist alley.**

The cool thing about getting a table is that you have space to really show off your work as well as sell stuff. It's not a bad idea to bring an assistant (your brother or girlfriend) to help you out so you can have a little time away from your table to do some business, as well as some portfolio reviews or panel talks. Make sure you have your sample packets and business cards to hand out to prospective clients.

Booths at shows can be expensive for an artist with limited stuff to sell to recoup the cost, but artist alley tables are quite reasonable ranging from $0 - $300. Go to some of the con's websites and look for exhibitor information to get an idea of what you get and for how much.

Convention Art Shows

Con goers love art! So a lot of conventions have some kind of **art show**, which is a stretch of panels with art hung on them like an art gallery. The art show is usually for the fans to enjoy, but ADs also check them out.

The show usually hosts a silent auction where patrons can bid to buy your art, or you can just show your art without selling it. Either way, it's a good idea to have a branded placard next to each painting and have leave behinds hanging on the wall near your name plate in a brochure, literature, or business card holder.

Even if you have a table at the con, you might want to hang in the art show as well since you're already there. They're usually free and you might get some extra sales or exposure.

There are tons of fantasy, horror, and sci-fi cons across the country (and the world) where you can actually mail in your work to their art show if you can't attend the show in person. What a great opportunity to have your work seen and sold!

At some conventions, the art show may be very prestigious like at World Fantasy Convention (www.wfc2013.org). This con is focused on published authors and while there are publishers there selling books, they don't have ADs at the show looking at portfolios. But they are often in attendance and looking at art. They aren't wearing name badges and are hard to find, so you might want to try to find their names *and photos* on the internet before you go.

There is no artist alley, but there is a wonderful art show where some of the biggest names in fantasy illustration hang their work along with up-and-comers.

WFC is a great opportunity to network with authors directly as well. They may have some influence over the cover art on their novels, especially if they are a big name. Plus a lot of authors are looking for re-envisioned covers for their previously published books now being released as ebooks.

Source Books and Directories

Art annual, **directory**, or **sourcebook** are interchangeable terms for paid advertising catalogs or books, issued annually, that contain pages advertising artists and their services. It's like a portfolio of working illustrators and photographers that you pay to be in.

The fees are pretty steep: you're looking at about $3000 a page. If you are repped by an agency, they may require that you buy a page in their section as part of your combined marketing efforts; or he may split the cost with you.

There are some valuable things you get in return for the high fee. The publishers of the directory send free printed copies out to creative directors, art directors, designers, and art buyers working in ad agencies, design studios, Fortune 500 companies, in-house art departments at magazines, publishing houses, record companies, and motion picture/television studios throughout the US, Canada and selectively in Europe and Asia. So you get a lot of exposure. Unfortunately, ADs are very busy, and just like mailed sample packs, the sourcebooks might not get looked at much.

Sourcebooks are beautifully printed and give you a level of prestige. ADs trust that the artists in their pages are pros. The sourcebook is also viewable online and you get a portfolio page on their companion website included in your paid fee. The idea is that the cost of advertising is quickly recouped by high paying advertising jobs. Your very first job (if you get one) can pay for the cost.

I've personally never done it. Mainly because of the kind of darker work I like to do, and the high cost. Also, most sourcebooks are geared towards a broad advertising and editorial marketplace, where fantasy artists are not in much demand. Although with the rise of superhero movies and fantasy heavy video games, there may be more call for fantasy artists in those markets.

Some of the Major Directories
- **Workbook** www.workbook.com
- **Directory of Illustration** www.directoryofillustration.com
- **Play** www.playillustration.com

There is a lot of debate as to whether or not advertising in art annuals or catalogs is effective, but they can be an excellent option, depending on the kind of fantasy art you do and what industries you want to get into.

If you do more cutesy fantasy, young adult book covers, or children's books, you might have a good shot.

Like most kinds of marketing efforts, the more often and more consistently you appear in the annuals, the more your audience with ADs will build, and the more work you will get.

Pros
- When you by pages, you also get time on their fully searchable websites, which is where the ADs likely search more.
- They send out thousands of free directories to art buyers
- You reach an audience you have little or no access to
- Trusted level of prestige and professionalism

Cons
- The price is quite high
- Low demand for fantasy art, especially gritty dark art, in the target audience
- You may not get much work out of it

Internet Saturation

The more you are visible out in the world, the more ADs are going to see your work and remember you. So it's important for you to have a strong presence on the web. At the very least you have to have some kind of online portfolio, preferably on your own website. After all, ADs surf the web for fun and for work just like you do.

Marketing can be time consuming and take time away from making art, so you have to weigh what you're trying to achieve and how much you want to do.

What do I mean by internet saturation? Google "Tom Baxa" or "Thomas M. Baxa" and you'll see the first results page is filled with my content. This is no accident. And I won't kid you, it takes time and effort.

Luckily, I have a unique name and that helps tremendously. If you have a common name, you may want to consider naming your company something unique and do all your marketing around the company name. It will be more effective in making you stand out.

You want to have enough content on the web so when someone searches for your name on search engines (Google, Yahoo, Bing), social media sites, YouTube, etc., a lot of info will come up about you. First of all, this helps them find you and gives them access to what you are selling, whether it's products or your services as an illustrator. It makes you look impressive, professional, worldly, and sought after.

And you want the content to be of *your* creation, not just news pages, company websites, or collector sites. If I didn't create all the content that I have (my website, my blog, my Facebook pages, my YouTube channel) then the main searches that would come up would be other people's sites with my Magic cards on them. Those kinds of sites are great, but they don't tell anyone anything about me other than I did some work on Magic. You want to control, the best you can, the information that you put forth about your services.

There is a practice called search engine optimization (SEO) that involves doing everything you can to get your sites to rank high in the search engines like Google. It's an important part of marketing, which is way too lengthy to get into here. You can pay people to optimize your site or learn on your own. There are tons of good sites and books on the topic.

Here a list in order of importance of the things you should focus on when building you web presence:

1. Your own website with portfolio
2. Your own Blog
3. Social media like Facebook, Twitter, YouTube
4. Portfolio sites like Deviant art

 Eye On BAA: I'll be covering SEO and other marketing strategies in an upcoming book and BAA blog posts: www.BaxaArtAcademy.com.

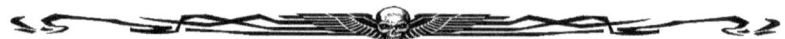

Patience and Persistence: The Follow Up

"I've done everything you said, why isn't my phone ringing?" If your work is excellent, believe me, ADs will take notice and get in touch. But there are many reasons why you may not hear anything right away.

You have to bump the competition

Unless his company is brand new, any AD you encounter already has a stable of go-to artists that he uses regularly. Sometimes more than he can handle.

You've got to make enough of an impression for him to call you instead of one of them. (Don't worry, ADs like to foster new talent when they can.)

Overworked and Overloaded

Art directors are people too, with all the flaws and weaknesses of anybody else. Plus, they're overloaded with work and bombarded with submissions. So you have to keep hitting them with your samples.

Stay in Their Minds

The most critical thing you can do for your career is to follow up on any business contacts you make so you stay fresh in their minds. Even if an AD loves your work, he might not have a project that is right for you at that moment; and six months down the road, you may have slipped his mind. You have to get used to continually following up with companies you'd like to work with.

Be Patient and Keep on Your Course

After meeting an AD at a con, or any other attempt to contact one, you just have to be patient. Even the ADs with the best intentions to look at new work are extremely overworked and seldom find time to look at submissions. Wait a couple weeks and mail a postcard to them, saying "did you get the samples I sent on Jan. 1st? Here's a new piece I just did" and keep following up whenever possible.

What can you do to stand out? How can you catch their attention right away and get them to act on it? How do you stay fresh in their minds? I'll give you some great tips in *SECTION 4: Working with Art Directors: Staying Connected with Your ADs* below.

Start Small While You Wait to Hear from the Big Boys

Always have your sights set high. Keep sending your samples to the big companies, but while you wait to hear back from them, you might want to try working for some smaller companies to get your feet wet. There are some real advantages to working for small companies, start-ups, or individuals when you're first getting started.

The pay is often low, but there is less pressure. It gives you a chance to learn about working with art directors, contracts, meeting deadlines, following art direction, etc., without blowing it with a very important client that may not give you a second chance.

But be cautious, small companies often have trouble paying their bills, especially in a down economy. They, too, are getting their feet wet on running a business, feeling out the marketplace, and meeting their obligations. Do small assignments to test the waters.

There are tons of resources in the *Artist's Market* and *Writer's Market* books and on various job listing sites.

Last Words

As you can see, being a freelancer can be daunting. It's a lot of work. Tracking down leads can be quite time consuming, but it's all part of having a business. When you're not working, you're looking for work. But don't forget to be an artist and paint, paint, paint!

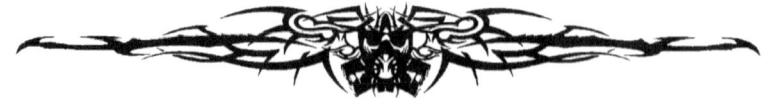

Notes:

SECTION 3: Assignments and Doing Business

This section if full of practical tips about the **business side of being an illustrator**. Remember I told you that even though you are making art and getting paid, it's still a job, and there are lots of business aspects that you are responsible for.

Most importantly, you need to be on top of Fees, Contracts, and Copyrights. After all, these are the things that bring in the money!

After doing hundreds of jobs over the years, I've come to learn a thing or two, and I'll tell you about the ins and outs of assignments, art orders, sketch approvals, delivery of final art, etc.

By taking action and reading this book from BaxaArt Academy, you're being handed info that has taken me years to learn and perfect. You're way ahead of the game, which will greatly improve your client relations and keep the jobs coming. It's just as important to know how to stay in once you break in!

I'll also give you some etiquette tips to help you gain favor with the people you are working with and leave them with a smile on their face. Which is what you want, so they call you again with another assignment.

What to Ask a Prospective Client BEFORE You Accept a Job:

Being offered an assignment is exciting! I know you want to dive in and make some art that you're actually going to get paid for – sweet! But before you leap, there are some important business points you want to consider. They are very important and should never be ignored. If you just can't deal with them, solicit the help of someone who can.

As a pro, there are certain things you need to know before you accept a job. And there's nothing wrong with that. No AD will get offended that you're asking these questions. In fact, he will likely respect you for your business acumen.

Before any company rep is allowed to discuss anything with you, it's likely you will first have to sign a NDA. A **Non-Disclosure Agreement**

(NDA) is a legal document where you agree not to share any forthcoming confidential information about a project with anyone until that knowledge is made public. Once signed, a prospective client will be free to talk with you about the specifics of the project, rates, business practices, etc.

Your first contact point is almost always email. If a client is interested in using me for a job, my first priority is to *call* the AD and get to know him a little bit in an effort to make more of a connection with him. You want to try to **get his number** so you always have it if you want to call him.

I may wait until an AD sends me some background info on the project, then email him and tell him I have some questions and would like to speak with him on the phone and ask for his number. I might also ask if we could set up **a phone meeting** to discuss the project and the terms of employment.

When you do speak on the phone, take the opportunity to get to know the AD a bit. Ask him about his background and how long he's been with the company. Be cordial and enthused (which won't be hard, because you will be excited about getting paid to draw monsters).

Ask him about the job, what is expected of you, some basic terms of your employment like your fee, when you will get paid, do you get to keep your originals, etc.

It's best not to rush to judgment and accept a job immediately. Take a little quiet time on your own to decide if the job, and the fee, is right for you. Hang up the phone saying:

> *"This sounds great! I'd love to work on this project, but I'd just like to read through the contract before I commit. Please send me a copy."*

No AD will ever have a problem with that.

Once you understand all the terms of the contract and the offer the company is presenting, then you can decide if you would like accept the job or feel the need to negotiate the terms of your contract.

Your Fee

When it's appropriate, ask your art director about MONEY. After all, that's why you're doing this. He understands that, and *will not be offended* by your asking. Quite the opposite actually, he'll see that you're a professional and that you value your time and skills.

Most often, by the time you're being contacted, the client has figured out their budget for a project and *they will tell you* how much they are offering for a job. Sometimes you have to take it or leave it. And sometimes the rates are negotiable. Sometimes the client will ask you what you charge; in which case you should be prepared to answer.

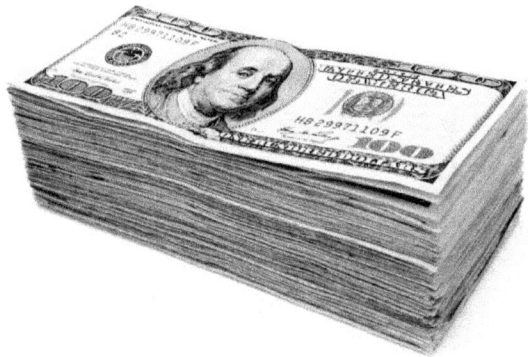

You need to be aware that some of the industries where you'll be doing fantasy art do not have high profit margins, so those companies do not pay very well, and won't cover any extra expenses. They certainly won't *offer* to, so you have to be bold and ask.

Large companies and lucrative industries like advertising, film and video games pay higher fees and cover some expenses. They are more apt to comply with your negotiation requests, especially if they are reasonable. Make sure you don't ask for the moon like some prima donna, especially if you are just getting started with a company. Again, it's best to discuss your fees upfront.

What Should I Charge?

Doing illustration for hire is a JOB. Sometimes it's best to think of it in terms of a job. A really fun and rewarding job, but a job nonetheless. Your main priority is to make money so you can support yourself and your family, and do the job in a timely fashion so you have time to enjoy the fruits of your labors. Life is about people - so do art, love it, ship it, and spend time with your loved ones.

When deciding whether or not an offer is acceptable, you must carefully weigh if the time it takes to do a particular job well is worth the money you are being paid. Sadly, in the arts, a lot of the time it isn't, especially early on. You have to decide if that's ok with you or not; if it's worth your time for reasons other than just financial gain.

Of course, you don't want to discuss any of these thoughts with you client. You just want to put forth how much you are excited to be working with them, while you negotiate for a fee that you feel is fair.

How do you know what's fair? Well, that's a tough question. It's important to do some research and get an idea of the typical fee structures for the industry you are considering. Some industries pay very well, some do not.

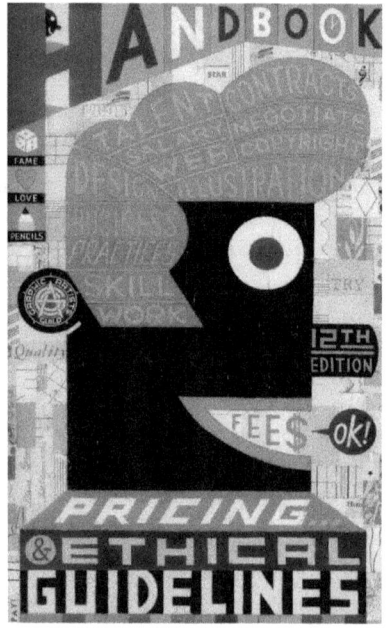

Graphic Artist Guild Pricing and Ethical Guidelines

One of the best starting points is the *Graphics Artist Guild Handbook of Pricing and Ethical Guidelines*. Use this link and buy yourself a copy of this book at Amazon immediately: http://amzn.to/1lycn2n! The GAG pricing guide is a comprehensive listing of the industries that buy art and what fees you should charge for what type of work you're being hired to do. It describes various pricing considerations, has sample contracts, it gives price ranges based on circulation and distribution size, and more.

You'll be surprised how thorough the book is. It's an excellent resource that no working illustrator should be without.

The other best resource is to talk to professional artist working in the field and find out what the standard rates are for the industry. They know because they've spent years doing the jobs and negotiating rates.

Bill Clients Based on Time and Rights

Your fee should be based on how long a job is going to take you, and the amount of rights you retain to the artwork. I'll explain why rights are so important in a minute, but just trust me for now.

Only you know how fast you can work and still get a decent result. So you need to determine up front what the job entails and how long it will take you.

It really helps to take a look at the numbers. For instance, a $1000 for a cover painting is decent, but $1000 for a cover painting where you have to read the manuscript, do 3 pencil comps, a color comp, and forfeit all the rights is quite low. A $1000 seems like a lot, but if it takes you ten - 8 hour days to do a cover painting, then you're making $12.50/hour. That's not so great.

Bill by the Hour vs. Flat Rate

You have to start thinking in terms of **your hourly rate** just like a regular job. It helps you put things in perspective and better value your time. Whether you are being paid a flat rate or hourly, they're really both the same thing.

The best way to come up with a rate for a client is to first determine the hourly rate you should be charging, then apply that hourly rate to the number of hours the job will take you to arrive at a final bid price for the entire job.

For example: A client asks you to do 3 color character concepts. You know it takes you about 7 hours to do one start to finish, so that's a total of 21 hours. I like to add a couple hours for changes or unforeseen problems. So let's make it 24 hours total. Through your research you've determined that a concept artist in the video game industry should make about $50/hour. So multiply 24 hours x $50 = $1200 flat rate for the job. If a client offers you a flat rate for a job, then you just figure things backwards: figure out how long it's going to take you and divide that into the flat rate to determine the hourly rate. Sometimes a flat rate is better if you know you can get the job done quickly and the fee is high.

If the job you are being offered entails a lot of tweaking, like concept art does, it's to your benefit to **bill by the hour**, that way if a job runs long or there are a lot of changes, you're covered.

If a client asks you for your **day rate**, you just multiply your hourly rate times 8. So in the example above, you would tell your client that your day rate is $400 for 8 hours ($50 x 8 hours = $400) and that anything over that is billed at $75/hour (time and a half).

Now you don't want to get too complicated with the client. They don't have to know all the reasoning you went through to come to your rate. Just give them a simple answer.

If you try negotiating your fee and the client won't or can't budge, then you can decide if you want to accept the job or not. I like to accept by saying:

> *"I usually don't do a job for this price, but I really want to work with you, so I'll be happy to accept your terms."*

Other Fee Structures
Most of the time you will be paid an hourly rate or flat rate, but there are all kinds of ways to negotiate your payment. For instance, you can take a smaller up-front payment with a royalty based on sales later. You can get paid an hourly rate plus bonuses if milestones are reached early. You can get a flat rate plus an additional flat rate when sales hit a certain number.

These are options to lower the initial costs for the art commissioner, and maximize profits for you if a product does well. But this is way more complicated than you have to worry about right now.

On top of your fee for creating artwork, there are other fees that you may consider as your responsibility as an artist, when in fact they are actually part of the job and should be billed to the client whenever possible.

Additional Fees you can ask for
- Shipping artwork to and from
- Rush fees
- Overtime + weekends
- Photo and model fees
- Excessive redraw fees

- Material fees (things above art supplies)
- Anything that is outside the realm of a normal illustration job that THEY ask for like fly to Bangkok to shoot photos of temples; in which case you would charge travel expenses, meal per deim, hotel, photo equipment and expenses, etc.
- Things that take a great deal of your time like going to a film location and waiting all day   to get access to a movie set to sketch. Bill them for your time.
- Things that are beyond what's stipulated in your contract
- Travel or gas expenses

When Do I Get Paid?

After determining how much you are going to get paid, the next question you want answered is *when* are you getting paid? You will most commonly see the phrase "Net 15" or "Net 30 days" in a contract or purchase order. That basically means you will be paid 15 or 30 days after you turn in the job and it is approved.

Net 15 is very common because it usually takes an accounting department a little time to get it together and cut the check.

Ask your AD if the company is actually hitting their payment schedule. If not, you can decide not to take the job, or take the job armed with useful information.

With companies being owned by larger corporations, things are done more professionally and there's more paperwork, so you have to stay on top of it to get paid. Review the *Payment Checklist* below for the skinny!

Partial or Milestone Payments

It is to your advantage to get partial payments as you are doing a job instead of waiting to get paid when you are all finished. Ask for it!

A commonly accepted partial payment schedule is to get **half up front, and half Net 15** after the job is turned in. Another good arrangement is **1/3 up front, 1/3 after sketches, 1/3 after finals**.

Milestone payments, usually reserved for longer term contract jobs, are based on hitting a certain deadline with work or being paid according to an amount of work being completed. For example, you get paid when you get 20 paintings done before Comiccon, or you get paid each time you turn in five completed pages of a graphic novel.

If you're working with a new client and don't know how reliable they are with payments, this helps you get paid. If they aren't reliable with a partial payment, you can stop working on the job without having lost tons of time and money. It's also good, especially for a long gig, to get paid in increments so you have some cash on hand to pay your bills.

Terms to Look Out For

Long payment schedules often mean that the company is waiting for the release of the product to get an influx of cash from initial sales to pay its vendors. That can be risky for you as a contractor because guess who is on the bottom of the list to get paid? First they pay their employee payroll, then they pay the printer who will hold product if they aren't paid, then they pay all other monies necessary to get the product out like shipping, marketing, advertising, warehousing, etc.

Net 60 days

Anything more than Net 30 days is excessive. You have to decide if doing a job for a smaller company that pays over 60 days is worth it or not.

After Publication or Release

Fee to be paid Net 60 days *AFTER publication*. Any production schedule is at least 3 months away from publication, so when you turn in the job you'd have to wait 3 months for release of the product then an additional 60 days to get paid. That's not good. I guarantee you the art director is not putting in a week's worth of work, then waiting 5 months to get paid!

Art Related Questions

Make sure you ask any questions that may impact the process you use to make your artwork for the job. The answers may sway your decision, or ability, to take a job. Once you do accept a job, get more specifics.

When is the deadline?
Can you do the painting traditionally or digitally?
Do they want digital art only? In layers? What color space?
Can you send them a painting to be photographed or a digital photo?
Do they cover photography fees?
Do they pay model fees?
Will they pay for shipping? Just ask for the FedEx number as if you full expect them to pay, like it's the standard that you've come to expect

Your Rights

[Disclaimer: I am not a copyright expert and do not claim to know the laws verbatim. The advice herein is only to be used as a guideline. I suggest you do your own research at www.copyright.gov and/or consult a copyright attorney.]

When I say your "rights" I mean the **copyrights** that are assigned to you *by law* when you create a work of art. Generally speaking, when you create an image, you own it, period, until you sell or grant ownership to another. This includes artwork, photographs, sculpture, fabric designs, logos, website designs, graphic design, and more. So everything you see out there is owned by someone and you don't have the right to use it. And no one has the right to use your work without your expressed permission.

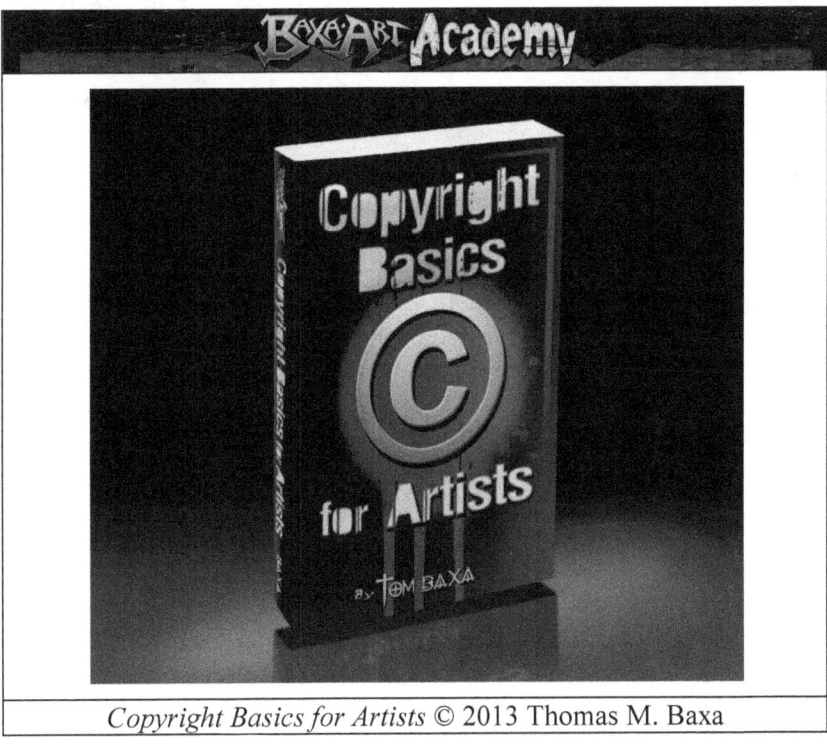

Copyright Basics for Artists © 2013 Thomas M. Baxa

The official copyright website is www.copyright.gov, but it's confusing. I highly recommend you get a copy of my ebook on copyrights *Copyright Basics for Artists* www.baxaart.com/BAA/books_index.htm. It covers all the important copyright topics in language that's easy to understand.

Why You Want to Hold onto Your Rights

Remember when I said that the two factors to weigh when deciding on your fee are time and rights? Here's why rights are so important: **When you own the rights to your image and the characters you create in that image, you can continue to generate income for years to come.**

You can sell the same image over and over to different licensing opportunities like posters, calendars, puzzles, lunchboxes, etc. You can sell prints and t-shirts. You can sell the original. You can develop the characters into a children's book, a comic, a movie, etc. You can sell the secondary rights for someone to use the image you created for one company on their company's product. Can you see the potential here?

If you own the rights, you can make more income down the road to offset a low initial fee. Even if the fee is pretty good, it's still likely not a fair price for your time and expertise.

Don't sign away your rights, because they may be very valuable some day. Look at what's happening with the surge of superhero movies. Those characters were created over 50 years ago and they're more lucrative now than they ever were. If you must give away your rights, try to get well compensated for them if you can.

Contracts Indicate Copyright Assignments

Contracts stipulate what rights you own to the pieces you are creating for an assignment, so it's important to get familiar with what rights you have and what rights you want to keep. In a contract, you and the company are *mutually agreeing*, in writing, to who gets what rights for the fee being paid. And the contract is bound by law.

Copyrights can be broken down into a variety of rights, which can be assigned or granted to parties other than the copyright holder. So you may get a contract that grants all rights to the company, but assigns you the right to show the work in your portfolio, and the right to make prints of the work. Or you can sign a licensing contract with Company A for t-shirts only, and a contract with Company B for prints, cards and calendars.

Work for Hire

As a freelancer, you will be offered many contracts that use the term "work for hire" in the language. A **work for hire agreement** means that you are assigning ALL copyrights to the party hiring you. They own it all, unless the contract grants you back some rights, for a term of 95 years from publication or 120 years from creation, whichever is shorter.

You may also get a contract called and **independent contractor agreement**. As a freelancer, you are an independent contractor as opposed to an employee. Read your contract carefully. It may or may not grant all the rights to the party hiring you.

If you are an **employee of a company**, in the absence of agreement to the contrary, your employer owns all rights to works created by you during your employment.

You want to avoid a work for hire agreement whenever possible so you can retain the rights to the images you create. If you are offered one, talk about it with your art director or legal department contact and tell him why you'd prefer some other arrangement.

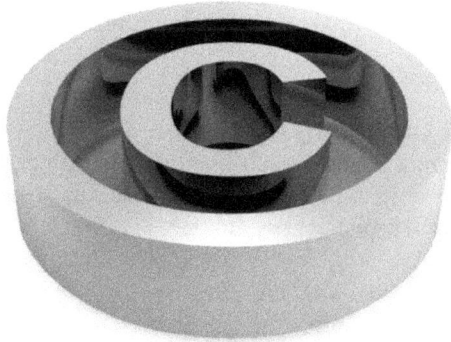

Copyright Notice
Contracts may grant you the limited right you to show the work you created, like in your portfolio or on your website, even though you may not own the copyright. In this case, you must attach a copyright ownership notice to any images you show in print, digitally, or otherwise, in the form of © or the word Copyright, the year published, copyright owner's name (for example: *Copyright 2013 Blizzard Entertainment*).

What should you put a copyright notices on? EVERYTHING. Your paintings, prints, social media postings, jpegs, blog postings, website postings, images in a book, images reproduced in your portfolio, merchandise you create with the image, etc.

Always put a copyright notice *on your own* work to help identify you as the creator and owner of the copyright. It's best to have the copyright notice on the actually image, instead of just on the page below the image, especially with digital copies. That way if someone borrows or shares the image, the copyright is already attached. I like to paint the © symbol with my signature on a painting that I own the rights to.

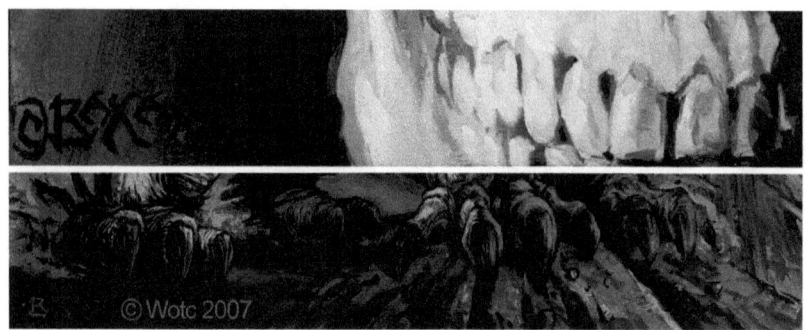

Copyright notice examples

Negotiating Your Contract

[Disclaimer: I am not a contract law expert and do not claim to know the law. The advice herein is only to be used as a guideline. I suggest you do your own research and/or consult a contract law attorney.]

Often you are presented with an offer by a company, and as someone who is not very familiar with the business world it's your tendency to think that you only have two choices: to either accept it as it or reject it. And sometimes that's the case, but you'd be surprised how often you can negotiate some of the terms of a contract. Even large companies are open to contract additions. It doesn't hurt to ask. Know what you want so you can ask for it.

One thing you can do to make things work smoother is to **prepare your own contract language** and include clauses that are pertinent to your needs as an artist. Put it in legalese language the best you can. I know you're not a lawyer, but there are some great resources in books and on the web about contracts for artists. The Graphic Artists Guild Pricing guide is one. Two excellent books in this area are Tad Crawford's books *Business and Legal Forms for Illustrators* http://amzn.to/1mED31x and *Legal Guide for the Visual Artist* http://amzn.to/1qRYf6R.

You want to make it very easy for the client to say yes. If your additions are ready to go, a company will be more likely to just accept your terms and put your language in the contract, especially a small company who doesn't want to pay a lawyer to re-draft a contract. At the very least they can see exactly what you are asking for, even if they have their legal department write the language.

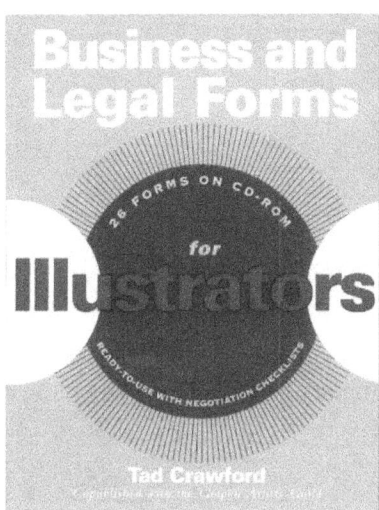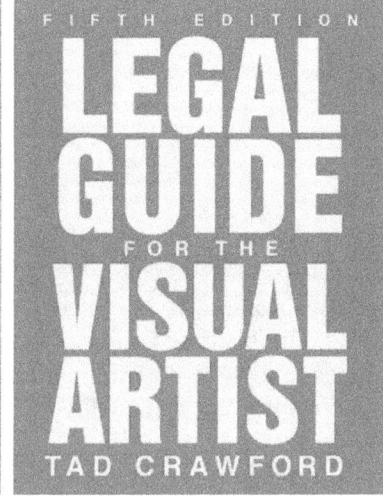

Educate Them

Small companies are often put together by gamers, not business men. They seldom have much business knowledge, and almost never understand artists' concerns, so they just do what they've heard other companies do. "Wizards of the Coast uses a work for hire agreement for its freelancers, so we will too," is the thinking.

It's your job to educate the as to why a work for hire contract is so detrimental to your livelihood. Don't do it in an asshole way, do it in the spirit of working out a mutually beneficial agreement. Kindly explain to them why you prefer another arrangement where you retain more rights, especially if they aren't paying you much money. I'll say to the client,

> *"I usually don't sign a contract unless I get X, Y, and Z, and here's why...." "I can send you some language to include in the contract if that makes it easier for you."*

Rights You Want

The best case scenario where copyrights are concerned is for you to grant the company **first time publishing rights**. This means that you own all the copyrights to the image, but you are giving the company you are doing the job for permission to be the first company to publish the work on their product. After a designated period of time, you can reuse or resell the work as you see fit.

With rights, there is the **grant of rights, the region they cover, what the work can be used for, and a time period the grant lasts.** So you would grant:

United States only [region], *first time publishing rights* [grant of rights], *for use on the "DragonWorlds" book cover and any marketing material used in its promotion* [use], *wherein the work will not be published by anyone else for a period of three years* [time period].

After three years you can resell the image if you like.

Generally speaking, if a right is not spelled out in a contract, then you own it. So in this case you own all other rights to the image. But it's not a bad idea to include the minimum rights language below in any contract, even though it is not technically necessary.

Minimum Rights You Want
If you can't negotiate for a first time publishing rights arrangement, and the company owns all the copyrights to a work, make sure you get the following rights assigned back to you in the contract:

1.) *Artist owns the original artwork, paintings and sketches, to do with what he sees fit.*

2.) *Company grants Artist the following rights, once any images the Artist created for the company are made public:*

   a.) *Display rights for the image and the original painting*
   b.) *Artist may publish the images, as a means of self promotion, in various forms of his portfolio, digital or in print, including but not limited to: online portfolios, websites, blogs, collections of his work, artist showcases, annuals, and other marketing outlets.*
   c.) *Artist is granted the limited rights to produce and sell Artist Prints.*
   d.) *Artist must attach copyright ownership notices to all images in the form of © Year, Company.*

3.) *If significant changes, other than resizing and color correction, are to be made to the artwork, artist is to do them.*

Terms to Look Out For

When you first get a contract to review, check for these red flag terms. If you see them, you may want to try to negotiate around them. Remember, your work might hit big, and when it does you want to retain as many rights as possible to capitalize on later.

"Work for Hire"

Not at all to your advantage (see below)

"All worldwide rights"

Not horrible, but try to limit the scope to regional or US only territories. Then *you* can sell the work in foreign markets.

"All rights in perpetuity"

This means they own the rights *forever* and they don't revert back to you or your heirs. Always try to have the shortest time frame possible on grants of rights. Two to three years is not unreasonable.

"Electronic Rights"

Electronic rights refers to any digital format that your work can be distributed in including, but not limited to, ebooks, dvds, cds, digital downloads, streaming, mobile applications, etc. This is an often difficult, but very important area to retain rights in, especially in this day and age. You might sell the rights to publish your art book in print to a publisher, but retain the rights to publish the ebook version.

"All rights in all formats, now and not invented yet"

This is bad because when a new format like dvd, or ebooks comes out and becomes popular, then the company also owns the rights to publish your work in those formats, and you've lost another opportunity to make future money on your work.

Full or Part Time Employee Rights

As a full time or part time employee under contract, the employer owns all rights to works created by you during your employment, unless there is some agreement to the contrary. So if you decide to take a job, know that going in. It makes sense because you are being hired to develop their intellectual property in exchange for money.

The other more insidious clause that is often in employee contracts from companies that deal with intellectual properties is language that states that **the company also owns ANYTHING YOU DEVELOP while employed by them.**

I know this sounds crazy, but the company is training you in their proprietary processes and business practices, so while you are employed by them you would be using their knowledge to develop your own, often competing, intellectual property. For example, you get hired by a video game company without any experience in video games, and during the term of your employment you learn how games are made, what assets you have to develop, how to sell a game to a publisher, etc. Is it fair for you to create your own game on the side using company knowledge? Maybe, maybe not.

For creative person, this clause feels like the kiss of death, so you want to fight to change that language if possible. You should know that **you are allowed to create IPs in areas that do not complete with your employer**. So if you work at a video game company, you can write a novel, etc.

When I got hired a Westwood Studios under a contract with this clause, I was also asked to provide documentation on any projects I was currently developing before I took the job. Since I started the projects before employment, the provision allows that I could continue to develop them. It was also documented proof for my protection.

Another clause you want to look out for in an employment contract is a **non-compete clause**. A non-compete clause basically says that after you leave the company for whatever reason you cannot work in the *same industry* for a period of time, like 2 years. This may be no big deal, or it may bring your career to a screeching halt. Try to get it removed, or boil the language down to very specifically name the type of company you can't work for.

Doing the Job
Be Professional, First and Foremost

It's important to remember that in addition to being a talented artist, you are also part of a team trying to get a project completed. And as a team member, it's important to play well with others. This is very much for your benefit. If you're difficult, acting like a prima donna expecting special treatment, or unreliable then you're not going to get repeat work.

Art directors have a lot of artists to choose from, and if you're causing them problems on any level, whether you're a big name or a nobody, they're going to drop you and move on to the next guy. So always be professional, do good work every time, be friendly, and more than anything else meet your deadlines. Let me say that again:

MEET YOUR DEADLINES every time.

ADs are super busy. They don't want to have to worry if you're going to turn in a job on time or not. In fact, they will often work with less talented artists if they have a good working relationship with them and can rely on them to turn in a job on time, every time.

When you turn in your art late, an AD might let it slide the first time, but if you make a habit of it, or you make up a bunch of excuses why you turned in a job late, then he will stop giving you work. Art directors are not your personal mentors and they don't need the hassle.

> **CAUTIONARY TALE:** I know an extremely talented artist who is accommodating and easy to work with, but had a little trouble hitting some deadlines with this one AD. Maybe it was two or three in a row out of many jobs – not horrible or anything, but for some reason that AD had it stuck in his head that the artist was late *all the time*. That was far from the truth, but a few late jobs caused the AD to form a negative opinion, and that's all it takes to miss out on getting more work. So make every effort to be on time.

Sometimes a job gets away from you, or you have an emergency. Look, ADs are people too. They'll understand. But you MUST communicate with them BEFORE you miss your deadline. Email and tell them what's happening and *ask them for a little help*. The two of you can discuss when you think you can have the job done and if the AD has a little room in the schedule to accommodate you. More times than not, they will.

Always be courteous and friendly.

If you go into discussions with an AD with a big chip on your shoulder, you're going to be in trouble. He doesn't want to hear your problems. How would you like it if you called your AD with a question about the job and he started telling you why he's depressed and how his boss is on his butt. As much as you want to care about your fellow human beings, you're trying to make something happen; you don't have time for that. Neither does he. There is a time and a place for those kinds of talks, and during business hours is not one of them. So keep it light and focus on the task at hand. And be nice. Everyone likes to deal with friendly people, including ADs.

Art Orders – the Assignment Comes In
What is an Art Order
An **art order** is the description of the artwork you are being hired to do. It can be quite informal like a description over the phone or email, or very detailed and specific. Sometimes you get really lucky and the AD says, "Come up with something cool!"

Art orders are usually written up by the AD, but sometimes they come from another department and the AD is your liaison for questions and reference needs. Wizards of the Coast has an **R&D (research and development) department** that is responsible for designing Magic set themes, cards, game mechanics, flavor text, etc. They design each card and work with the art director to determine what art should go on the card. Other companies may call this department "brand development", "game design", "new product development", etc.

Here's an example of a typical Magic: the Gathering art order:
ART   ID: XX.XX.X   title: [Maelstrom   Wanderer]
SIZE: 2 1/16" (52mm) wide by 1 1/2" (38mm) tall   PRICE: $XX.XX.
SKETCH DUE: 5/11/2011 ART DUE: 6/7/2011
ART DESCRIPTION:
Color: Red, blue, and green legendary creature -- one of a kind
Location: A steeply inclined landscape, swept by a very strong wind
Action: The Maelstrom was the point at which the five shards of the plane of Alara merged -- a huge, roiling, crackling whirlpool of mana, aether, and magic. The Maelstrom is mostly gone now, but it remains a site of bizarre, flaring magic and strange winds. Show The Wanderer, a towering elemental creature borne of the Maelstrom. Its body is composed of green veins and vascular structures, fire and rock, and ribbons of blue arcane energy. It's easily 60 feet tall. It wanders the former Maelstrom's rim, into the wind, trailing blue plasma and licks of flame as it goes.
Focus: the huge "maelstrom elemental"
Mood: A walking storm of quasi-living magic, purposeless and ceaseless

Info you get in an art order:
Art Description
Describes the scene you are to illustrate. The description can be simple or very complex, depending on the function of the illustration. Sometimes you get actual text from the product.

Due Dates for Sketches and Finals

Card or Illustration Name

Color / Factions / Races
In combat based games there are opposing sides, indicated by these factors.

Dimensions
Given in terms of final output or print size, then you can work proportionately larger. You may also get dimensions in terms of a minimum art size, either in inches at 300dpi, or as a pixel dimension like 2300 x 3200 px at 200 dpi.

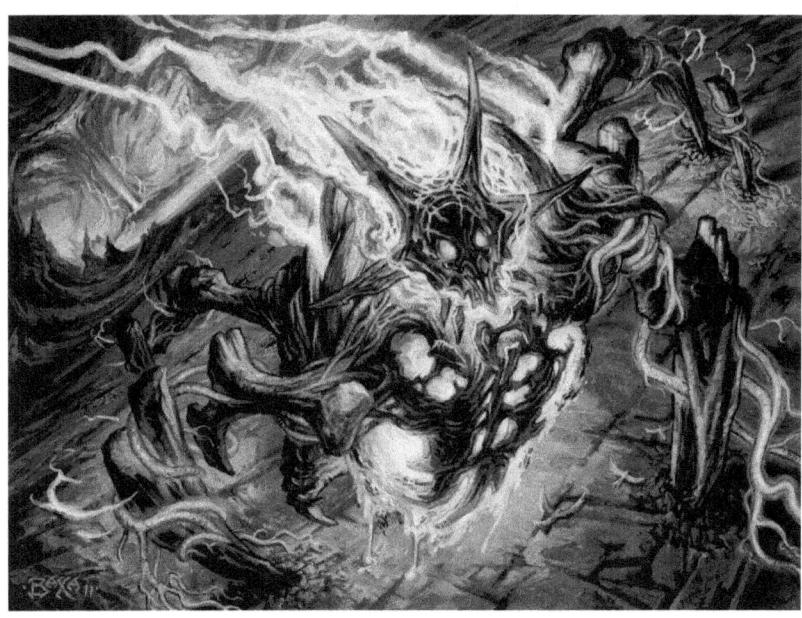

My solution based on the above art order. *Maelstrom Wanderer* ©
Wizards of the Coast 2011

Style Guide

You may be supplied with a style guide, which is a reference manual created by the company that illustrates some of the major elements of the product for you to follow. Sometimes you must follow the style guide very precisely, and other times it is more of a flavor guideline.

Reference Material

Usually visual reference of animals, locations, weapons, textures, vehicles, etc., that the AD wants you to use as inspiration for your illo. It may be an earlier painting of the character you're supposed to incorporate, photo reference, text from a story, video or cinematic footage, you name it.

Mood / Action / Focus

The AD may indicate what he wants you to focus on in your illustration like "focus on the somber mood of the hero king as he holds the corpse of his fallen brother."

Any Other Specifics That Might Be Important

Such as: the illo is going on a transparent film backed by light, it needs to be vector art so it can be scaled up, the colors have to be saturated, and so on.

Art descriptions in art orders are usually meant to be a guideline and are open to your interpretation and your artistic license, especially if you think you can solve the problem visually in a more interesting way.

Use your AD. Ask him questions about the material. He has his eye on critical factors that come from the marketing team and management when artwork, especially a cover, is being planned. Show him your take on things in the sketch phase.

As soon as you get an art order, read through it carefully to see if you understand what the AD is looking for in each illustration. Do you need reference? clarification? more info on the universe or characters? text from the actual article to help you with flavor? Ask your AD. Also, here's a legitimate excuse to call your new AD. Take it. Call him, rather than emailing him, to clarify questions you might have about the art order.

Illo size

Art orders usually list the dimensions that the final art will be printed at. You obviously need to know them before you can start any project.

It's common practice to work larger than print size and then reduced the art after it is scanned or photographed. A good rule of thumb is a 60% reduction. Working larger makes it easier to draw without trying to render everything tiny, and when you reduce the art the image tightens up and becomes a bit more cohesive before going to print.

The Proportion Scale

There's a handy tool that you must have to help you with this. It's called a **proportion scale.** You can get a proportion scale for about $5. First you set the wheel so that the percentage of original size, or the amount you are going to reduce the art [in this case 60%] is in the center window.

Then locate the printed art dimensions on the *outer* ruler, let's say 7 1/2 inches. The *inner* ruler shows the exact size the art should be so that it reduces down by 60%, in this case 12 1/2 inches.

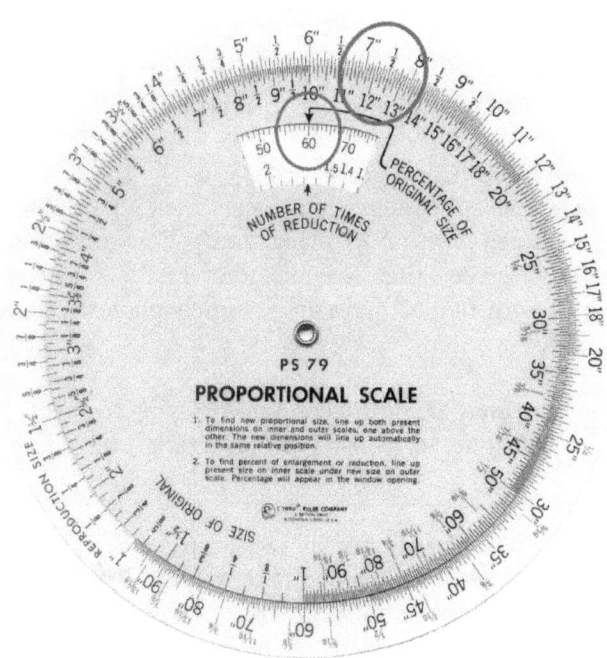

Proportion scale.

This 60% reduction rule can also be applied to digitally created artwork. Some amount of reduction helps tighten things up. However, for digital work 60% might be a bit high. I like to go with about 20-30% so more of the stroke marks are retained, but it all depends on how you work, so experiment.

> **CAUTIONARY TALE:** When you are working for an *online only* magazine where the art will only be published on the web (which means at a small size and 72 dpi), the client may want a full size version of the art. That means you have to paint it the size you would as if it were going to be printed at 300dpi. This way the client can have a full size copy for their archives in case they want to print it later in another format; which is fine, as long as they're paying you for that size. Ask your art director if they need the final art to be full print size *before* you start painting.

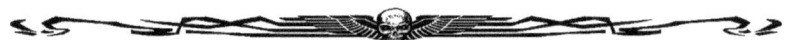

Reference:

Your AD will likely provide you with reference specific to his product's universe. But as an artist, you will want to use your own reference to help get a more natural look to your figures, add more believability to your environments and accessories, capture different lighting states, create believable nature elements, and to simply get you inspired.

Scrap: Reference Not Content

Scrap is another name for reference photos. The term originally referred to "scraps" of paper torn out of magazines. Your **morgue** is another name for your reference files, whether they're file folders filled with pictures you've torn out of magazines, digital photos, or files off the web.

Scrap can be extremely helpful when you're trying to invent something believable or authentic, or when you're trying to render something realistically.

But remember, the images you've saved in your morgue are ALL copyrighted and owned by someone other than you, so you have to be very careful not to copy them in your work.

This one student at the college I went to heavily referenced a photo out of *National Geographic* and got sued. It crushed him early in his career. You may think, "the photographer or copyright owner will never see this illo I'm doing for a small game company." Well, you never know. The game might take off and be bought by a big company with a huge marketing budget, then all of a sudden, your image is posted everywhere. Especially in this day and age of internet sharing.

Don't risk it! If you feel compelled to closely follow your scrap reference, make sure you change it - a lot! The law gives a guideline that you can use 10% of a copyrighted work, but that is not reliable and a judge can always determine you infringed. Use scrap as *reference*, not as *content* for your images.

If you enjoy doing photo montage artwork, do not use images off the web; you're asking for trouble.

Digital Scrap
With all the awesome art and photos being passes around via social media and all over the internet, it's easy to get a great collection of "digital scrap". I have a library of reference photos well organized in folders and subfolders.

I caution you though, don't spend your life collecting jpegs instead of making art. You know how easily "I'll just look at this one site," can turn into hours of your life burnt surfing from site to site downloading reference. If you use your jpeg morgue a lot and are in a habit of going to it often to get inspired, then that's great. But chances are those jpegs you saved of rhinoceroses having sex, while stunning, will never help you with your work. And you'll likely forget you ever saved them. When you have a project, go find the reference you need, when you need it and spend your time making art.

That being said, some good places for finding photos you can use as reference are:

Search Engines
Google Images is a great way to find what you need quickly to get started. It taps into all kinds of sites, including user uploaded photo sites like Flickr. But everyone, and I mean everyone, uses Google Images, so the chances are great that you and a bunch of other artists are all using the same pose of that polar bear in your art.

Stock Photo Sites

Stock photo sites like www.corbis.com are excellent for reference and you can easily search for what you need. The photos are high quality and often quite interesting and inspirational for composition, color, texture and poses.

Photographer's and Artist's Sites

You can search for individual photographer's sites as well as artist's sites. Photographer's sites are full of their best images. Again, very inspiring and good for reference. Portfolio sites like DeviantArt also have a lot of photography galleries on them.

Anatomy and the Figure

There a number of excellent anatomy for artist sites on the web that have photos of nudes from multiple angels like www.posespace.com. Some are free, and some are pay sites, and some have dvds with large photos for sale. Body building and fitness sites are great for human anatomy, as are adult sites. Medical and plastic surgery sites have photos of the body in various stages of health and disease.

Specialty Sites

There are websites for just about every interest in the world and they are great resources for reference: sites about fashion, jewelry, historical costumes, military gear, vehicles, robots, medieval weapons, you name it.

Photograph Your Own Reference

It's *always best* to take your own photos. First of all, you're the copyright owner and can do anything you want with the photos. Secondly, you can control the pose of your figures and the lighting, which is helpful when planning a painting. Also, your photos are original, not some Googled image that everyone pulls up in a search.

You reference photos don't have to be super high quality, although today's cameras and smart phones are quite good. Don't get bogged down in all the photography lingo – it will just prevent you from getting started. Shoot some photos of friends and get to painting.

Of course you can get quite sophisticated with your photography if you like, in which case a high end SLR digital camera and good lights are important.

You may want to shoot video as well. It can help you better understand anatomy and the way the body moves.

Drawing from Life, the Best Reference

Drawing from life is always the very best reference you can have. Your subject does not need to be translated and figured out from a flat photo – it's right there in front of you for you to interpret as you like through your own artistic expression.

I discuss the benefits of drawing from life in the *BOOK 1: Seeing: Drawing from Life* section. Do it whenever you can, either as a learning experience or for reference for a painting.

Get together with some of your artist friends, chip in and hire a model, and go to town. I'm sure lotsa local artists would love to join you. There are likely groups like this in your area that get together once a month and draw from life. Make a day of it: bring snacks, have guest artists come and talk, share your experiences and have fun.

Buy cool still life items at garage sales and flea markets for cheap and use them as props for your life drawing sessions and in your art. It's also a great place to get magazines and books dirt cheap to tear up for scrap.

AD Supplied Reference

After reading the art description, ask for reference from the AD if you feel you need it. Has the character appeared in a previous book or card set? Is there something out there that they are thinking of for the character – like "it should have an Indiana Jones feel?" Once you get the reference, study it along with the art description and ask questions if you need to. Know what it is you're supposed to draw before you start.

Your art director is going to supply you with reference. It's helpful to understand some of the basics of the industry you're working in, to help you grasp what's happening in the reference. Remember, if you're ever stuck, just contact your AD.

For example, the Magic: the Gathering card game has five card colors. Aside from being required to have the color of the card you're assigned the predominant color in your illo, you must also understand that each color has attributes and psychologies behind them. Knowing this about the product will further help you interpret the reference and make more on point illustrations.

Know What You're Looking At

When working on illustrations based on a video game property, like the World of Warcraft, you're often supplied with in game screen shots from video game itself as reference. It's often hard to determine what materials something is made of in a screenshot. On a low resolution textured polygon model, leather looks like metal looks like bone looks like cloth. Sometimes you can tell the difference, sometimes you can't. The same can be true with painted concept art reference. Ask questions until you know what you're looking at.

Another time it helps to have some basic understanding of the elements of a particular industry you are working in is when you are given renders of low poly 3D models as reference. In this case, when you see reference for a gauntlet that is hexagonal in shape, you shouldn't draw it as a hexagon. It's a hexagon because of bandwidth limitations of the game engine, not because it was designed as a hexagon. In a realistic rendering, that gauntlet should be rounded; the model just doesn't have enough polygons to make it round.

Style guides
Style guides are larger universe "bibles" or comprehensive guides that cover the major elements of a product line. They cover character races, classes, abilities, weapons, clothing, gear, personalities, psychology, society, culture and more. They may also contain descriptive writing or fiction. They may contain technical details, diagrams, or schematics of product manufacture, design, or packaging. They might have page templates for you to follow and anything else that would help you do your job.

Instead of a style guide, you may receive a **style board (or design board)** which is kinda like a large bulletin board image with lotsa inspirational photos on it that relates to the topic. Style boards are widely used in the fashion and interior design industries. Style boards might have photos, fashion photos, swatches of actual fabric, color schemes, textures, illustrations from other artists, etc. Style boards are more for general flavor than reference to be followed to the letter

Sketch Approvals

Sketches can be done anyway you like: pencil sketch on paper, charcoal, tonal wash, line drawing, digital sketch, etc. Some clients may want sketches done a certain way, so ask. And some clients may require a color comp as well. Sometimes I do a color comp if I think that will help sell my concept or make it sing.

It's a really good idea to draw a box that is proportional to the dimensions of the final art on your paper before you start drawing to get your composition working in the right frame. Use your proportion scale!

I like to put the illo specifics on the sketch like illo name, identification number, my name, etc., including any notes like "grey storm clouds here," or "blue glow coming from the eyes." If your notes are in an email, they won't get seen down the chain of approvals. Put it right on the sketch.

When your sketch is done, you just have to digitize it, by scanning or photographing it, then email a jpeg to the client for approval. You want to keep the file size down to about 2mb, but you want it to be big enough to print on a piece of 8.5" x 11" paper because ADs often print sketches to show them around the office in the approval process.

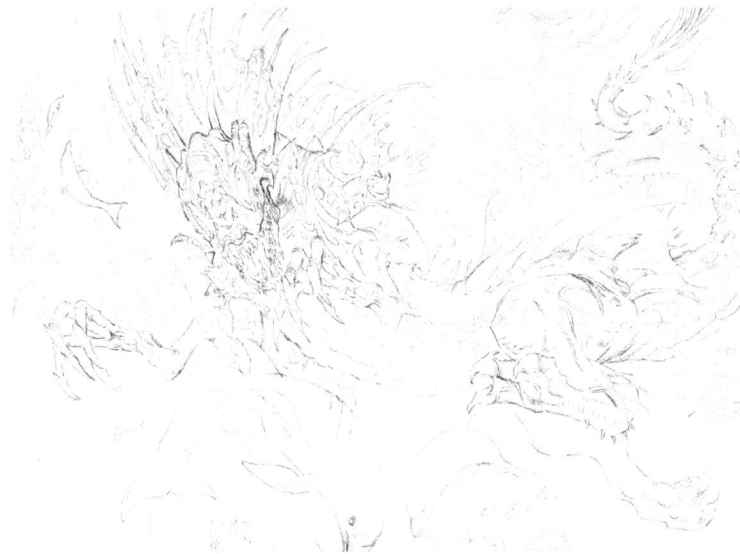

Quagnoth sketch © Wizards of the Coast 2006

Minimizing the Chance of Revisions

I like to do pretty finished sketches. This serves three purposes. First, with more detail an AD can more easily understand what you're showing them. Secondly, a finished drawing, tonal or line, looks more impressive to them and whoever else they have to show for approval than a sketchy thumbnail. And thirdly, they will be less apt to ask for changes. If you turn in a sketchy thumbnail, the AD knows it didn't take you long and won't take you long to do another. But if the sketch is more polished, they will likely go with it, or just ask for minor changes as you go to final.

Remember, every time you make changes, it takes up your valuable time. Unless you are getting paid for changes, you're losing time and money. So you want to minimize the amount of changes however you can. The main way, is to do good work the first time.

ADs love when you do multiple thumbnails or simple layouts for them to choose from. This is one way to minimize changes: by getting input from the AD at various pre-stages. This can be a pain though, especially if the AD you're working with is not very decisive or good at design or able to communicate what he's envisioning to you.

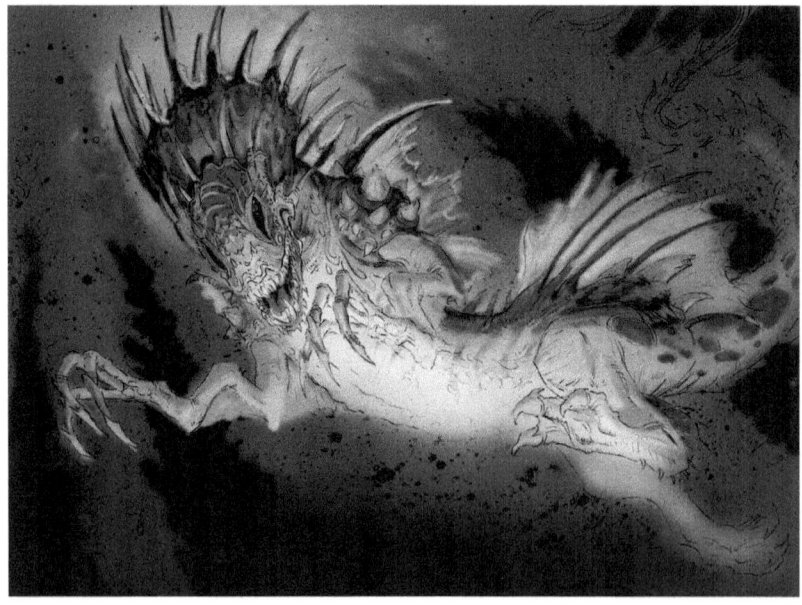

Quagnoth color comp © Wizards of the Coast 2006

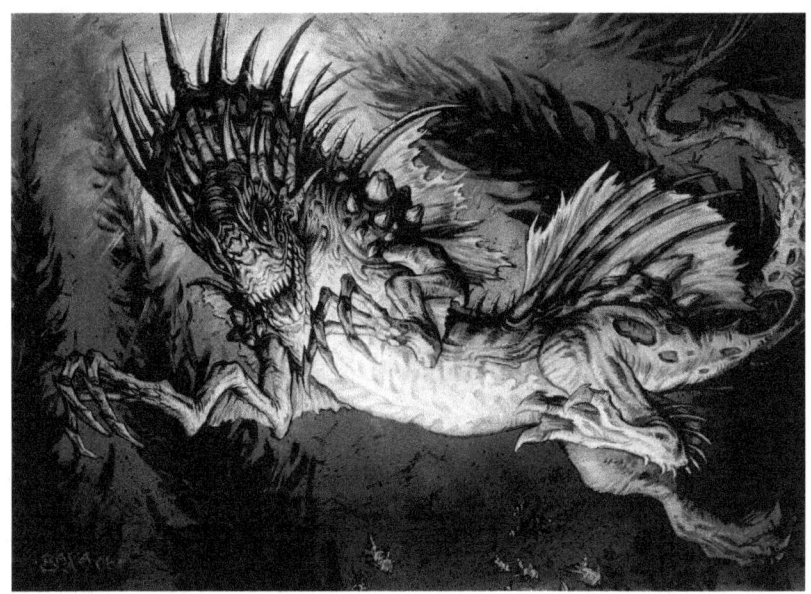

Quagnoth final painting © Wizards of the Coast 2006

If part of your normal process is to do multiple layouts for yourself until you get something you like, that's great. You may want to show the AD a couple to choose from if you're already doing them. Do whatever you have to do to create a great piece and make the client happy.

However, one thing to remember is that the "rules" that you establish for your working relationship with someone will be the standard that is expected of you from then on. So if you do three layout thumbnails and some character design concepts before your final pencils, then your AD will likely expect that same approach every time

I feel that doing multiple preliminary sketches is a lot of extra work, and it slows down the approval process because you're waiting for the AD to respond to thumbnails, final pencils and final paintings.

They are hiring you because you are good at what you do. Do it, and give them something dynamic and on the money the first time.

I like to turn in jobs right at the deadline, even if I finish an illo early. This way the art director will be less apt to ask you to make changes because they have to go to press. This can be risky though, because they may not like what you've given them and still want you to make changes in a short time. It's best to do this only once you're a proven quantity that is, you've worked with that AD and they like your work. This may seem adversarial, but as long as you're on deadline, the AD will not hold it against you.

On the flipside, if you're working with a client that often gives changes, or you work a bit slow, you may want to turn sketches in early to give *yourself* more time for fixes if requested.

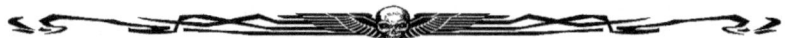

Final Art

Once your sketch is approved, it's time to paint! If you're going to paint digitally, just bring your sketch into your favorite painting program and have at it. If you're going to do an oil painting, the following is what I do to preserve my sketch and save time.

Mounting a sketch

I print out my sketch on Epson Ultra Premium Matte Presentation Paper (#S041341) 13" x 19". That's the largest sheet they have, but it's plenty big for most of my jobs.

Next I mount the paper sketch onto either heavy weight illustration board or a piece of masonite which you can get at Home Depot and cut to size. Illustration board will warp a bit, so masonite is the best choice and it's sturdy for shipping. Masonite is *not* acid-free, but you'll be coating the entire board and paper with an acrylic barrier, so you'll be fine.

You're going to use Liquitex Acrylic Matte Medium as a glue to mount your paper sketch to the masonite, kinda like doing decoupage. I like Liquitex, because it leaves a little tooth when it dries. Have your board, sketch, matte medium, a 1 1/2" paint brush, and a brayer (rubber ink roller tool) ready at a big sink or by your bathtub. You'll want to put your board on a piece of cardboard to protect from oozing medium.

Soak your sketch in cool water for the length of time it takes you to brush on a coat of matte medium on your masonite. (Note: archival inks won't run in water, others will.) Pull the sketch out of the water, let it drain a bit, then squeegee off excess water with your hands. You want the paper to be damp, not wet.

Lay it on the wet matte mediumed board where you want it, then roll it down with the brayer, wiping up excess medium. Then brush on a coat of medium over the whole surface and let dry overnight. Add a second coat of medium, let it dry, and you're ready to paint.

This process is excellent, but takes a little practice. I highly recommend you watch my video on how to mount a sketch by clicking the link or image below:

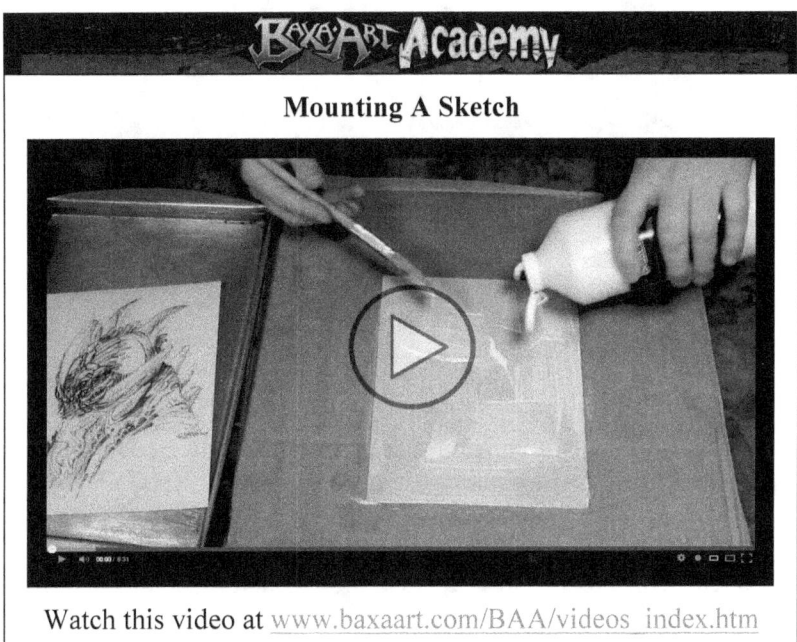

Mounting A Sketch

Watch this video at www.baxaart.com/BAA/videos_index.htm

Work in a Timely Fashion – Speed Revisited

To me, doing a job in a "timely fashion" is defined as doing the amount of work necessary to appease the client, feel good about putting your name on the work, leaving time for your personal life, and making the effort worth the fee.

Let me say that again: Is the time you're spending on a job WORTH THE FEE? Sure sometimes you want to just spend hours on a painting because you're having way too much fun, or you want to make it really good for your portfolio, etc. But you have to weigh the cost of doing that.

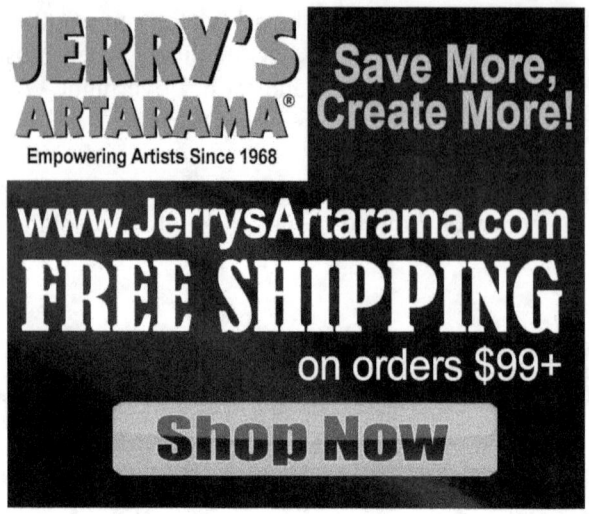
The supplies you need to mount a sketch are available at most art stores. I always shop at Jerry's Artarama online (www.jerrysartarama.com). Their prices on Art supplies are super reasonable!

Timely fashion can mean different things for different jobs. For example: Working for 3 days on one concept of a character is way too long; in this case working quickly to flush out broad stroke ideas would be considered working in a timely fashion.

As I stated before, being fast at illustration is helpful. And that comes with time and confidence. However, if you're fast, but you're not delivering the quality level expected by your clients, then speed is useless. So find a balance.

Being fast is also about making decisions quickly, like what camera angle to use for a certain illo? What time of day should it be? What background elements will help sell the concept? Grab an idea and run with it. Don't spend a ton of time mulling over all the possible choices you can make for the image.

Establish your Baseline

As I mentioned above, it's important for you to establish some personal "rules" around your working relationship with a client. This is not something you want to discuss with the client; you just want to figure out some guidelines for yourself.

However you operate with a client, they are generally going to expect that same behavior every time. You want to do a great job and wow your new client, but you want to be careful not to overreach.

If you stay in the studio working until 2 am every night, the client is going to consider you a work animal and expect you to put in that amount of time *on every job*. You wouldn't work until 2 am every night at an office job would you?

If you help out on a rush job, guess who they're going to call next time there's an impossible deadline? Guess who has to work nights and weekends to get it done? If you get a spot illo job that pays $50 and you spend a week creating a cover level painting, they're going to expect that every time, and you're getting paid peanuts for the time you're putting in.

See what I'm saying? You have to find a happy medium. Put in the hours and do good work, but don't kill yourself. When you're first getting started or working outside your comfort zone, it's hard to gauge how long a job is going to take you. That's ok; it gets easier as you do more work.

When in doubt, err on the side of caution and do more to make the client happy. You can pull back later when you have a working relationship and the AD is comfortable with you and confident that you will come through with the goods in the end.

For instance, once you've established a strong working relationship with an AD, and he feels confident that you will turn in final art that is at the level he needs, you can do rougher layouts that take you less time, or start to render a bit less in non essential areas, etc.

Let me remind you to NEVER tell your art director this is what you're doing. Let them think that you're rockin' it hard all the time.

Know When To Say When

I'm like you, creativity is a passion and I love making art. It's easy to get wrapped up in a painting, watch the hours fly by, and love every minute of it. It's good for your soul and tons of fun. But life is about people and about love. Know that, and seek it out.

If you stay in the studio working until 2 am every night you neglect yourself by not spending more time loved ones or missing out on some of the great stuff of life. Most of your friends work 9-5. If they're calling you to hang out in the evening and you're still working, you miss out.

My point is that you have to know "when to say when" as the saying goes. Illustration is a job, and you have to have a quitting time for your own sake.

You can rework a composition, change the color scheme, and render until you're hands go numb. But what does it really get you? Is your piece really *that much* better because you rendered the snaps on a uniform? I think not.

For your personal work you can go nuts, but for illustration jobs get in the practice of doing just what's needed to get your point across, no more, no less. Do great work while applying an **economy of means** by putting your energy and attention on what's most important. You can do this by simplifying your style just a bit and not rendering everything in the scene up to the same level of detail. Focus on what's critical in the scene and render that, and suggest the rest with broader strokes and implied detail.

Painting with an Eye on the End Product

What is the end format that your painting will be presented in? This is an important question and can have an impact on the way you approach a painting. It's good to make some adjustments in your work depending on the final output destination.

This isn't something to obsess about. It's another one of those things you get better at with experience, but you're getting a head start with this book.

Your client will have experience in knowing what adjustments to make to get the best results; that is providing they have a quality control person or department. Small companies don't and your art may be handled by a non-artist, so you want to do your best to get close in the art and any digital files you provide the client.

The more spot on your paintings and digital files are, the less time the client has to spend to get your art to "look right" and the better you come off looking. They might not even know why, but they'll be happy that your art looks great every time.

Painting for PRINT

If the final output for your painting is going to be in print on paper, there are some adjustments you can make to the way you paint and/or in the way that you color correct your digital file to improve your final images. It's a good idea to adjust your paintings because they will be all that much better when initially photographed. Then you can make some final adjustments on the digital file compensating for CMYK printing and printer color space (see below).

Paper absorbs wet ink and colors bleed into one another on a minute level, causing **mid-dark values to skew darker**, especially on cheaper paper stocks. So you'll want to work a bit lighter with a bit more contrast and a bit more saturated colors. This will keep your image from getting muddy or going too dark. You want to also create clear value and plane separations in your compositions.

Detail is lost when printing in general, and more so the more your image is reduced. Putting in a ton of tiny detail is a waste of time because it will not have much impact in print as it does in person, especially at a small size. Save yourself some time and detail only what's important. Keeping your compositions bold with strong focal points and a good range of values will help retain a powerful impact in your work, even in print.

Subtleties in value and color are greatly diminished so you want to push the value ranges in your paintings. Remember that an actual painting is being affected by light. Glazes and translucent colors come to life with light, but those inner glows will not translate when photographed, reduced, and printed.

I like to do paintings that sing when you look at them live with a certain amount of detail to make them gritty, evocative and exciting. I know that some of the detail and color subtleties will be lost when it goes to print, but I think it's important that the work you turn in continues to impress your AD in person as well as in print. You have to find a balance.

One thing that most of us don't think about is that **cameras and scanners actually see some colors differently than the human eye.** Cameras are notorious for over saturating red for example, so a hell scene filled with reds, red-oranges, and yellow-oranges tends to lose contrast as the tones all over saturate with red. You want to heighten the value contrast in predominantly red paintings to compensate. Paintings also tend to flatten out a bit. Mainly because the eye can actually detect depth in translucent paint on a canvas and the camera cannot.

A huge factor to consider is that ALL printed matter is limited to the CMYK color space, because of the inks and processes used in printing. Also called "process color" or "four color", CMYK printing is based on a model of four colors, Cyan – Magenta – Yellow – Black, that when mixed in all possible combinations, gives you a set number of colors that can be accurately printed.

CMYK has a huge range and will reproduce most images quite well, but it does have a few deficiencies. For example, there is less value range in the greens, blue-greens tend to go more blue-purple, and reds skew darker.

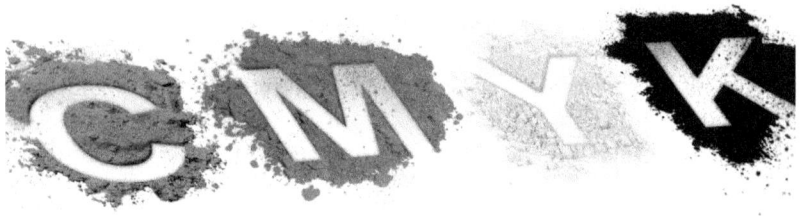

These variances are subtle and usually not of too much consequence, but if you plan on doing an underwater scene full of blue-green, aqua, turquoise, and blue-purples for the shadows, most of the variations of hue will print the same and your work will flatten. So a little knowledge in advance and adjustment in your colors could help a lot.

In a digital file, every pixel has a color assigned to it and that information is stored in the file and displays no matter what that file is used for. You can adjust that pixel color data to suit your needs.

Since all work is digitized first before printing, you may want to color correct your digital file yourself before sending it to the client. In Photoshop, you can put your file in the CMYK color space and get a good idea of how it will print and make some color adjustments. Same is true for digital paintings; they also need to be color corrected for CMYK.

See *Delivery of the Final Art: Digitizing a Painting for Delivery: Color Correcting* below for more about CMYK and color correcting your digital files.

Painting for SCREEN

All computer, smart phone, tablet, or television screens display colors in the **RGB color space**. RGB uses three colors, Red – Green – Blue, in combination to create a spectrum of colors. RGB is commonly thought to have 16 million colors, so it is extremely precise, and covers all the nuances of color quite nicely.

Because a computer screen is back lit with light, it is generally more vivid than print and colors are more vibrant and bright, so you can paint in a bit darker palette if you like because the value ranges in the darks will hold up, especially if you do the painting digitally to begin with. The RGB color space and monitors can display some more saturated colors as well, so you can do very electric paintings if you like.

Just as when you paint for print, you'll likely paint larger than the final output size, so you want to have an idea of how small the image is being reduced and for what type of device. If your art is going on smart phones, you don't want to work too big or have way too much detail because it will get lost in reduction. However, many clients will ask for files larger than final output size so they have an image they can print or use later as technology improves and game resolutions grow.

If the final output destination for your artwork is a screen, like for a video game or mobile app,
you'll get the best results if you paint digitally because what you see on your screen will translate pretty closely to the end product, whereas a painting has to be scanned or photographed and some detail and subtlety will be lost.

A critical tool for getting your artwork look right for output and syncing up with your client's system is ICC color profiles. See *Delivery of the Final Art: Color Correcting: ICC Profiles* below for more info.

Delivery of the Final Art

Now that technology has given us the convenience and control of being able to photograph and scan our own work, we also have more responsibilities. We have to have the knowledge, hardware, software, and time needed to create and properly format digital files for delivery to the client. The great thing is that as artists we have more control over the color correction and preparation of the digital files.

You always want to provide a flattened uncompressed TIF or Photoshop PSD file unless the client asks for something else. I always provide a flattened file so they don't feel like they can mess with the layers in Photoshop.

Jpegs and other compressed files are NOT suitable for print because the compression algorithms, while magically reducing file size, cause visible "artifacts" or visual errors when printed at high resolution.

Questions to Ask Your AD

The following questions will help you determine if you have to prepare the digital files yourself or not. If any of the services you are asking about seem spotty, then you may decide to do it yourself at your own expense. You may opt to anyways, to maximize control.

If you are sending in an original painting, photograph it yourself the best you can anyways, just in case it gets lost or damaged in shipping, that way you can still deliver the job if your photo is decent. It beats doing the painting over.

- Do you accept paintings and photograph them?
- Who photographs the art?
- Are they photographing oil paintings or scanning them?
- Is the photographer using polarized filters on the lens and lights?
- When do I get my original painting back?
- Do you only accept digital files? What size and format?
- Will you cover my cost of photographing the art myself?
- Who is color correcting the digital files? Do you have an imaging department?
- What ICC profile/color space should the digital file be delivered in? (see below)

Digitizing a Painting for Delivery

If you decide to send in a digital file instead of your original painting, you need to digitize it by photographing it or scanning it.

Photographing Art

If you do an oil painting or a mixed media piece, you'll get the best results if you take your painting to a professional service bureau that specializes in photographing artwork, especially if the artwork is large. They are pros, have tons of experience, have the right gear, and will get you great results.

Digital photos are often priced out by the megabyte (mb), averaging about $1 per mb, and a high resolution digital photo is about $35-$50. (Note: a 40mb tif file is about 11" x 14" at 300dpi (or 3300 px wide x 4300 px high). That's a good price for a cover painting job, but if you're doing 10 card paintings, that can add up quickly, in which case you may choose to photograph the art yourself. Either way, you'll still have to do some color correcting.

You can choose to photograph your own artwork, and with today's digital cameras you can get good results. To get professional quality results, it's a bit more complicated. Too complicated for this book, but keep your eyes peeled for a detailed blog post about it at my BaxaArt Blog (http://baxaart.blogspot.com).

Until then, here are some basics:

Diffuse Light

To avoid hot spots on the photo, you want diffuse light. Your best bet is to shoot inside in a controlled environment with photo lights. You should have two lights positioned at a drastic angle so the light is "raking" the surface to avoid glare. (If you can't afford a lighting set up, you can get decent results outside on an overcast day). Your painting should be fully upright with the camera on a tripod parallel to it. Set your camera ISO to 100 or 200 to avoid grain, and shoot in RAW file format, because it retains the most digital data and has no processing.

Polarizing Filter

Oil paintings get the best results when photographed with polarized lights *and* a polarizing filter on the camera lens. Polarizers help reduce specular highlights that occur when light hits the peaks of glossy brush strokes. Polarizers are not always used with digital cameras, so ask your service bureau pro about it.

White Balance
This is crucial for artwork. White balance is adjusting your camera so that white objects you see with your eye photograph white without a color tint. Normal "tungsten" light bulbs create a very yellow cast to objects and fluorescent bulbs create a blue-ish cast. Digital cameras have some auto settings to compensate for different lighting conditions and a custom setting for more pro applications.

Photography Supplies
You may want to Google around for some solid tutorials on photographing your artwork before you begin. Beach Camera (www.beachcamera.com) and Samy's Camera (www.samys.com) are a couple of excellent pro photo stores that will have the tools you need and the expertise to talk you through your purchase.

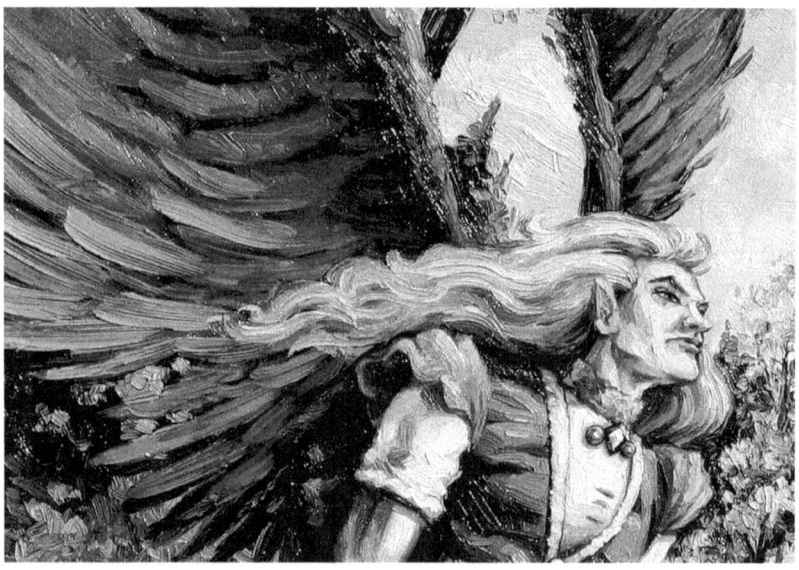

Flying Elves © Thomas M. Baxa 1998. Photo shot *without* polarizing filters. Same thing would happen if you tried to scan an oil painting. Notice the white dots and lines where light reflected off the strokes.

Scanning Art

Scanners are an excellent option for art that is not too reflective, like drawings, watercolors, etc. Most don't work well with varnished oils, however some do. My friend has an older scanner, the Umax Powerlook 2100XL which is supposed to be good at scanning oils without glare. I took a 24 x 36" oil painting to a service bureau once, and they actually scanned the painting on a huge flat bed scanner and got perfect results. So it can be done. But most consumer level scanners produce a specular highlight mess.

Scanners capture a high level of detail. But their laser lights can be harsh and can overpower or wash out subtleties in the highlights depending on the surface of the work. One great advantage to scanners is that they can be calibrated to your work environment's color space and ICC profile. Unfortunately, most scanners are small in which case you have to scan your painting in pieces and stitch them together in Photoshop.

BAXA ART Academy

TIP: Removing Specular highlights on oils scans in Photoshop
Here's a good trick for using the "Dust and Scratches" filter in Photoshop to remove specular highlights from a photographed or scanned oil painting.
1. Original painting photo is the background (lowest layer)
2. Make a copy of that layer
3. Apply dust and scratches to the new (top) layer
4. Here's the key: Now make the top layer a DARKEN layer, (shift the darkness or opacity of layer if needed)
5. Merge down

The "Dust and Scratches" filter finds all the white/light dots and by using it as a darken layer, it only affects the dots and fills them in without blurring more of the original painting than necessary.

Color Correcting

After you scan or shoot a digital photo of your artwork, you'll have to adjust the colors so that what see on your monitor matches your painting. Trust your eye and get the digital version as close to the way you see your painting (under the lights you painted it) as possible.

There are several important factors to consider when color correcting in a digital environment, which will greatly improve the chances that your artwork will be reproduced as you intend it to. If you do all you can then the client will only have to make very minor adjustments based on their system.

Color Correcting Factors and Tools
1. Color Space
2. Calibration of your system
3. ICC Profiles
4. Color Guides
5. Color Match Prints

Color Space

For this discussion, **Color space** is loosely defined as the set of colors that exist in your working environment, that is, the colors that show up on your monitor, printer, scanner, camera, etc. Color space can be used to describe your whole set up, or the color space of each device. Color space also refers to a global color system like RGB or CMYK.

Obviously colors can vary quite a bit between devices. Your monitor can run warm and appear a bit yellowish, and when you *print* that slightly yellowish image it seems a bit magenta. And that's just in your studio. Your monitor is different than the service bureau's monitor, than your client's monitor, than the book printer's monitor.

An effort has been made to standardize color spaces so there can be a degree of consistency in various output mediums. These standards are called **ICC profiles**. More on that in a minute.

Since color spaces can be so different, you need to minimize the differences and provide your client with some indicators or guides to help them color correct to your wishes.

Calibration of Your System

One of the first steps is to calibrate all the devices *in your studio* so they are producing colors in a similar fashion; so that when you scan something, view it on your monitor, then print it, all the colors are the same (or darn close).

Calibration is a bit involved and you need to buy a monitor calibration tool, which comes with software, and go through some steps with all your devices. Spyder brand colorimeter is well reviewed and a lot of pros use it.

Calibration is very helpful, but remember your system is calibrated to itself, not to your client's. ICC profiles to the rescue again.

ICC Profiles
An ICC profile is a data file that defines the color space of a device or the way an image file will be viewed on a device. ICC profiles are an attempt to emulate color spaces and standardize them to create a degree of consistency across output devices.

So if the digital printing press being used to print your client's book is using the ICC profile *U.S. Web coated (SWOP) v2* and you convert your digital photo to that same ICC profile in Photoshop (PS) and color correct it, what you see on your monitor should be close to what will print on the press because you are both working in the same standardized color space.

But ICC profiles are only an interpretation, so nothing is exactly the same, but it gets you pretty darn close. Devices usually have a default profile, and many allow you to assign one.

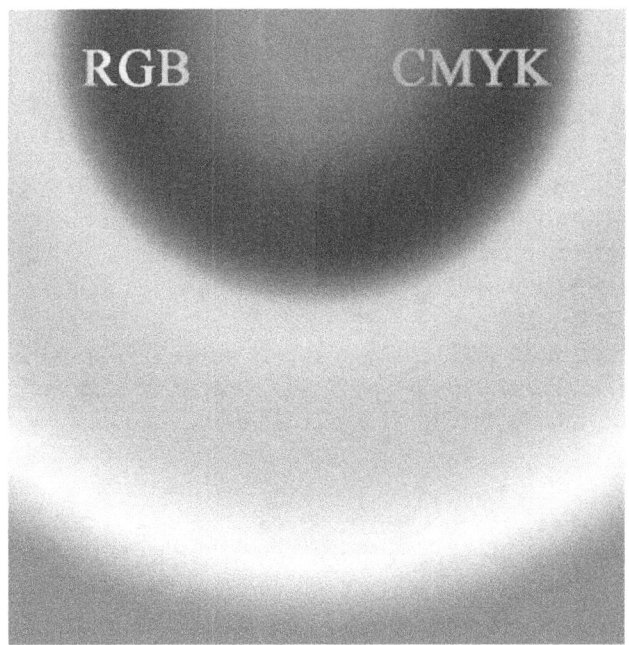

Side by side, CMYK seems dull in comparison to RGB, but on its own it has all the richness and range you need.

Ask your client what color space/ICC profile he wants the digital files to be delivered in. Most often they want something widely accepted like *Adobe RGB*, and they will make the conversion to the ICC profile they need for their printer. This is good because you can get your art looking good, and they have the expertise to get it looking good at press.

Sometimes it's helpful to know the actual profile of the output device because a profile for printing in CMYK like *GRACoL2006_coated1v2* can look drastically different than *Adobe RGB*, so it's good to have the option to color correct for yourself in the proper color space.

ICC Profiles in Photoshop
Go to **Photoshop > Edit > Color Settings** and you will see the current color settings for the Photoshop work environment or color space. Set the RGB working space to *Adobe RGB (1998)*. This is the standard for the art and graphics industry. (Don't use *sRGB* because it is a color space with much less colors so files are smaller for the web). If your PS color space is set to *Adobe RGB*, then that ICC profile will be assigned to any image you create in PS.

Every image file has an embedded ICC profile from the software that created it. When you open an image file, PS preserves the embedded ICC profile by default, unless you change it.

Open a tif or psd file in PS (not a jpeg). Go to the **Edit > Convert to Profile** and you will see in the dialog box that the **Source Space** shows you the current embedded ICC profile of the file, and the **Destination Space** allows you to assign another ICC profile to the file if you like.

Device drivers have ICC profiles and may insert them into the PS list of profiles. For instance, my Epson Stylus Photo 2200 inkjet printer's ICC profile is available in PS so I can sync PS's color space with my printer's.

Checking CMYK
When a client provides you with their CMYK ICC profile, change your PS CMYK working color space to that profile. Now when you got to **Image > Mode > and select CMYK**, PS will assign the profile you set.

Toggle back and for between RGB and CMYK and you'll see colors shift. You may want to make some minor adjustments before you send the digital file to your client.

Should I Paint Digitally in CMYK?

Trying to paint in CMYK is tricky because as you are picking colors to paint with, you may be picking colors that are **out of gamut**, or not printable in the CMYK color space you have selected. Luckily, PS lets you know in the color picker dialog box.

Even more strange is when you've already done a lot of painting, then switch it to CMYK and try to paint. Because of the way printing ink creates black, it is usually represented in PS CMYK as a 90% grey and that can really throw off your eye and painting sensibilities.

It's best to finish a painting in RGB, then switch to CMYK for color adjustments.

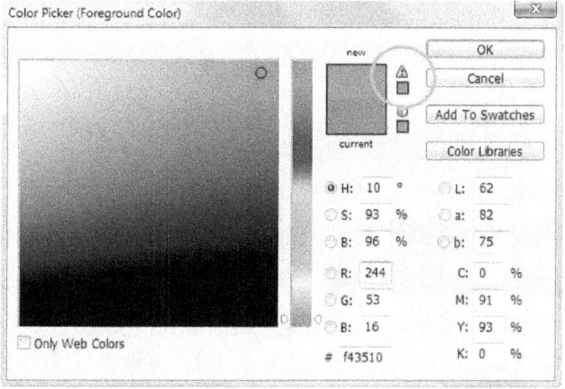

Photoshop out of gamut indicator (circled in green) in the color picker dialog box: a triangle with an "!" in it.

Color Guides

Since all monitors display colors slightly differently, it is important that you include some form of color guide on your digital file. A color guide provides "absolutes" of color for anyone to color correct to.

You want to attach a store bought color guide, like the one pictured below, next to your painting before you photograph it so when you bring the digital photo into Photoshop to color correct, you'll have a guide. When you have a service bureau photograph your work, ask them to include a color guide well.

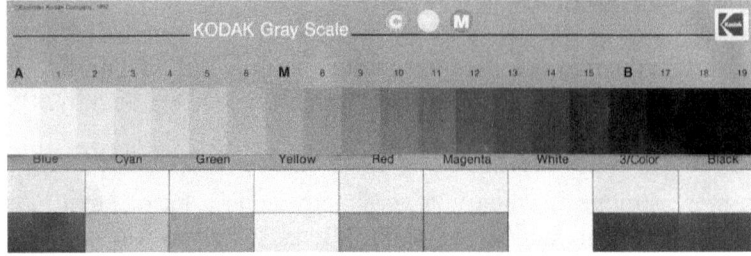

Color Guide by Kodak/Tiffen

If you paint digitally or are correcting a photo with no guide on it, first adjust the digital photo to match the painting *on your monitor*. Then you attach your color guide *afterwards*. This tells the client what black and white and 100% colors look like in relation to your artwork. Now they can adjust the colors in *their* color space and on *their* monitor to look very close to how *you* intended the painting to look.

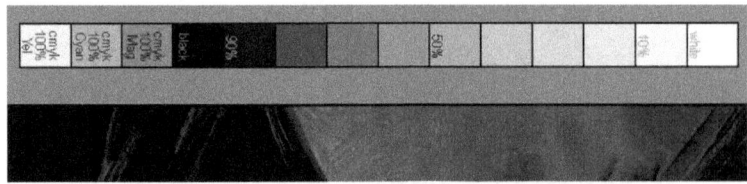

This is the color guide I made that I attach on the edge of my digital files. Make sure you include at least 100% white, 100% black, and 100% CMY.

Color Match Prints
If you're delivering a digital file to your client, and no original, you should snail mail them a **color match print**, which is a printout of your painting that is as close to accurate in color as you can get to the original.

This way, no matter what's happening with color spaces, monitors, and ICC profiles, the client will have a physical print of what the art *should* look like and they can do their own color correcting to match it.

Actual Delivery of Assets and Tracking
Shipping
Remember I told you to ask your client if they photograph paintings and if they pay for shipping? These two factors will determine whether or not you spend the time and money to get a digital photo shot and color

correct it yourself, or ship a painting for the client to shoot. Remember, that if you paint big you may have to build a crate to protect the painting which can be quite costly to ship if you have to pay for it yourself.

Regardless, it can be nerve wracking to worry about your artwork being shipped back and forth to a client where it can get damaged. Always make some kind of copy of your work before you send it out, just in case it get's damaged beyond repair – you can still deliver the goods to your client.

UPS vs. FedEx
If the client is paying for shipping, he will give you his account number with his preferred carrier. Use that, and don't ever abuse the privilege. If you're not sure what you need as far as labels or boxes, call the carrier for advice.

In my opinion, UPS and FedEx are equally reliable and have comparable services. Both have package tracking, which is a must. UPS's rates are a bit cheaper. There are UPS Stores and FedEx Office/Kinkos Stores in most areas. Get to know the latest time you can drop off a package and it will still be picked up and go out for delivery that day, for those times you are up against a tight deadline.

The critical difference lies in the amount of insurance coverage they allow. FedEx only allows up to $500 insurance on artwork. Period. That's not much. UPS insures as high as you want with some minor restrictions, so that's a better bet.

USPS
The U.S. Postal Service is quite reliable as well, although I don't use them much for shipping original paintings. Got to your local branch and ask them about their services. Priority mail is fast, considerably cheaper than UPS and FedEx, and has tracking.

I like to use the USPS for international shipping, because it's waaaaay cheaper. International First Class is good, but has no tracking. Express International costs more, but has tracking. But the best option for artwork is Registered Mail. Registered mail is checked in at each arrival point so it can be well tracked.

Our postal service delivers packages to foreign countries' postal services and they take over from there. Most are pretty good, but a word of caution: in some countries their postal services are horrible and wrought with theft. Do a little research, and when in doubt use a private carrier like UPS, FedEx, or DHL.

Packing Up Your Art

I know you envision a kind and considerate UPS driver gingerly handling your package marked fragile with kit-gloves. No such luck. The drivers certainly don't want to damage any package, but they're not reading "fragile" and "do not bend" notes you scribbled on the package. (Btw, use fluorescent pink fragile stickers and plaster them all over the package instead of hand writing on the box). I had a friend who worked and FedEx and witnessed firsthand how they literally pour packages out of an airplane into bins. Pack it well, my friends!

Most of the time I ship my illustration board paintings in a FedEx box – flattened. And, believe it or not, I've *never* had a piece of artwork damaged in 25 years (knock on wood). It's pretty unbelievable actually. I feel like I shouldn't temp fate by even writing this! I have heard horror stories though, so I pack better nowadays.

This is important: it is the job of any insurer NOT to pay you. So cover all your bases, follow their rules and pack your stuff well. If you make a claim of a painting being damaged during shipping, UPS will closely examine the way you packed your package. They will look for any excuse to say that it was not packed well enough to warrant reimbursement.

One of their sneakiest denies is when you use an old box. They claim that a reused box is less stable and provides less protection. They also require 2" packing of either bubble wrap or packing peanuts around *all sides* of the item being shipped. Incidentally, if the UPS Store packs it for you, they make a note of that in the computer and you have a better chance of being covered.

Packing Tips
- Cover your painting with tracing paper first that doesn't stick to the surface
- Add a protective raised lip on anything that might have a bit of tack like oils or acrylics
- Then put a sheet of masonite or strong cardboard on both sides of the art. Save strong boxes like the ones computers and TVs come in, for their double thick, sturdy cardboard
- Bubble wrap it several times around. Note: Do not bubble wrap directly on the surface of an oil painting because it will off-gas and leave a pattern in the varnish.
- Put that in a taped up plastic garbage bag to waterproof it against rain and snow
- Put that in a box wrapped in 2" of bubble wrap or packing peanuts

- Make sure your box is packed tight. A soft corner will dent and could reach the art.
- Use strapping tape, aka monofilament tape, for extra hold

Return Shipping from the Client

You have to hope that your client understands that artwork is delicate and will take the same measures in packing it as you do. If you're lucky, they'll save the packaging you sent your artwork to them in and return it the same way. That doesn't always happen.

You might want to connect with the shipping department and make nice, just like you would the accounting department. Ask them to please pack it up your artwork well upon return. Also ask them for a tracking number if possible.

A company will claim responsibility for artwork damaged while in their possession and during return shipping to you, but it's not a bad idea to put wording to that effect in your contract.

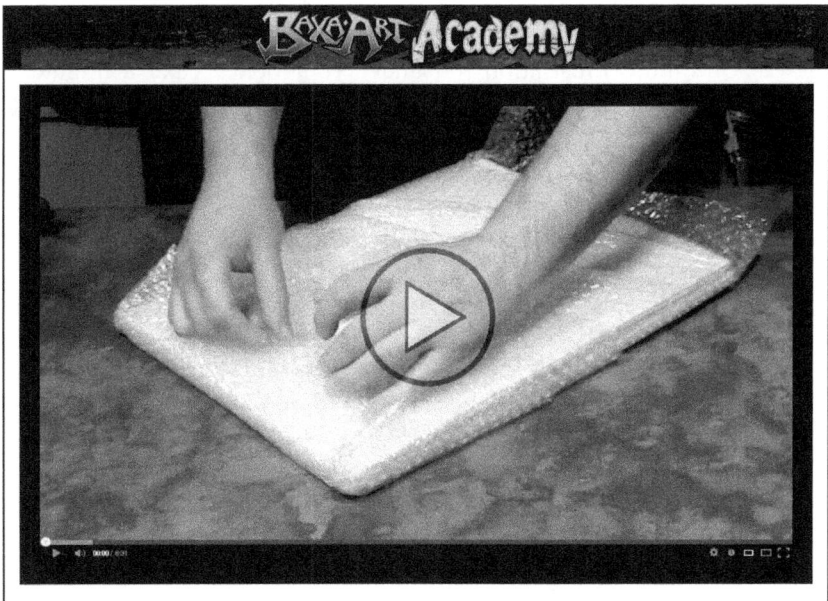

Check out the free video on **Packing Up Art to Ship**, you might pick up a tip or two: www.baxaart.com/BAA/videos_index.htm.

Digital Delivery

These days, most companies have some procedure in place for you to deliver digital files. At the very least, they will have an FTP site available. FTP, which stands for file transfer protocol, is a secure way of transferring data from one computer to another over the web. You need an FTP program (usually a free utility) and some log in and password info from your client to send your files.

There are data transfer/upload services that are free or inexpensive like YouSendIt, DropBox. They are very simple to use and have good email notification systems. Many companies use these services or have their own proprietary software that does the same thing.

FTP is secure. Email is not. But if you're sending files that aren't sensitive and are small enough for an email server to handle (around 2mb -5 mb) then you can use email. And you can always snail mail a disc or thumb drive to your client, although it's not done much anymore.

Once you've uploaded a file via FTP or other means, email your art director and let him know to look for the file. This lets him know that you've turned the job in on time.

Pat on the Back

Phew! One more illustration job under your belt. Take a minute to congratulate yourself on a job well done. Seriously, take a minute to realize what you've accomplished and feel good about it. You are the source of your own power.

Don't look to external sources for your validation. You'll likely be let down. Reflect on all that you've done to reach this point and know that you made this happen and when the job was in your hands you did your very best to rock it out.

We all want to hear that we did a good job, but in this busy day and age, it's unlikely that you will hear from your AD after you turn in a job. It's just the way it is. Even if he loved your illo, he won't even take the time to email you. So you have to be ok with that and be your own cheerleader.

You can email him and ask for a little feedback, but as you know ADs get hundreds of emails a day, and they just can't do their job and answer all their emails. Ask some very specific questions so the AD can give you quick answers and you may hear back.

Payment Checklist

You've already determined the terms of payment when you took on the job. So now it's important that you do your part to make sure payment happens. Small companies are usually pretty informal, but larger companies are sticklers for the right paperwork, so it's best you know what's required of you. This is part of doing business, even as an artist. Don't worry, it's not too scary.

Art directors seldom handle payments and contracts, so find out who to talk to in accounting from your AD. Then email or call the accounts payable department or the staff accountant and ask them what forms they need from you *before* you're waiting for a check and it's causing delays. They will have emails ready to send you with the necessary forms.

No one will mail you paperwork anymore, you'll get it all as digital files over email. Nowadays, most legal documents are accepted in digital form. So once you fill out and sign your documents, you can deliver them to the client digitally. You can also print them out and fax or snail mail them back if you like.

On the Job

Using the Pencil Tool in Adobe Acrobat to Sign a Document
Open the pdf contract the client sent you in Adobe Acrobat (not Adobe Reader). Go to Tools > Comment and Markup > Show Comment and Markup Toolbar > Choose pencil. Now you can write anywhere on the document, fill in fields, and sign it. Then SAVE it for the pencil writing to stay in the document. Then send it to your client.

To change color of pencil, line widths, etc., right click on the Pencil Tool icon in the toolbar > Tool Default Properties > adjust to taste. I like to use a blue line so it stands out from the black document text.

Check with your client to see what they accept, but here are some possibilities: Paper documents, pdfs or Word docs with a "digital signature", printed document with your physical signature scanned in and sent as a jpeg or pdf. I like to "write" in the pdf they provide and send it back (see the *"On The Job" Using the Pencil Tool in Adobe Acrobat to Sign a Document* box below).

Remember, these documents have your address, phone number, social security number and your legal signature that can be used for identity theft, so protect it as you would any personal info. Email is not secure. Send at your own risk. Fax and FTP are secure.

Keep track of your paperwork, get it in quickly so you're all set and can focus on your art. Make sure you get a copy signed by the company rep returned to you for your records.

The reason I'm spending so much time on this stuff is that, despite the fact that we just want to be artists and paint, we must also be business people. Unfortunately, ALL of these things *must* be on file with the company before you get paid. If you don't send an invoice for example, you will *never* get your check, so get on it. The following is a list of some of the paperwork you can expect.

W9 Form
> This form is required by the government for you to get paid from any company. Simple to fill out. Required only once at the start.

Contract
> This is the agreement between you and the company outlining the terms of the job. It would behoove you to get up on basic contract lingo. But you need to know that when you sign a contract, you are bound by law to what you've agreed to in it. So READ it and if you don't understand something in it, ask the company to clarify for you. Contracts are usually drafted for each job and they require your signature.

Master Agreement
> You may encounter this with your more corporate clients. The Master Agreement is a main contract with all the terms spelled out that you fill out once when you start your relationship with a company. Instead of generating all the same paperwork over and over for each job, the company considers the Master Agreement on file the guts of the contract and they just send you a **Purchase Order** or a **Statement of Work** document requesting deliverables for the particular job. Requires your signature only once.

Purchase Order or **Statement of Work**
> Usually one page that says what they want from you for any particular job. It spells out how many illos, fees, deadlines, and some other details. POs are always issued under a master agreement, and often with regular contracts as well. You don't have to sign

them, but you do have to reference the PO number when you invoice for payment.

Invoice

An invoice is basically a bill that you send a company for your services. Your invoice should include: Your contact info, your social security number or federal tax number, who you are billing, the product you worked on, what you did for them, the purchase order number of the job, the amount due, the payment terms (always write "Due Upon Receipt"), invoice date, and an invoice number to differentiate it from other invoices in their system.

1099 Form

If you are working on a contract basis, instead of receiving W2 Forms (like when you're an employee) you will receive 1099 Forms from each of your clients. 1099s tell how much you were paid during the fiscal year by that company. Companies are required by law to issue these to you buy January 31st for the previous year, so you can use them to do your taxes.

The process for getting paid usually goes like this:
- Verbal agreement to do the job
- Contract or Master Agreement is read, amended if necessary, signed, and turned in to client
- W9 is emailed to you, you sign it, and return it to the client for their files
- Purchase Order is emailed to you while you're working on the job
- You turn in final art
- Art Director must sign off internally that the art is approved, then email you saying it's ok to invoice
- You email your invoice to the Accounts Payable department
- You get paid in the amount of days your contract stipulates, like Net 15 days
- Keep track of how long ago you invoiced. If your payment is late, email the accountant to see what's up, and/or issue a friendly reminder or past due notice

Remember, if you forget to turn in your signed contract or the invoice, *you will not get paid*. As you can see there are quite a few things that can delay your payment, so be diligent about your part. If you just suck at this kind of stuff, get a friend or your spouse to help you out.

Some companies will cut you a check, even if some changes to the final artwork are requested; mostly companies or ADs that you've had a relationship with for a while. Some companies will not allow you to invoice until the job is completely done.

Some companies allow your payment to be direct deposited into your bank account instead of having a check mailed to you. This saves you some time and a trip to the bank. Ask the accounts payable department about it.

See *SECTION 5: Some Tricky Stuff: Getting Paid* below for some good strategies around payments.

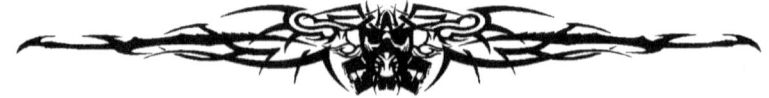

Notes:

SECTION 4: Working with Art Directors

Art directors come in all shapes and sizes. Aside from personality differences, the way they think about their position and the way they look at artists can vary greatly based on the job they are tasked with doing.

Most ADs are artists themselves, who have decided to take a job for whatever reason, usually for a steady paycheck and benefits. Sometimes it's because they are truly good at art direction and love what they do. Just like you don't want to be judged for your choice to be an artist, no one should judge them for the choices they've made.

This section of the book will give you some insights into the way ADs think, their motivations, the job they have to do, how to work with them, how to get on their good side, the different types of ADs, and more. All with your number one goal in mind: getting more work.

Just Talk to Them
Art Directors are just people like you and me. And they are art lovers, so you have that in common right off the bat. I know it can be a bit intimidating when you're just starting out in the biz, but it shouldn't be. Just chat with them a little like you would with anyone you're trying to get to know. And never be afraid to bring up business related topics, your AD is there to help.

Art Directors are Artists
If you talk to any art director, you'll quickly find out that they too are artists. They've often had long careers as working artists and moved into an art director position, or do both. Many ADs hold art sacred and have chosen not to do it for a living, but have instead chosen to keep their passion private and do it on their own terms. They may be preparing a series of paintings for a gallery show, they may be writing their first novel, they may be putting together a collection of paintings about dragons, or planning a painting trip to Greece!

If they're not artists, they certainly love art, in all its forms! They love looking at art, going to galleries, surfing for art on the web, buying art books, buying original art, you name it. Don't forget that, more than anything, ADs are art lovers just like you!

Shadow Artists

Julia Cameron, in her book *The Artist's Way* [a brilliant book which I highly recommend that helps keep your creativity flowing despite unseen blocks (available at Amazon http://amzn.to/1lyk0G7) coined the term "shadow artist" and describes him as a person who is an artist at heart and would love to make art for a living, but has chosen not to for various fear based reasons.

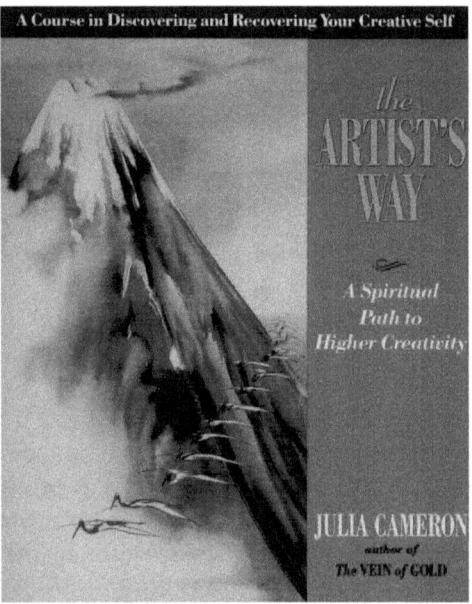

All people are driven to create in some form or another. All too often, when a young person expresses an interest in being an artist (writer, dancer, singer, musician) for a living, their dreams are met with well meaning "realistic" advice of their parents. They are told, and come to believe, that it's too hard to make a living as an artist, so they decide not to try. Parents and friends mean well, but they are just afraid for you, and truly can't understand the passion that boils within you. But often, the nay-saying is enough to crush the dream.

However, shadow artist love art and love to support the arts in many ways! We need shadow artists because they help keep the arts alive in our culture in ways that we as artists cannot. They raise money for the arts, they donate collections to museums, they attend art openings, they buy art, they talk about art, they lobby congress for the arts and on and on. Just like you and me, they are an important and enthusiastic part of the art community!

It's sad when a person decides not to pursue their dream of being an artist, but totally understandable at times. They are often afraid that they are not good enough to make a living at their craft.

> *But you are not afraid! You're going to go for it! I know this because you're reading this book and preparing yourself to succeed! And if you feel like you're currently a shadow artist, it's never too late to pick up and nurture your artistic passion!!!*

Shadow artists often choose careers that are close to or support the arts, like a museum curator, a gallery owner, a volunteer at a fundraiser, and (you guessed it) art directors. If you view an AD as a shadow artist, you may lead with a "those who can't do, teach" attitude. **Don't.** It's just not a fair or kind outlook, and it will only get you in trouble.

It's good to be aware of the type of AD you are dealing with, but if you fail to view them as your ally, you will likely form an adversarial relationship and that won't be much fun, and definitely won't help your career. Isn't it better to have a little compassion for all our fellow art world friends and approach them with understanding rather than contention anyways?

Your AD may be a shadow artist, and wishes he was making a living as an artist, but that is no reason to look down your nose at him. If fact, it would do you well to find the greatness in what he is doing. He chose to set aside his dream of being an artist for another equally noble dream of nurturing and supporting his family with a steady income. He helps other artists get better; he gives artist work, he supports fantasy and other forms of art, etc. And he likely still pursues his passions as an artist in his off time.

The Non-Artist AD
In your career, you will work with some ADs are not artists *at all*. This is sometimes the case in small companies with a small staff where everyone has multiple responsibilities. Sometimes the AD is someone who got promoted to the job from a non-art related position.

This can be frustrating because it may be difficult for non-artist ADs to understand what it is to be a creative person or what it takes to make art.

Yet they are in a position to dictate terms to you, request changes to your art, and decide whether or not you will get more work from their company.

One of the potential difficulties with non-artist ADs is that they don't truly understand what you need to do your job better, so that makes them poor advocates for the artists working under them with the higher ups.

If you're working with an AD that you know is not an artist, it may be difficult to accept criticism from him. Stay calm. You're the artist, so it's your job to explain your choices to them and why you feel they work for the assignment. Do your best, but in the end, you still might have to make the changes.

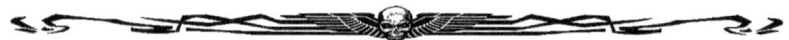

Types of Art Directors

An art director is the person in charge of the overall visual appearance of a product. He or she will spearhead visual design and/or oversee any artists (freelance or in-house), vendors, or departments that contribute to the visual aesthetic; as well as liaison between clients, management, and artist to keep the vision consistent and in line with the company's needs.

Even though a person might hold the title of "Art Director", his actual role and views concerning artists may vary greatly depending on the needs of the company he works for. Larger companies often have several art directors with different titles or responsibilities.

Art Director Types
Management
These AD positions are more like department heads or managers that oversee a staff of creatives, aid in workflow, handle scheduling, lead meetings, liaison between staff and upper management or clients, etc. They may be involved in the art approval process behind the scenes as part of the art team, but you will not likely deal with them directly.

Concept and Global Art Design

These ADs are responsible for conceptualizing products in early in their developmental stages. They may lead a team of artists, assure product continuity, aid in concept design, and are responsible for more global art concerns such as world building. You may or may not deal with them directly.

Art Managers

They have similar roles as ADs, but they really just assign the art, keep track of who's doing what, get your questions answered, catalog and organize the art when it comes in, get art to the right department, ship the originals back to you, etc. They are sometimes tasked with giving art feedback themselves, or just relaying feedback from the senior art director or the R&D team.

Production Managers

These types of ADs are a subset of the art manager type, and in some cases may not be creative people. As the name implies, production managers are more concerned with product production than the art itself, which may be perceived as just another step in the process of getting a product on the shelves. Consequently, they might perceive you as an easily replaceable "pair of hands".

Excellent Art Directors

A truly great art director knows how to walk the line between artist and management and marketing to help contribute to a really great product and create an atmosphere of camaraderie, fun and creativity. He understands artists and what makes them tick. He likes working with artist and doing all he can to get them what they need to do their job the best they can. A great art director knows when it is important to go to bat for the artist with his bosses, especially when his advocacy would bring about a result that is best for the product and the working relationship. He garners respect from the artists he hires and his management team because he works hard to ensure that the visual parts of the product are exciting, pertinent, creative, and evocative in the marketplace.

True Collaborators

This is very rare, especially if you're a freelancer. Due to the nature of commerce where faster is better, it is seldom that the illustrator is involved in the creative process when a company is initially developing a product. Jobs are segmented, and the artist is usually brought in later solely to visualize a world or product that has already been created by writers or a product development team.

On occasion, artists are brought in as part of the initial product design and development. You may be part of a team with other artists, writers, game designers, and management. An art director involved in this scenario will actually want your input and value your perspective as a visual person. He oversees the team and has final say, but his role is to collaborate with artists and bring in ideas from several sources in a creative brainstorming atmosphere.

Guys Who Fell Into the Job

This guy worked in the mail room and moved up to an art manager position because no one else wanted to do it and now they're making decisions about art. Sometimes they are artists themselves and can be very knowledgeable, but most often they are not artists and really don't understand the creative process or the technical aspects of creating art. They may admire your skill greatly, but likely view you as a vendor or asset creator. They are quite adept at keeping schedules, organization of assets, team communication, making sure products ship on time without mistakes, etc.

Even if they lack artistic ability, they still deserve your utmost professionalism at all times (especially if you want to keep getting work from them). One benefit you may find with this type of art director is that they often trust your judgment and leave you alone to do your job.

Different Industries Have Different Art Department Structures

Every company is different, and so is each industry, so it is helpful to understand their structures a little bit so you know who you want to show your portfolio to. Don't worry, you'll often work with one or two people on a job, so you don't have to know the entire corporate structure up the chain in order to do your job or have a healthy relationship with your AD. The following is an overview and will be helpful, but is by no means comprehensive, so do some research on your own.

More times than not, the art director is the person you'll be working with. In different industries, the person with the title of "Art Director" has different responsibilities, so sometimes the art director is not the right person for you to solicit; he's not the person that hires artists. Sometimes the true art director simply has a different title in a particular industry. There's a wide range of people who may be responsible for hiring you as an illustrator like:

Art Directors
- Creative Directors
- Production Designers
- Producers
- Editors
- Art Buyers or just Buyers (fashion)
- Lead Artists
- Generalists
- World Builders
- And more…

Hierarchy

The AD may hold a different position in the hierarchy of a company in different industries. For example, on a feature film the AD is not the top guy in the art department, the production designer is, but oddly enough, he is often your competition because he is creating the look of the film and doing concepts. On a big movie with a big art team, so you may be hired to do concept work under the production designer. You may also want to solicit producers because they pull together a concept team to pitch films or in the pre-production stages of a film.

In video games, sometimes it's a producer who is heading the team and has final say-so when it comes to art or character design, although he usually defers to the AD. This can be scary, because while producers are very adept at many things, they are seldom artists. They're the guys who say "I'll know it when I see it," which means draw it over and over until it looks like something they've seen before in a movie and feels "right" to them. But they are likely the person who will hire you.

In advertising, the AD is not the head of the art department, but they are part of a team that comes up with the overall concept for a campaign. The creative director is the lead who hires and oversees the entire visual art team.

Here are some art department structures in different industries:

RPG, small
Art director, staff artists (sometimes), freelancers

RPG, corporate
Senior Creative Art Directors or Managers, R&D world design teams, Art directors, staff artists (sometimes), freelancers

Video Game Cos
Producer, Art Director, Lead Artist, Concept Artists, Art team for 2D textures and 3D modeling

Ad Agencies
Creative Director, Art Directors, Designers, Production Artists, Comp/Concept Artists

Special FX houses
Figure Head/Company owner, Shop Manager, 2D Concept Artists, Sculptors

Films
Producer, Director, Production Designer, Art Director

What ADs are Worried About

I've talked about what ADs are looking for when they look at your portfolio, and that's closely related to this section where I discuss their fears and what makes them hesitant to try out a new artist.

If you take a minute to put yourself in their shoes and **try to understand their needs**, you'll have a better grasp on how to talk with ADs. If you know what they're worried about, you can alleviate their fears right off the bat and make them feel confident in having chosen you for the job.

The best way to do that is to deliver the goods, and deliver them on time, every time! ADs want artist that can do the kind of art that they need for their product line, so it looks awesome and pleases their bosses, with the least amount of worries or hassles. If an AD already has artists that are filling these needs, it would take a pretty good reason to change. It's always easier to stick with what you know than to try someone new and open yourself up to possible issues.

Notice I included that ADs want to please their bosses. Yes, ADs have bosses and they have to answer to them. Ultimately, the number one fear ADs have is that their bosses will not be pleased with their choices and they will get fired. So there's a lot on the line.

When an AD does see something in an artist's work that inspires enough him to hire that artist, he's taking a big chance, because he's never worked with him and there are a lot of unknown factors that come with any new working relationship.

Even if what they see in an artist's portfolio is exactly what they need, that doesn't guarantee that he can consistently produce the same level of quality for an assignment. Portfolio pieces are not done on a production schedule. Artists take weeks to do one piece. You can do an excellent piece if you have 2 months. Can you do the same thing in 1 week?

Which brings us to deadlines. ADs have no way of knowing if an artist can get a job done on time, and that worries them quite a bit because they have production deadlines that they have to hit. If the artist is late, then they're late, and the product is late, and the makes them look bad.

ADs are also worried that although an artist can do a cool portfolio piece, are they capable of extrapolating and visualizing strong illustrations from an art order? When an artist makes a portfolio piece, he's the AD, he's coming up with ideas that he's excited about and fully understands. Can he produce a strong piece with a topic that isn't his favorite? Can he *tell a story visually* based on a few lines of text?

ADs want to know that an artist is up for the challenge and is willing to work with them to find a visual solution that's effective. They want someone who is open to feedback and approaches an illustration as a problem solving process with a collaborative mindset. It shows them that the artist is willing to put in the time to get things right.

There are so many concerns: Does this artist really get the genre enough to deliver the right flavor needed? If he's not that passionate about the genre, will he still give 100%? Will he perform professionally so I won't have to babysit him? Does he understand contracts or will I have to spend a lot of time emailing with him? Will he pester me a lot or will he do the job seamlessly? Can I rely on him this time, *and* next time?

Then there's the risk of personality conflicts. Artists are notorious for being moody, flaky, egomaniacal, prima donnas, and not that good with details. Of course, these are generalizations, but an AD never knows what he's going to encounter when he hires someone. Obviously ADs have to take risks, hoping that an artist will do a great job.

Occasionally, an AD will see a piece in your portfolio that fits a slot he is currently trying to fill and pay you to use it. When I was still in college, I had already started sending out sample packs to companies I wanted to work for. To my surprise, I got a call from the AD of Dragon Magazine saying that he wanted to use one of my portfolio pieces for an article about magic. It was my very first published piece in 1988!

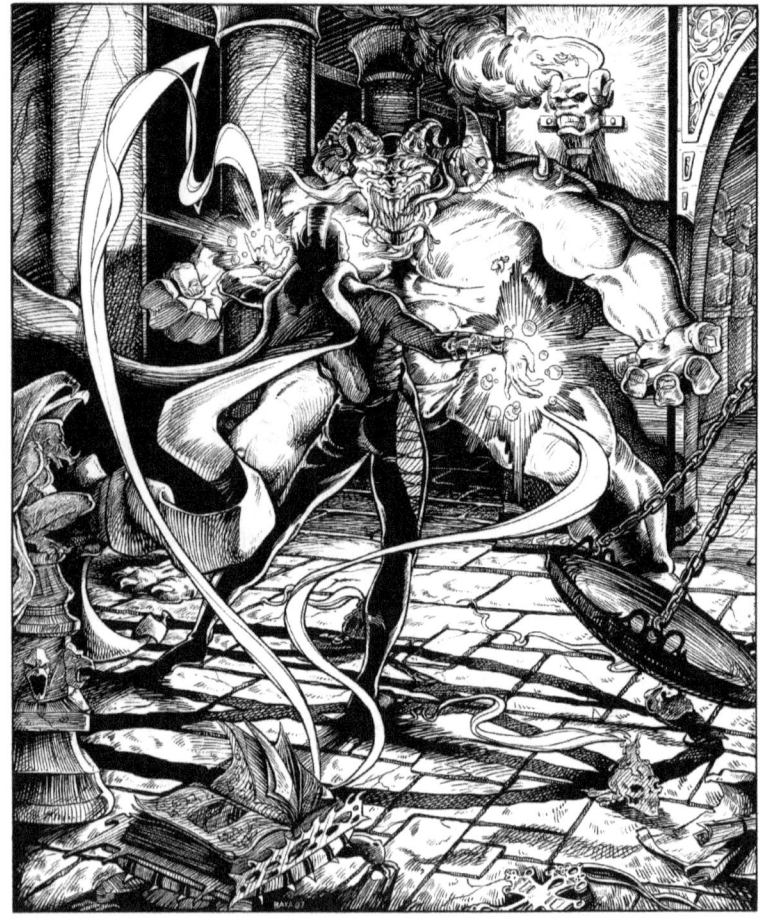

Dragon Magazine #132 © Thomas M. Baxa 1988.

When Will an AD Hire a New Artist?

For the most part, art directors are already working with a lot of good artists. And there are also plenty of times where they aren't; such as when an AD is new to the position, the company is new, or the product line is new, or they want a fresh look to a product line, etc., so don't despair. If they do have a go-to stable of artists, you have to give them a reason to not use one of them, and use you instead. Hopefully your art will do that.

There are millions of reasons why you might get hired for a job, and why you might get passed over, but here are some common ones to help you put things in perspective:

Reasons Why ADs Don't Hire the New Guy:

More possible headaches and they're already overwhelmed
It takes more time to break you in. They have to talk with you more, explain things, etc.
Not sure what they're going to get from you
They have a tight deadline, and need to go with someone they can rely on
Already using artists they know well and like personally
Loyalty to older artists and industry pros
If you fail, they have to scramble
It's hard for them to delivering bad news, if you didn't hit the mark
Artists can be a sensitive, and strange. They don't know if you're a weirdo, quirky, a bad listener, argumentative, etc. and they don't want to take a chance and deal with that noise
Didn't have time to look at your work
Never saw your submission
Your samples never made it to their desk

Reasons Why They DO:

You're good!
You have a unique style that can add some zing to their existing product line
Your art style is perfect for a project they are working on
They want a new or specific look for a product
Many of their go-to artists are busy (like during con season+ holidays)
They simply need more artists
They have a lower budget, so they hire young artists
They're tired of the guys they work with all the time
You have friends in common
Another art director recommended you to them

They love supporting new artists and fostering fantasy art in general

They remember what it's like trying to come up, and like to cut guys a break

They appreciate an artist's initiative and persistence in contacting them

An artist is building a large fan base on his own and could bring his fans to their product line

They are new in their position and want to make a splash and shake things up with new art. And more....

Don't get discouraged. Just keep putting your stuff out there and following up and things will break.

Art Directors – Friend or Foe?

Answer: Art Directors are ALWAYS your friend.

Even when you think they're completely wrong. Your job is to be Switzerland and stay neutral, calm and professional at all times, even when it's difficult. Remember, this is just a job. Yes, you love making art and you put a lot of your heart in to each piece, but you're also being hired to perform a task and deliver a product that has a specific purpose. The AD is your client, and it's your job to do your best to give them what they need, while also using your creativity to give them something special and exciting.

Nothing, and I mean *nothing*, can be gained by you viewing your AD as an adversary that you have to best and prove wrong. It will only aggravate them, hurt your working relationship, and cost you jobs. There's nothing wrong with having a discussion about what might work best for the project, but being stubborn and pissy will get you nowhere.

Listen to What They're Telling You

I know. You're a kick ass artist – you know it all. No one is going to compromise your craft. I know you're thinking "this guys just an AD, he doesn't know what he's talking about." Guess what, sometimes he does.

You can always learn something new, and an art director has a wealth of things to teach you. In most cases, an AD has *years* of experience in the industry over you. That experience is something that you can learn from. You can learn a lot about how to behave as a professional, how to tailor your art to fit the marketplace, how to survive in a company with a corporate structure, who is the big cheese, etc.

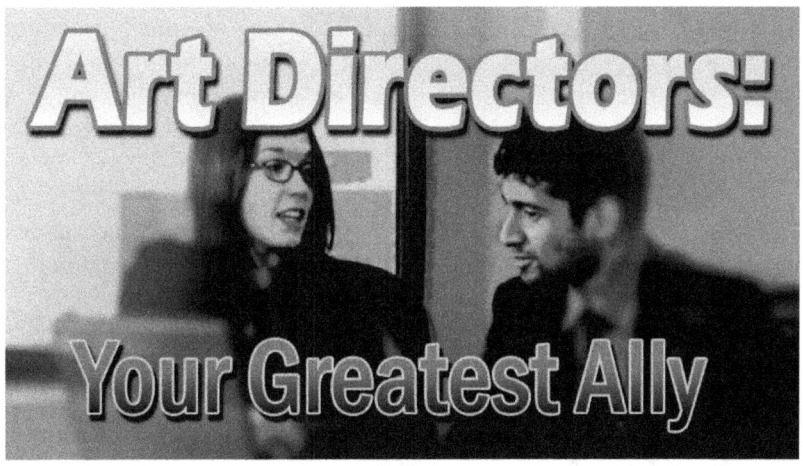

Aside from business knowledge, an AD's advice about you artwork can actually be very helpful. A fresh pair of eyes and some objective input can really help you see things in a new light and improve your art.

Also, if an AD is saying something to you, he's actually giving you insight into what you need to do or produce in order to make him happy and to keep getting work. He's giving you all kinds of clues about how to work with him and work around him without his even knowing.

Don't Take It Personally. It's Not Personal, It's Business

Artist are taught to believe that art is a very personal thing; that it is near and dear to their heart; that every painting is like one of their babies. Ok, that is true to some extent, especially with your own personal artwork. You put a lot of creative energy into a personal painting and you imbue it with feeling and all kinds of thematic content that is very important to you as a person and an artist. So your artwork feels very special to you.

But when you're working on an illustration job, let me say that again, illustration JOB, the client isn't in your head experiencing all the sweat and tears you are. They just need a very cool picture to fulfill their business needs. They don't care that you were feeling blue about the death of your grandmother and painted this work as a tribute to her. That kind of personal motivation is fine: it's an important part of who you are as an artist, it's part of what you want to say with your personal artwork, but it's not part of the artist/client relationship.

So when an AD tells you that the painting is a bit moody for the article and that you need to rework the colors, it's nothing personal. He's not saying that your grandma was a deadbeat and not worthy of your attention. He's not saying that you suck. He's not saying that you're a bad artist or a bad person. He's simply saying "this doesn't suit the needs of this particular assignment."

When you're gardener trims the hedges back a bit too much based on his aesthetic choices, you don't think he's a bad person do you? No you just ask him not to trim so aggressively and you move on.

You can be any kind of artist you want to in your own studio, but when you agree to do a job for a client, you need to deliver based on *their* needs, not yours. And, don't kid yourself, it's a game of compromises. But that's ok, if you can keep your head about you. If you want mommy to hang your art on the fridge, then don't be an artist for hire. Some of the feedback you may hear can be brutal, and that sucks. But do not take it personally. It only makes you upset for no reason, and you still have to make the requested changes. You can do that all pissed off, or you can say "oh well, that's part of being a pro" and have fun reworking the painting.

Look at the bigger picture and remember that you're just part of a much larger process when you are creating art for a client. There are game designers, writers, research and development that deal with continuity, the AD who jobs out the art and brings it together, the photographer, the color corrector, the graphic artist, layout artist, and all the business people too. Not just special, talented little you. Get the picture?

You're part of a team all working to achieve a goal of creating a final product. If you keep this in mind, it will help you be a bit more objective and not be crushed by criticism about your work.

ADs Can Be Your Greatest Ally

Art Directors are generally on your side. They love artists and are often artist themselves. So they get you. They know what you're going through. They get what it's like to fight with the paint, struggle with a composition, etc. They also understand what you face as a working illustrator.

On the Job

There have been several times when I went to a company that I've had a long relationship with to ask for some help. I always start with my art directors, and they have been more than happy to help me out. One of the main things I needed help with was getting permission to use copyrighted artwork owned by various companies to include in my art book *Blood Rituals: The Art of Tom Baxa*.

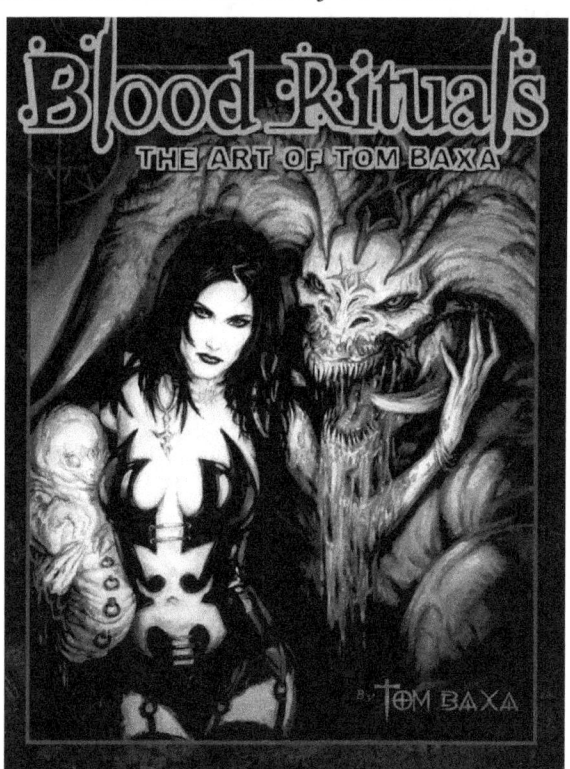

Blood Rituals: The Art of Tom Baxa © Thomas M. Baxa 2011. You can buy a copy at www.baxaart.com/Blood_Rituals_Index.htm.

But they do have a job to do, and they have to do it, while keeping their bosses happy. So the AD is the guy who straddles the line between the artistic side of things and the needs of the company. The AD is often shielding you from all kinds of bullshit, even when you don't know it.

A good AD will champion your art, meet management half way, and run interference between you and the non-artists in charge. They can be your greatest ally.

They can help you liaison with management or the design team if necessary. They can help get you in touch with other departments of the company like legal or licensing. They can connect you with the right people to contact within the organization to approach if you what to pitch them your own game. Most importantly, they can help you coordinate with the accounting department and help you get paid.

ASK, Don't Tell
Art directors can be quite understanding if you don't blindside them. If a job entails more than you thought it would and it's taking you a long time, talk to your AD, tell him you could use more time. Tell him you want to do your best work for the company, and ask him if you could have a little more time.

A key strategy here is to *ask* for what you need. If you come at the AD with an attitude of "I'm such a good artist, you'll just have to wait until I finish," he's going to get turned off. He might put up with it the first time, but he'll likely not hire you again no matter how good you are. And if you're enough of a pain in the ass for whatever reason, he might just cancel the job and assign it to another artist and you're out of luck. And remember ADs talk to other ADs and you might get a bad rep out there with other companies.

But if you are genuinely interested in doing right by the company and you need some extra considerations for whatever reason, open a dialog with your AD and see what can be done. *Ask* him if he has any ideas as to how you can work things out. He'll often try his best to meet you half way and help you both come to a solution that is best for all.

Also, if you're having a problem with an AD, something isn't sitting right, he's not using you as much, or any other issue – instead of making assumptions, just email them and ask them what's up. It's always best to go straight to the source.

AD's Blog and Social Media Pages – A Hidden Gem

If an AD has a blog, read it. If he has a Facebook account friend him and pay attention to your news feed. You can learn a great deal about the ADs you are currently working with and ADs in general. They are giving you insights straight from the horses' mouths.

Like any other person, an AD writing a blog is doing so in an effort to share his knowledge, inspiration, and ideas. Most often he's not going to filter or scrutinize what he is writing. He's going to "talk" to you candidly as if he was talking to a friend, and he's going to spill the beans. He's going to tell you exactly how *he* likes to be approached with a portfolio, how *he* likes to be contacted for work, and what *his* pet peeves are. He's going to tell all his secrets about how you can get work with him; sometimes directly or somewhere between the lines.

And, again, ADs also have a lot of extremely valuable things to say, so you might just pick up something that could change your whole outlook, not only with him, but with the way you do business as a whole. And that's great for you! And its FREE advice from a pro.

This also hold true for his Facebook page. Read your AD's posts. Like most of us, he feels like he's just talking to a few intimate friends in his circle on Facebook, and that can work to your advantage, because he will often speak candidly and reveal more insights into his personality for you to learn from. He might go on a rant about how much he hates getting submissions on his Facebook page; and you learn, not to approach him that way. He might say how much he enjoys meeting artists at cons, and mention which ones he's attending so you can meet him.

I saw one fiction editor's Facebook post about how much he hates when writers solicit him by messaging him on Facebook. He felt that Facebook was for socializing and not the proper venue for manuscript (and art) submissions. If you submit to this particular editor this way, you will be deleted and possibly black listed in his mind.

I've seen other art directors actually post that they were looking for artists to hire on their Facebook page and to contact them there with a link to their portfolio.

In social media exchanges, you'll also see the ugly side of ADs. Yeah, you can say "see I knew he was a jerk," or you can say "what can I learn from this?" Listening carefully to what an AD is bitching about in his blog will arm you with a lot of information so that you will be better prepared to deal with him in the future.

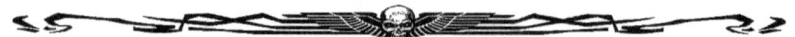

Communicating with Your AD

Your two main goals in communicating with your art director are to 1.) Get clarification on an assignment and 2.) Build a relationship with him so you continue to get work.

You want to use any means at your disposal to "talk" with your ADs as frequently as possible without being a nuisance. That means email, phone, social media, their blogs, etc. This section will give you some clues about how to communicate professionally with ADs and tips on how to stay in their minds so that when jobs come up, they haven't forgotten you.

Email

As you know, language in emails can easily be misconstrued because there is no context, vocal inflection, or body language to tell the recipient that you're joking. So keep your emails clear and professional.

And leave out your personal opinions on things. You never know the position of the person on the other end, so you don't want to jeopardize your livelihood by offending your AD with some snide remark. You're doing business. Save the comedy routine for your friends.

One thing you must remember though is that if it's in an email, it's in writing FOREVER. Email is like written proof and an implied contract, so watch what you say.

Good talking to you today, your input of the job was quite helpful. [make him feel good]

I wanted to be clear about the offer you made me as per our phone conversation on 1/8/13. [say when and where the offer was made] *I'll be doing 4 full page color illos for $XX. by Jan. 24th.* [spell out the terms]

Is that correct? [Call to action to respond]

Let me know, [2nd call to action to respond]
Thanks, Tom

This can work in your favor when you want to document an interaction. If an AD offers you something on the phone, send a confirmation email spelling out the terms of what he offered you after you hang up. Prompt him to respond, and if he does, it's like he agreed in writing.

Get in the habit of saving and organizing your business emails. You never know when you might need them. It's best to use an email client program like Microsoft Outlook and download your emails to your computer, that way you have them locally, can copy them, and archive them. If you leave them on a server like Gmail, one day they might just go away, and you're out of luck 5 years down the road when you need proof for a lawsuit or something.

Social Media Messaging

If someone it communicating with you over social media or some other means, prompt him to email you at your official email address. Social media messages can be out of your control and cannot be filed away on your personal computer. Your personal communications are logged on the site's servers and are public property.

Take control of important communications and do them over email. You can resend emails to remind someone of what they said to you. You can't do that with social media messages or IMs. It's better do talk on email, and that way you also get the other guy's email address so you can add him to your mailing list and follow up in the future.

Pick Up the Phone

Look for any excuse to CALL your art director and get to know him better. It will show that you're are interested in doing a great job and that you care enough to get it right. It also helps the AD remember you above the guys who only send emails. And who knows, you might get to like each other.

But don't pester him. Call with a specific reason in mind. And remember that they likely don't have much time to gab. Once you have him on the phone you can chit-chat a bit on a personal level, but not *too* personal.

Be careful not to ask too many questions like you have no idea what you are doing. Ask your artist friends for that kind of help.

Reasons to Call:
- Questions about the art order or reference
- Questions about contract terms or fees
- Topics too complicated to type a long email
- Seeking feedback on the job you did for a client
- Want to refer the AD to a possible business partner
- Come up with more business related reasons

Most ADs are so inundated with phone calls on a daily basis, that they usually won't answer their phone at all. Many companies have systems that differentiate internal calls from external calls, so if an external call comes in, the AD will almost always let it go to voice mail.

No sweat – you're friendly, you're courteous. Leave a brief message and your number and ask him to call you. Be sure to mention any reference or documents the AD might want to pull before they call you back.

He may just email you back in response to your phone call and answer your questions. At least you got a quick response and you can keep working. He just didn't have time to chat.

If you really need to talk on the phone, you may consider emailing him first and asking to set up a phone meeting. Give him a time range when you are available and wait for him to email you back with a specific time that is convenient for him to talk. Then confirm that you will call him at the time he specified. Be on time, like any other meeting.

This may seem like a bummer that you can't get your AD on the phone, but you know what, it's actually to your advantage as well. You're just as busy with things that are critical to your life, like painting!

And remember, having a client's phone number is a privilege that should be appreciated and respected, not abused. Don't call him too much. Don't give his number to anyone. Don't post it on a forum. Treat his number as you would your own home phone number.

Staying Connected with Your ADs

You know how it is; you meet someone at a party, instantly forget their name, and don't see them again for a year. What are the chances that you'll remember them? Or you get a pamphlet in the mail, and you throw it in your "I'll look at that later when I have time" pile, and you never do.

It's human nature to move from one thing to the next, especially in this day and age. ADs are no different. They are constantly bombarded with information like you and me, and it is not uncommon for an AD to lose sight of artists they met at a con, or even artists that they've worked with for years when it's time to assign a job.

It is your job to stay in their minds!!!

This can be time consuming, but it's all part of marketing yourself as a freelancer. Fortunately, in this information age and the Web 2.0 era, we artists have greater access to ADs than we ever did in the past. We can interact with them on social media by commenting on their posts or messaging them. We can follow their blog or forum and also comment there. And there's always email. If you're popping up everywhere they look, they're going to remember you.

Above all else, be genuine!

When approaching ADs, try to adopt a mindset of genuine interest and friendship. ADs know you're out there trying to market yourself, and they will actually respect you for it. But no one likes to be worked. And I don't want you to work them. Business, just like life, is built on genuine relationships. You want to be authentic in all your dealings and by building real relationships that will last, you will get more work and have more fun doing it.

Email Your ADs

Email is the best way to stay in touch with ADs. You would do well to focus your efforts there, because it's a *direct pipeline* to your AD. Everyone checks their email every day, so it's likely that your email will at least be read. As I said earlier, the best time to email anyone is early Tuesday morning at the start of business.

The key is to find any excuse to be in touch with them on some level, whether it is very directly like having a conversation over email, or more indirectly by popping up in their social media arenas.

The concepts behind the tips I'm laying out here can be applied to email or social media. You may just have to tailor your approach a bit depending on the forum you're using.

In any case, you ALWAYS want to include some form of **call to action**. Be clear and make it easy for them to do what you are asking by including a link directly to where you want them to go. Or give clear instruction about the destination like,

> *"I'll be at GenCon in the art show, table 35, come by and see my new line of Dragon paintings like the attached jpg!"*

Remember to entice your recipient with some snappy language and intriguing mystery to get them to take action and click over. Think as if you were on Twitter all the time. You have only a sentence or two to grab them and send them somewhere.

> *"If you like blood oozing out of every orifice, click this link:"*

Btw, never let an opportunity drop. If you're at your computer and get an email from an AD that means that he is sitting at his computer answering emails. So it's a good time to have a "conversation" with him. Email him back, if only to say thanks for getting back to you. Ask him a question to prompt him to continue talking with you. Ask him for feedback on your work; nothing too lengthy, just a quick question, but one that beckons a response. Don't expect more than one or two email responses.

Follow Up

When you try to make first contact with an ad, you may not get a response right away. Or you may get a response like, "I like your work, but it's not right for our current project, but I will keep you on file." That's great, but it's easy for an AD to lose sight of you in a slew of artists. So you have to follow up on your leads, especially prospects that seem interested. Make note of who you've contact and who was receptive, then contact them again in a couple months. Don't be a pest, but be persistent and professional.

Remember, they are moving along getting their job done with artists that are in front of them as they are passing out assignments. **Be the artist that is forefront in their minds.** You'll get work ahead of the guys who just stay quiet and don't do any marketing no matter who they are, what they've done in the past, or how good they are.

In *Section 2: Getting Work*, I discussed some strategies for initially submitting your work to an art director via mail and email. Use those same strategies to follow up with clients you already have, as well as with clients you haven't secured yet.

Ping Them with News of What You've Been Up To

This is probably the very best way to follow up with art directors. Show them some new artwork and or talk about some interesting things that you've been doing related to your life as an artist. As an artist, you're always making new art, especially if you're trying to find work in new areas, so why not send a postcard or email showing off your latest masterpiece. ADs love seeing new art that inspires them. Show them yours.

With art, it's good to just send an update and leave it at that. That does the job of keeping you fresh in a person's mind. Or you can ask for work at the end of the mail like this:

> *"I'm just finishing up a big job, and I'm going to have some time in my schedule coming up. I was wondering if you had any assignments that I might be right for?"*

Make it sound like you're constantly busy, but as soon as a spot opened up, you contacted them. It's all in the way you phrase things.

If you send emails too often, and the AD wasn't all that excited about your past ones, he will start deleting them without opening them, so be careful not to send too many. This is especially important if you are a young artist and your work is still in the formative stages. Spread your updates out and give yourself time to get better at your craft, then hit them up.

Aside from showing them new work, you can tell your ADs about some of the exciting things you've been doing, what cons you're attending, new product releases, books you're in that just came out, etc.

Your very best practice is to be posting this stuff on your website or blog, then sending ADs and potential clients there.

Kill two marketing birds with one stone: write a short blog article about your latest piece. That way you continue to build your blogging presence on the web, attract more followers, and can direct your ADs to your blog in an email. They can see your new art and might follow you.

On the Job

I did some concepts for a miniatures company that I was stoked about, emailed them, and didn't hear a peep. I was a perplexed because the owner was very cool on the phone, and the company has been around for a long time. I sent some follow up emails, and never got any feedback. I did get paid. Well, I figured the illos weren't right for them and he chose to blow me off instead of giving me a decisive no.

But I still had a good feeling about the company, so I thought I'd keep in touch a bit via email. A year later, I sent an email to the guy to show him that I colored one of the illos. To my surprise, he said that he had tucked the illos away in his "to do later" pile and just never got around to them. My pinging him with a friendly email update prompted him to pull the illos and get them sculpted!

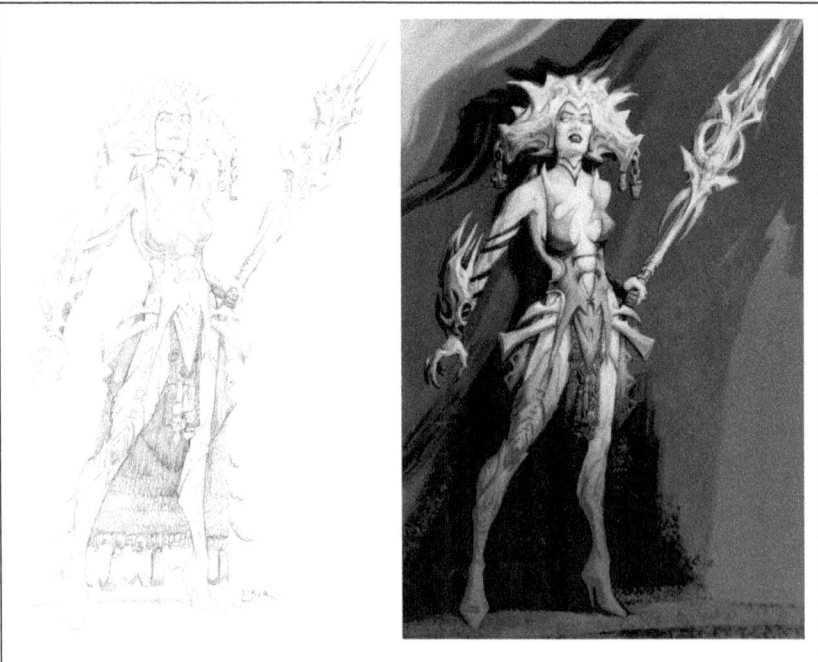

Mini design: *Sorceress* © Thomas M. Baxa 2012.

Again, use a snappy teaser to get them to click over. Every mope says "check out my new blog article." That's boring. ADs don't have time for that. But if you say, "Flames engulf the witch before her beloved can save her from a fiery death in my new piece – click here," they're more likely to take a look.

Make Your Client Feel Special

Make your ADs feel like theirs is the only job that you're thinking about. It's your number one priority and it's very important to you that you hit the mark for them. Don't talk about other jobs you're doing for other clients. You're giving them 110% all the time.

Your ADs don't have to know how long it takes you to do a job or what shortcuts you take to get it done. They don't need to know that you traced your photos to speed things up. They don't need to know that you limit the hours you spend on a spot illo as opposed to a full pager. Keep this stuff to yourself, but make them feel like you always give them your best effort.

Whenever possible, let them know how much you love working with them and on their product line. This won't be hard to do, because you probably do enjoy it. But take the time to actually say it. Let your ADs know that it has been a positive experience for you and that you appreciate them and their efforts.

Always Say Thank You

Whenever you get an email from one of your ADs, be sure to shoot them back a quick thank you. Keep it brief and genuine, and be enthusiastic. Everyone likes to be appreciated, and a little good will, will go a long way.

"Thanks so much for the assignment. I've been a fan of Magic for a long time, and I'm psyched to be working on it!"

"Thanks for the feedback on my sketches. Your comments helped make the composition stronger."

"It's been great working with you on Forgotten Realms, I hope we can work together again soon."

"I appreciate you going to bat for me about this issue. It's a true mark of a good art director who can walk the line between

helping his artists and giving the approval team what they need. Well done. "

Butter Them Up

Everyone loves flattery and wants to be appreciated for the job they're doing. Don't you? Well so do your ADs. Tell them that they're doing a great job choosing artists, that the product line has really improved since they took over, that the last advice they gave you about your artwork really helped.

If you really feel this way, share it with them, they'd love to hear it. Regardless, your goal is to get more work, and staying on good terms with your ADs is important. Some kind remarks go a long way, believe me. Most of the time they are getting pressure from their bosses, have way too much on their desk to handle, feeling pressure to hit their deadlines, and are getting bitched at by other artists that are much dumber than you and don't mind burning bridges. A nice compliment can make their day a little brighter, and help them feel good about working with you. And that's a good thing.

Tell them they are better than other Ad's you've dealt with (without naming any names, of course). Gaming is a small industry and ADs have a competitive nature. They love to hear that they are better than the other guy.

It's important to be sincere. Take a moment to remember some actual positive experiences that you had while working with them. If you're laying on the flattery in a forced way, they will sense that at be turned off.

10 Things ADs love to hear:
- You're better than other AD's I've worked with
- Your advice about my work has helped me grow as an artist
- You were so right about the changes you suggested
- Thanks for taking the time to help me out with the legal department
- Your dedication to the project shows in how excellent it has turned out
- You've done an excellent job assembling the right team for this project
- The way you've pulled all the elements together is impressive
- That article on your blog was very insightful and inspirational
- Your name comes up a lot when I talk with other artists as being one of the good ADs
- I'd recommend you to any production in a heartbeat

Currency

In this instance, **currency** is not money but rather emotional currency; it's the thing that gives a person a boost or makes them feel good about themselves.

It's always a good thing to identify the currency of any person you are in a relationship with whether it be your family, your spouse, work mates, or your art directors. Being aware of your own or another's currency is not a tool to manipulate them, it's a tool of self awareness to help us understand the things in life that give us joy. Currency applies to all areas of life, but we're going to zero in on some currencies that might apply to artists and ADs.

What is each of your AD's currency? What are they into? What interests do you share in common? If you don't know, you're not getting to know them enough. And each person may have multiple currencies, but focus on their primary currency. If you don't have an opportunity to actually determine an AD's currency, some of the ones listed it chart below are a pretty safe bet. Try some.

Their Currency Is	Send Them Links To:
Information	Art books, reference, articles, videos
A job well done	Success stories by other industry leaders: ADs, designers, artists, company owners
Prestige in the marketplace	Articles or mentions *about them* on the web, blogs, etc.
Compliments	Flatter them. Send them articles about bad ADs and say "thank god you're not like this."
Finding cool art	Send them jpegs and links of art they may like, fantasy related or not
Working with up and coming artists and students	Send them opportunities about workshops, art communities, art competitions, etc.
Charity work in the arts	Notify them of great art organizations to support

Send them cool stuff in the mail or links via email and social media that they might be into that fits their currency: links, reference, books, YouTube videos, dvds, etc. Get creative and playful with it.

Blog and Social Media Strategies

Social Media is for being sociable. It's not a place you want to do business like asking for work or soliciting professional advice. Don't message your AD and ask him questions about a job you're working on, and definitely don't discuss NDA material in a public forum like Facebook. Use email for any questions related to a job.

Use social media is for a more subliminal approach to stay connected and fresh in the minds of ADs you currently work for and those that you'd like to work for.

Find ADs you'd like to connect with and send them a Friend Request. Once you're Friends on Facebook, they will pop up in your News Feed and you'll see their posts. Comment on their posts often and they'll get used to seeing your avatar photo on their page.

A good strategy is to post a comment with a link in it. This way, the person begins to interact with your comment and this increase the chance of them remembering you because you give them interesting links to explore. Make sure the links are on topic. Use your call to action language in your posts and prompt them to go where you want them to. Of course, when you post stuff on your Wall, it will appear in their News Feeds as well. So be active on Facebook and post new work and news about what you're doing.

The more they see you, the more likely they are to click over to your Facebook page where you will have a portfolio of your work in your Photos section.

Get active on your favorite AD's blog too. They spend a lot of time and energy creating articles and posts for their blogs and it means a lot to them if people are enjoying what they have to say. Comment on some of their articles in a meaningful way. Again, if you are a member of an AD's blog mother site, then you will have a branded avatar that the AD will see along with your posts. Now they see you on Facebook, and on their personal blog. Then next time you email them, they'll already be familiar with you and want to take a look.

Freebies

Everyone loves getting gifts in the mail. Create some marketing freebies and snail mail them to some of the key ADs in your life as a thank you for the assignments they've given you over the past year.

Aside from being a nifty gift, these "marketing" freebies are designed to be reminders of you, your art, and your brand. You want to send a gift that they use at their desk everyday like a calendar or a mug. A calendar is great, because if they use it, they'll see your work every day for a year. Every time they take a sip of joe, they'll be reminded of your work and drink to your success! Include your artwork, logo, and url on any item that you give as a gift. If they dig you're art, they'll use the item.

Café press (www.cafepress.com) is an excellent way to make low run, print on demand products with your art on it. Send them a copy of your latest sketchbook or art book. Cool art related items like a branded lead holder or imprinted eraser.

You can also give them digital based freebies like ebooks, coupons, gift certificates to your site, or a free print on demand product that gets shipped to them, etc. Free gifts can be a very effective subliminal strategy.

Other Strategies

- Befriend them; chances are you have a lot in common
- Hang with them at con dinners and social events
- Invite them to events you are planning like life drawing night, etc.
- Invite them to your gallery opening
- Tell them that you're going to be at SDCC, when and where, ask them to come by your booth or table
- Ask if you can come and see the company offices/studios
- Get in a habit of dropping off finished jobs in person if possible
- Send a thank you email or card for no reason – it makes you feel grateful for them and the work you've gotten so far
- Branding helps. Put your logo on everything you send them, including emails and social media posts

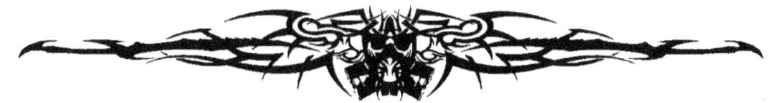

SECTION 5: Some Tricky Stuff

Well, you can't say that BaxaArt Academy doesn't deliver the goods! You've worked your way through a lot of great information and I hope you've been taking action on it along the way. This section has a few more bits of advice can help you with some hard to navigate terrain.

Calling for More Work

So you've gotten a cool assignment from a company that you've always wanted to work for. The project was fun, will be high profile, and it paid well. You nailed it and the AD was happy with your work. Now you want to do more work for this company. How do you get a follow up job?

If you're lucky, the AD will contact you on a regular basis when jobs come up. However, that's not always the case. Or it happens for a while and then the jobs come less frequently. It's up to you to take initiative and call your AD for more work.

As you've been getting work, hopefully you've been applying some of the techniques outlined above to stay in contact with your AD. This goes a long way to keep the lines of communication open so that when you do email or call him, he will respond, because you have an established rapport and you've done your job of keeping it going.

You can try emailing your AD and using some of the statements below. Email takes the pressure off the AD and can often get you an immediate response. And email may be the only way to reach some ADs. If this is working effectively, great.

Unfortunatly, emails are easy to blow off, so a phone call will be much more effective and get you more information because you can ask questions.

You may want to prepare just a little bit before calling. Check their blog, as it may reveal how they like to be approached. But as usual, just be cordial, friendly and brief. And enthusiasm goes a long way; it says that you are eager to do a good job and really like the company, the people and their properties. Start with a little chit chat, compliment them on something they've accomplished then try one of these approaches:

"Dungeons and Dragons is such an awesome property! I love working on it, and would be thrilled to continue to be a part of it. Are any up-coming projects that I might be right for?"

"We worked so well together on project X. I'd love the opportunity to work with you again!"

"You seemed pleased with the way I visually solved the problems in our last collaboration. I enjoy challenging assignments, and would love to work with you again!"

"It's been a while since we worked together – let's do it again. I have some time in my schedule, so please give me a call if you have any assignments that you think I could do a great job on?"

Remember that some ADs may be awkward at confrontation or find it difficult to say "no" to you, so they may opt to not answer you at all (easiest for them), or give you a standard line like "I'll keep you in mind for a project in the future." And they may mean it, but it can feel like a blow off to you. It's not. It's just a kind, and often truthful, way of letting you know that there is nothing available for you to work on right now.

Unfortunately, that kind of response doesn't give you much information. Is there work, but I'm not right for the assignment? Is there work, but the job is filled already? There won't be work for one year? The project is cancelled? The AD is getting fired? See what I mean, you really don't know when you might get work again.

Try to pry some additional info from your AD about some specifics. **At the very least, ask when would be a good time to contact them again about work.** You might learn that the AD sends out all assignments on the first of every month, that they are developing a new card game and will need 100 artists soon, that there will be no work for 6 months and you should concentrate your efforts elsewhere during that time, etc.

If you are working with an AD that has a hard time with communication, don't press too hard, because it will only make him uncomfortable and drive him away.

Do Rush Jobs

When an AD is stuck and needs someone to pick up the slack, this could be a good opportunity for you to get some work and more importantly get on his good side.

He's in a bind because someone turned in unacceptable work, flaked out (as some artists are known to do – but *not* you!), or the bosses threw a monkey wrench in his machine. But they still have their deadline and they need to get some illos done. Try this approach:

"I'm pretty quick at visual problem solving, maybe you have an assignment that another artist dropped the ball on that you need done in a rush. I have some time in my schedule right now where I would be able to help you out."

Whether you asked for the job, or you got it because you've been following up with that AD and were in his mind at the time, he might shoot you a rush job. If you can do it in the time allotted and still do good work, take the job.

When you come through and save his butt like this, he's going to remember the big favor you did him, remember who you are, and be grateful. As a thank you, he might give you an assignment with a normal deadline.

He may, however, think of you as the guy who can bust ass and do things on a short deadline. Maybe you are. It is a way to get more work. It can also be draining killing yourself on every job just to hit a tight deadline.

Whenever you are offered a rush job, kindly and confidently ask if you can get a little more money. Say:

"Since you need this job by this date, I'd consider it a rush job. I usually ask for an additional 15% rush fee."

Say it confidently like it's something you always do as the pro that you are and like it's expected. Never be afraid to ask for a rush fee, especially if you're working for a big company. They're used to this kind of request and will likely grant it.

Definition: A **Rush Fee** is an additional fee added on top of the illustration fee that you are entitled to because you are doing the job on a very short schedule. It means you're putting in extra hours or weekend hours to hit the deadline, so you are compensated for the overtime and grueling schedule.

Your AD might say that it's not in their budget, but that's ok. Take the job anyways, saying:

"Well, I usually get a rush fee, but I'd really like to work with you, *so I'd be happy to do the job without additional payment* this time.*"*

If you don't get the rush fee, it's ok because you're doing the rush job for the other reasons outlined above. Just by asking, it makes you seem much more professional and shows that you value your time and ability.

Getting Back in When an AD Stops Using You

This can be tough, which is why it's so important for you to follow the guidelines I've laid out for you in this book. Doing so will greatly improve your chances of getting repeat assignments from your clients. You've got a huge advantage because you've taken action and bought this book!

So, what can you do if the phone doesn't seem to be ringing and your clients have slowed down on the amount of assignments they give you, or heaven forbid, stop using you all together?

First of all you have to understand that there are many reasons why a client might stop using you, and it may not have anything to do with the quality of your work. Sometimes the reasons are the same as when you're first trying to break in like they've simply lost track of you because you're not marketing yourself enough, or any number of other reasons.

The first thing you want to do is try to *identify why* an AD has stopped calling. We sensitive artists often get a little paranoid and make assumptions that simply aren't true. Remember, it's nothing personal. No AD is sitting around thinking, "I'm going to make Baxa's life hell." He's just going along doing his job.

There are many reasons why he might not need your services. When we don't hear anything, we tend to think the worst. Don't. Go on a fact finding expedition instead.

Look at the product line. Has the artwork taken a new direction visually that is different than the way you work? Are there less products being released? Talk to your peers. Are they still getting work from that AD with the same regularity? Look at news about the company. Has it been bought and going through a reorganization? Has the AD you worked with left the company? For you to sit around making it about you and thinking, "I must suck since he's not calling me," is just silly. Get some info.

You have to take some responsibility here though. Take a careful look at your performance with the client. Were you late with your final art? Were you kind of a pain in the ass to work with? Did you put forth your best effort on jobs recently? See if you can't identify some of your weaknesses and improve upon them.

Sometimes the reason an AD has stopped using you is more closely related to your actual artwork, in which case you'll want to talk to your AD and try to determine where things went wrong. Email him and ask for a phone meeting to discuss the issue:

> *"I've noticed that you haven't sent any assignments my way lately. We seemed to work very well together on previous projects, and I'd love to do more with you. I know this can be hard to talk about, but I'm a pro and I welcome feedback on my artwork and my performance."*

> *"I was wondering if we could set up a phone meeting to discuss where I went wrong and what I can do differently to show you that I'm committed to doing a great job for you. When is a good time for you?"*

You want to let him know that you love working on their property and that you are willing to hear his feedback and change your approach to suit his needs.

If you're a dick and come at him like "Hey, why'd you stop giving me work? I have bills to pay you know," you're not going to get anywhere. Maybe ever again.

Don't just walk away – try to find out why he is using you less and what you can do to reverse the situation. Be delicate, professional, and genuine. Approach your AD with an attitude of learning and tell him that you really want to improve your skills and that you greatly value his opinion. **Ask for his help** by letting you know what is and isn't working, then follow up with him with some new samples that demonstrate that you listened to his advice and have implemented the changes he recommended.

The AD You Work With is Replaced

A change of art directors is disconcerting because you don't always get the news or know who is moving into the position. It can be like starting over, especially if you never had any contact with your AD's replacement.

But all companies try to make transitions easy. Many times, the replacement is someone who is already working at the company and is moving up the food chain, in which case, he may be fully aware of who you are and the work you've already done for the company. Even if he is a new hire, he might be totally into the product line or required to get up to speed on it, in which case he may see your name and work.

Previous ADs handing over the reins, like any job, will help the new guy transition into the job and may provide a list of artist that he has worked with for the new AD to reference.

Sometimes ADs will send out an email to say goodbye and notify all his hires that he is leaving. Sometimes it's on the day he's leaving, and sometimes you get some notice. If you know your AD is leaving, ask him for the contact info for his replacement, if he didn't put it in his email.

Contact the new AD *immediately* and make a connection. You want to do it right away and get out in front of artists that don't make the effort. Start with email and try to get him on the phone:

> *"I worked on this and this for Bill, I look forward to working with you as well.* [phrase it like it's a given] *I was wondering if I could give you a call. Are you free for a quick chat?"*

You will have to make some effort to connect with the new AD, as if he were a brand new client. Use the techniques I've laid out in this book and make contact.

Sometimes the game or product that you're working on moves to another company with a new AD. Same thing. Make contact.

Also, keep track of where your old AD lands, because he may be in a position to give you work at his new company. Now you have your old AD giving you work and your new AD giving you work!

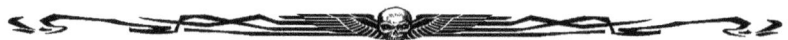

Getting Past the Gate Keepers

It's not always easy to reach the person you are trying to contact. In fact, it's very often deliberately difficult. It's the job of the gate keepers to protect their coveted bosses and keep you out.

> **Definition:** A **gate keeper** is a person who screens solicitors for their boss. It is their job to either outright keep you from contacting the person, or determine if you have a valid reason for calling.

Bullshit, right? Well, not really. You have to appreciate the position of the high level person you are trying to reach. They are busy doing their job. Their schedule is very full meeting the demands of their higher ups, so they just can't take the time to talk to everyone who would like to speak to them for advice, an assignment, or anything else.

Look at it this way, what if the next time you sit down to do a painting you get 15 calls that day that take 10 minutes each. That's 3 1/2 hours you could have been painting and working on your goals. That's a lot of time out of your important day! And you're not nearly as hotly sought after as the art directors you're trying to reach. So try to understand their position – it will help you keep a level head and better understand how to get around the gate keepers.

Types of Gate Keepers
Voice Mail System
Some companies don't have a receptionist at all – they have an automated system instead, or use it to screen calls. This is tough because you can't ask voice mail questions or ask it for a favor. Sometimes you can get through by spelling the person's name. If

not, you'll have to do more research and try to find an actual phone number or extension for the AD you are trying to reach.

Secretary / Receptionist / Assistant
Many receptionists are *not* gate keepers and will put you right through. If they don't put you through, they may give you some helpful information.

Second in Command Type (Assistant AD, Producer, someone junior)
This is a pretty good connect. The Assistant AD is often a person that is in the know and although they may or may not be in a position to make the final decision, they have the ear of the head cheese and their word carries a lot of weight. So if they like you, they may recommend you to the art director.

What You're Up Against – Their Tricks to Recognize You as a Novice
The gate keepers are a sly bunch. They have a lot of subtle ways to figure out if you're a novice who is cold calling their boss out of the blue.

One technique they use is to answer the phone by simply saying, "Studio." They don't say the name of the company or their name so you don't even know if you've reached the right place. If you ask, "Is this Legacy FX?" then they know you haven't called before and that you don't belong. When they answer, just say, "Can I speak to Mr. Big please." If you introduce yourself, and the gate keeper doesn't know you, you might be in trouble.

Gate keepers will usually be intentionally gruff to put you off and make you feel defensive. If you stammer or get intimidated, then they know you're not a pro. Like a wild predator, the gate keeper can sense fear. Speak calmly with authority and don't be afraid to ask for what you need.

They will likely ask you what your call is regarding. Have a planned answer that is direct and confident. Don't use salesman talk like, "I have an amazing opportunity that he'll be interested in." They can smell salesmen a mile away.

How To Get In

Make Nice with the Gate Keeper

This is crucial and applies the first and every time you are calling any office. Befriend the gate keepers and they may be willing to help you. For a while, they may be the *only* people you can reach. Treat them with respect and speak to them as you would the art director you are trying to reach. Use all the tools you've learned here to get through to them. They're not your enemy, they're just doing their job. You want to turn them into your ally. Your main goal is for them to act as your advocate, your pal, who will introduce you to the head honcho. *Ask* them if they would be willing to *help* you.

Be Armed With Info

Know who you are calling *by name.* Try using just their first name like you're already friends.

Lead with Your Artwork or Impressive Client List

Can the gate keeper view your artwork as you talk to them? A strong portfolio or resume of past work experiences and clients can be your foot in the door.

Sound Like You're a Big Wig

If you speak in a calm and confident tone and don't say much, the gate keeper may consider you to be senior or management. They won't risk offending you by asking too many questions.

Young Gun Approach

You can certainly try the young gun approach. Be earnest and truthful: "I know I'm reaching for the stars here, but I'm a young artist trying to make my mark and I hoping for a break. Can you please help me?" It might work. But the bigger the person you're trying to reach, the more unlikely you will be successful.

Be His Equal

Have your girlfriend pretend she is your assistant: "Tom Baxa, calling for George Lucas"

Kill Him with Kindness

"Are you having a bad day? You sound a little overwhelmed?"
"I can appreciate it must be tiring having deal with so many people all the time."

"I'm sorry you're having a rough day – I'm sure you're a lot of fun when you're not buried with too much work. Am I right?"

Have a Power Play Line Ready
When the gate keeper asks you, "What is your call regarding?" have a planned answer that is direct and confident, and make it sound like you're already in business with the AD or his associates: "I have some things about the project I need to discuss with Mr. Big."

Fib, Just a Little
"I'm working on the production team and I need to run something by Mr. Big"

"Mr. Big #1 recommended that I call Mr. Big #2"

"Is he expecting your call?" "Yes, I sent him some info and we need to discuss the details before the close of business today." (creates urgency)

Ask for the AD's Voicemail
If all else fails: "Not that I don't love talking with you, but I've bothered you enough. Why don't you put me through to Mr. Big Name's voicemail and I won't have to bother you anymore.

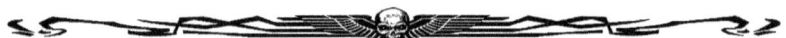

Getting Paid:
Unfortunately, sometimes you have to deal with employers that are having trouble paying you. Sometimes, they downright refuse. But more times than not, the people you are dealing with are good people with the best of intentions that love fantasy just like you. They likely have every intention of paying you, but just can't. At least not right away.

Being patient is helpful. Depending on the company you accepted work from, you may have known going in that they might pay slowly, so that's ok. You can wait, providing they will pay eventually. Just don't wait too long.

There is nothing wrong with asking for your money. You've earned it. I'm sure the person you are talking to doesn't expect you to work for free, just like they don't expect to go to their job, work for a week, and not get their paycheck. You did the work, you deserve your pay.

You are a professional, and even if you're not, here's a chance to practice being a professional and asking for what's due to you. It's actually less scary than you think.

Take Small Assignments

If you've never worked with a company before, test the waters by doing a small assignment. This is actually good advice for all levels of companies. You can get screwed by a big company, just like a small one. See how they are to work with, if they pay on time, etc. It lowers your risk.

If you bust your hump spending two months on a big job doing 30 illos and get screwed, you're in big trouble. If you do two illos that take a couple days and you don't get paid, then you won't have wasted too much time.

Ask What the Terms Are Up Front

The key here is to gather some information on the credibility of the company that is offering you work **BEFORE** you accept a job. Once you decide to move forward, minimize your risk by doing a small test assignment. Before you officially accept the job, ask about the payment terms and keep the lines of communication open with your AD and the accounting department.

How Long Are They *Actually* Taking To Pay?

Btw, before you start a job, ask your AD what the payment terms are. If you've heard some buzz about this company paying slow, ask him if they are *actually* hitting that schedule. If not, you can decide not to take the job, or take the job armed with useful information.

Ask other working artists if the company is just paying slow and are reliable to pay eventually, or if they are in serious trouble and might not pay at all. Word also gets around the internet pretty quickly too if a company is not solvent.

Sadly, some companies are shifty and may have an unspoken policy to screw people over while they are funding one of their other projects. You want to avoid this situation at all costs.

If you take on a big job, ask for **incremental or milestone payments**. This reduces your risk of getting screwed and is a good practice with all your clients. This way you're getting paid every two weeks as you're doing the job and not having to starve and put off your landlord until you finish a 4 month job and waiting two more weeks for your check. Also, if your payments stop coming, you have some leverage to stop working on the job.

Make Sure You Do Your Part
Once under way, remember to ask your AD or the accounting department what you have to do in order to get paid. Actually, it's ALWAYS your responsibility to do your part in getting paid. It's your business, it's your livelihood, it's you're paycheck. Know what you have to do to get paid, and do it in a timely fashion. If you don't, your check will get delayed, or you simply won't get paid at all until all the ducks are in a row.

For example, if you don't send in an invoice (your bill) for services rendered, the accounting department won't have a bill from you, won't know you finished the job, and won't have any idea that they're supposed to pay you. Let them know with the proper business documents.

It is good practice to keep track of your jobs: the date you turned them in, the date you invoiced, and when your payment is due based on the agreed upon terms.

Get To Know the Accountant
When you accept a job, you're almost immediately contacted by an administrative person, like a **production manager**, that sends out contracts and other documents. In a smaller company the AD might take care of this, or you may be dealing with the **accountant** directly. A larger company usually has a production manager who is your liaison to the legal and accounting departments. They are your friend!! Be nice to them, they are the ones who help you get the things you need.

If you're working with a production manager, you don't have to contact the accounting department unless there's an issue. If there is a problem, ask to talk to the accounting department. Make friends and play nice with the accountant. Believe me it will go a long way, and you will get paid before someone who is being an asshole to him. Trust me!

I recently had some confusing ups and downs with a client about contract points, additional payment terms, and a lost check. All I can say is that the production manager at that company is fantastic. She really went above and beyond to help me solve the problems over several months. From the get go, I was always genuinely appreciative of her efforts and she went to the mat for me. It pays to be nice.

What To Do When Payment Is Late

Companies, especially smaller ones, wait until their product is released and they start making money on it to pay you. This is the case when you get terms like 60 to 90 days. Yes, this sucks, but it is often the case, especially in the publishing industry. It's an indicator that a company is small and doesn't have enough capital in the company to pay its contributors until their product starts showing returns. Guess what, if their product doesn't sell well, they don't have money to pay you. So be aware of the risks when you take a job.

Don't get me wrong, a lot of companies pay well and on time without you ever having to check up on them. Even if they are paying slow, but definitely pay eventually, that's money in the bank.

Remember your goal is to keep getting work and get paid for it, so you don't want to piss people off. But you DO need to speak up. The squeaky wheel gets the oil. Be persistent, but always be nice and professional. Ask for your money with a smile. **Your strategy is to get the company to pay *you* BEFORE someone else.** You do that by asking and being nice.

If your payment doesn't arrive on the exact day it's due, give it a week or two before you take action. You may have miscalculated, or there may have been minor delays in the accounting process. If your payment is overdue, send the company a *gentle* reminder or a past due notice via email. If it gets to be a couple weeks, give them a call.

Sometimes your main contact, be it an AD or production manager, will run interference and not allow you to talk to accounting or legal. Try saying, "I don't want to keep bothering you with this accounting stuff, can I have the email address of the person responsible for sending out checks?" You'll get it. The AD doesn't want to hear artists beg for money any more than you like doing it. If they insist on keeping the chain of command, roll with it.

Advocate
If your courteous proddings are getting you nowhere (although they are almost always effective), one good strategy is to have someone else other than you be "the bad guy" around asking for money. Have an advocate that can play hardball, so you aren't the heavy, your "agent" is. I use my girlfriend. Have your advocate call on your behalf and be stern.

This way, you maintain your good working relationship with the company as an artist, and your representative is taking care of business and can apply a bit more pressure if needed. This is a great perk of having an agent: he takes care of collecting money, and you are just the friendly artist.

Your representative can be your wife, girlfriend, a friend, etc., if you don't actually have an agent or accountant. A helper can be a bit more of a pest or push the boundaries a bit more to get things moving. But, as always, if you helper is jerky and belligerent, nothing will happen. They should lead with the utmost professionalism and represent you as you would carry yourself.

Stepping It Up
Ok, emails and friendly phone calls aren't working. Now what? Well it's time to get a little more assertive. You're getting more proactive and confrontational here, but you still want to remain professional and courteous.

If you live close to the company, go into the office to turn in your next job. Give them a call and say, "Since payment has been spotty in the past, I'll be coming into the office on Friday to turn in the job and I'll expect payment in full upon delivery."

Any time you are in the office, make it a point to introduce yourself to the accountant and say "hi" each time you're in the office. They like that because they love art and no one ever visits them. If you're having issue getting paid, set up an appointment with the accountant and go see him with an attitude of trying to work things out amicably.

Unfortunately, it's usually out of their hands as to why people are not getting paid. They may not even know why, they just get an edict from the boss as to who to pay and when. But what they can do for you is put you at the top of the list when they finally get the go-ahead to pay the artists.

Struggling companies often pay small amounts to a lot of vendors before they pay big debts. You can try arranging to get paid in smaller amounts, so that at least you're getting something instead of waiting until they can cut a $3000 check.

One trick that can yield results is going up to a company's booth at a convention. At a show, they're there making money. There is money in their cash register. Try to find a principal person in the organization, and ask to get paid on the spot.

You can also ask a company to pay you in trade for product instead of cash: "Give me 20 books and we'll call it even." They like this because they have product on hand that they're trying to move and it's cheaper for them to give you product than cash.

Last Resorts
Now they've just been dicking you around for too long by making empty promises and not delivering on them. It's time to get more drastic.

DO NOT START HERE; these are desperate measures to employ if you just don't think you'll ever get paid and you've made a decision that this is a company that you just don't want to work for anymore. Why work for a company that isn't paying you? There is no reason that would justify that.

I personally don't believe that you should ever approach any business contact by getting in their face and yelling at them. You may feel differently. But the way I look at it is you don't want word to get around that you are an angry, pain in the ass person. It will only hurt you from getting work. And, believe me, the fantasy community is small enough that word will get around. There's a difference between being assertive and being aggressive. Know the difference. Be nice, be stern, and get paid. You worked for it, you deserve it.

Give Me One Million Dollars, or I'll Kill Your Artwork
You can try holding your art hostage if a company has been delinquent paying you in the past. When you finish an illustration, send your AD a low resolution jpeg to tease him on the day of the deadline. He'll email you back and say, "Looks good, upload the high rez version." But in this case, you're going to hold the art hostage until you are paid in full and you're going to tell him so. He's going to be pissed and call you unprofessional. And you're going to say, "I am professional, I get *paid* for the work I do, so pay me."

Sick a Lawyer On Them
Most of the time, you've turned in the assignment based on the terms of your contract and have waited your net 30 days in good faith, so there is nothing to hold hostage. So it's time to send a letter from a lawyer. Don't have one? You're an artist, make some fake letterhead and scare the company into paying you first. Or actually get a lawyer.

There are some free or inexpensive law advocacy services around that can help you. Here is Los Angeles we have California Lawyers for the Arts. They have a reasonable fee for legal help and lotsa other resources. Take a look at their site and try to find a similar service in your area. Believe it or not, those cheap legal service companies you see on TV can also help you out. Your goal here is to apply some pressure without spending an arm and a leg.

Ask your art community for recommendations for a lawyer. There are many lawyers that love fantasy art and would like to help you out for free or take paintings as payment for their fee. Have the letter you want to send to your client already drafted and ask them to put it on their letterhead. Make it easy for them and it will cost you less.

Expose Them for the Rats They Are
Companies value their reputation just like you do and they don't want word to get out that they are a bad company to work for. This can be a powerful "negotiation" tool. Begin by informing the company that if they don't pay you, you will be "forced to use all resources available to you to make sure other artists don't get treated the same way you're being treated." This of course is a veiled threat, and they may recognize it as such. You may get a check in the mail very quickly.

You do have to be very careful about what you say, especially if it is documented in writing and/or stored on a server somewhere. I am not in any way advising you to slander anyone or speak ill of them in public forums like the web or social media. I do not know the law or the difference between a truthful accounting or slander, so be VERY careful about what you choose to say.

Even if you are totally right, totally truthful, and say things totally within the letter of the law, a company can still *sue you*, and then you're screwed. So again, be very, very careful.

However the mere threat of bad publicity among the fan base or other artists, on Yelp, fantasy art forums, pro or non-pro websites, etc. may be enough to get you paid. Certainly the threat of reporting the company to the BBB carries a lot of weight.

BBB, the Better Business Bureau

The Better Business Bureau or BBB (www.bbb.org) offers reviews and a rating system of the performance of businesses. If the business has been shifty, customers, associates, and other professionals can lodge a complaint. Checking the BBB in the state that the business resides can give you a good indication if a business is not performing admirably.

No business wants a bad BBB rating, so they will likely make every effort to make you happy if you happen to mention that you're going to lodge a complaint against them.

Collection Agency

A collection agency is a company whose sole purpose is to collect delinquent debts for a fee. Before you hire one, check them out. If they are too aggressive or evil, you may want to find a more professional outfit to use. If the collection agency works on a commission basis for a part of the debt recovered, they will hustle to get your money.

With most small companies in the gaming industry, one call from a collection agency will do the job. A corporation might not be as scared.

I have never personally used a collection agency, but I know some artists that have had some success with them. The minute you take real action that can damage a company's reputation; you'll be surprised how quickly they find some money to pay you.

Lawsuit

Ok, sometimes you have to take it to court. But honestly, as a freelance illustrator you'll probably never sue someone, mainly because of the massive expense and time suck of a lawsuit is just not worth it. Sometimes it is. That's something you have to decide.

For example if you do a job and your contract says you own 50% of the characters and J.J. Abrahms picks up the property, makes a film that brings in 500 million dollars, you may want to sue.

Usually a letter from a reputable law firm, or the mere threat of a lawsuit will bring about a quick out of court settlement. Big companies rather pay you to go away and be quiet than risk negative exposure.

Check Yourself
If you find yourself in a position that you're owed so much in lost fees that you're considering suing, then consider that it is you who is doing something wrong. You're taking on too big of jobs without doing your homework on companies, or you're taking a second, and third assignment when you're not getting paid for the first.

It's true that most of the time you're doing things right and it's the company that is failing to live up to their part of the deal. Sometimes things happen that are beyond your control. More times than not, you're going to do a job and get paid, no problem. Don't anticipate problems. Focus on making good art and communicating with your art directors and accountants and you should be just fine!

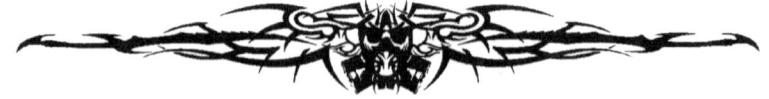

Notes:

CONCLUSION:

Awesome – you did it! You took the time to invest in your future by soaking up all this great information. I hope it has inspired you to take action. It's time to get out there and get some jobs. Good luck!!!

This is what BaxaArt Academy is all about – helping other artists soar! I hope you found the book enjoyable and stimulating.

Keep tuned in to www.BaxaArtAcademy.com for more cool stuff. And check out BaxaArt Blog http://baxaart.blogspot.com, the place where all things converge and I share more industry info, trade secrets, strategies, art talk and more.

Feel free to contact me with any burning questions that will help you with your growth path and career as a fantasy illustrator or feedback on the book at FreelanceFantasyArtistHelp@gmail.com. Any testimonials or comments you offer would be helpful! Plus, just like with my art, I'm always looking for feedback on how to keep raising the level of my work.

Pay it Forward

During our studies as artists, we all get advice from those who have gone before us. The pros who took the time to offer you advice or a leg up did so in the spirit of giving back to a community that they love. So it's important for you to help others out as they begin their journey as well.

This idea of paying it forward is not just for old pros, the same holds true for you. When you learn a new tip, technique, or business approach share it with your artist friends and share it with me – I'd love to learn something new. We have to look out for each other and foster fantasy art any way we can. That's what this book and BaxaArt Academy is all about.

Some things you can do to pay it forward: Open doors for those starting out, view portfolios and give feedback, email your artist friends when something hot is happening, blog your thoughts, share your art, tell your buddies about a big job that you can all get in on like a 300 card set, put links to their websites on your site, share their posts on Facebook and Twitter, go to their art openings, visit them at a con, contribute to their Kickstarter campaigns, and anything else you can think of.

Be of service in any way that you can to help your fellow artists and nurture the fantasy art community as a whole. If you take a minute to think about all the folks that have helped you out, you'll likely be surprised how many there are. Be grateful for that help and do the same for others.

We know what we have, how important the arts are, and we have to support each other and keep the artistic spirit alive in ourselves, in our friends, and in society as a whole.

Spread the Word

Start paying it forward by spreading the word about this book. If it's been helpful for you in any way, tell your artist friends! Put the link www.freelancefantasyartist.com on your Facebook page, tweet it, email it, and mention it in your blog.

We artists need to support each other, because no one else is looking out for us. It's important to spread any valuable info that we find like good books, reference sites, tutorials, and incredibly useful informational gems like this book. If you know of any excellent blogs or podcast sites that might be interested in the book, let them know that the book is available for review and that I'm available for interviews.

Good artists and good resources like *Get Work as a Fantasy Artist* and BaxaArt Academy can use your support. You know how it works – talk us up on social media and share some of the links below.

Thanks and keep making art – for all our sakes!! -- Tom

Here are some links to share:

Get Work as a Fantasy Artist ebook: www.freelancefantasyartist.com
Blood Rituals: the Art of Tom Baxa artbook: http://www.baxaart.com/Blood_Rituals_Index.htm
Websites: www.BaxaArt.com , www.BaxaArtAcademy.com
Facebook: www.facebook.com/baxaart
Blog: http://baxaart.blogspot.com/
Twitter: www.twitter.com/BaxaArt
Café Press Store: www.cafepress.com/baxaart
Ebay Store: http://stores.ebay.com/BaxaArt
Baxa on Amazon + Kindle:
www.amazon.com/Tom-Baxa/e/B0030NBSLY

Ebook of Get Work As A Fantasy Artist

You can purchase a *full color* ebook version of this book that you can read on any computer or mobile device at www.freelancefantasyartist.com. There's even a free bonus section called *Advice from the Pros* with advice from some of my pals in the industry that is only available in the ebook version!

If you feel that the info in this book was helpful to you, recommend this material to other artists you know. They'll thank you for it!

Please help others appreciate the value of this book, and write a review for it on Amazon, or email me your comments at tbaxa@baxaart.com.

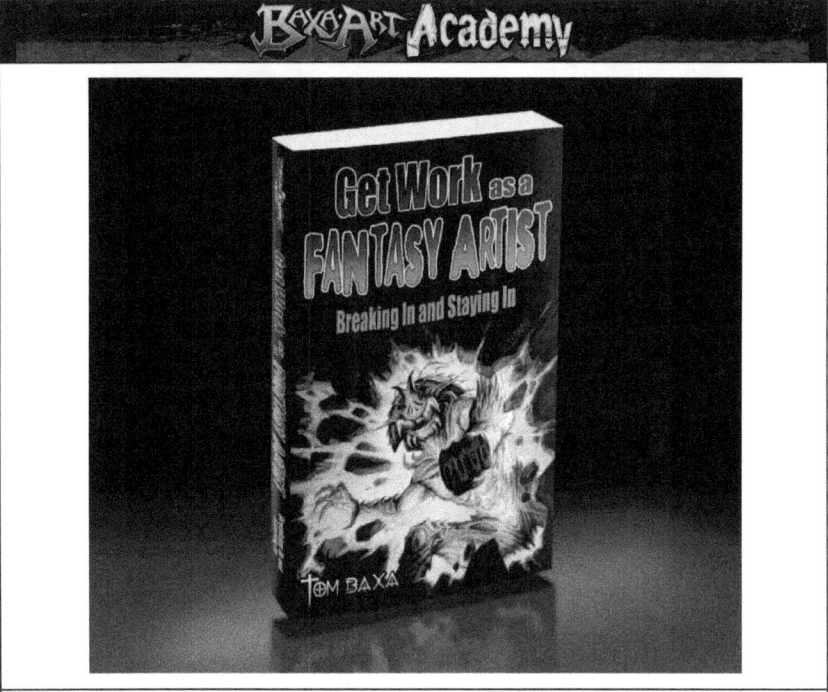

Get Work as a Fantasy Artist Book 2: Breaking In and Staying In
eBook © 2013 Thomas M. Baxa at www.freelancefantasyartst.com

Special Thanks

If you're as lucky as I am, you have someone in your life that fills you with joy and shows you all the amazing things that life has to offer. Susie opens up my heart up and shows me new things and new ways of thinking that make me a better person. She knows just what I need and how to give it to me right when I need it most. I'm so grateful to have you in my life and I love you dearly! Thank you for every day together.

I'd like to thank some special friends who helped me with this ebook: John Rheaume, Jim Nelson, Mark Nelson, Randy Asplund, Chris Beatrice, Randy Gallegos, Michael Kaluta, Jim Pavelec, Brian Snoddy, Sean Chandler, Jim Edwards, and William Hammock, Tricia Maxx. Thanks to all of you for your inspiration, excellent work, and friendship.

I'd also like to thank all the art directors that have given me jobs over the years.

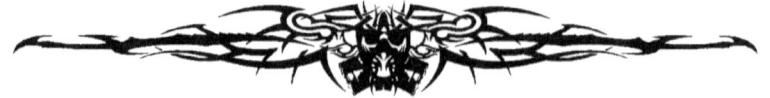

Appendix A: Resources

BaxaArt

BaxaArt website
  www.BaxaArt.com
BaxaArt Academy
  www.BaxaArtAcademy.com
Get Work as a Fantasy Aritst ebook
  www.freelancefantasyartist.com
Dynamic Fantasy Painting With Tom Baxa dvd
  http://www.baxaart.com/gnomon_index.htm
Copyright Basics for Artists
  www.baxaart.com/BAA/books_index.htm
Blood Rituals: The Art of Tom Baxa
  http://www.baxaart.com/Blood_Rituals_Index.htm
BaxaArt Blog
  http://baxaart.blogspot.com
BaxaArtUpdates eNewsletter
  www.baxaart.com/BaxaArtUpdates_sign-up.htm

Baxa on Amazon + Kindle:
  www.amazon.com/Tom-Baxa/e/B0030NBSLY
Books that Baxa's In: www.baxaart.com/Baxa's_Picks_index.htm
Facebook: www.facebook.com/baxaart
Twitter: www.twitter.com/BaxaArt
Café Press Store: www.cafepress.com/baxaart
Ebay Store: http://stores.ebay.com/BaxaArt

List Services

Art Marketing.com http://artmarketing.com/shop/index.php?cPath=27
Agency Access www.agencyaccess.com
Creative Access www.creativeaccess.com
ADBase www.adbase.com

Art Annuals

Spectrum www.spectrumfantasticart.com
Society of Illustrators www.societyillustrators.org
Communication Arts www.commarts.com
Expose www.ballisticpublishing.com/books/expose
Infected By Art www.infectedbyart.com

Books
Avengers: The Art of Marvel's The Avengers
Elysium: The Art of Daarken
AVP: Alien vs. Predator: The Creature Effects of ADI
Art of Darksiders II
Art of Blizzard Entertainment
Andrew Loomis List of Books (rereleased)
Burne Hogarth Books
Step By Step magazine
Imagine FX magazine
Writing without Teachers by Peter Elbow
Licensing Art & Design by Caryn R. Leland
Business and Legal Forms for Illustrators by Tad Crawford
Legal Guide for the Visual Artist by Tad Crawford

Printers
Digital Printers
Generally less expensive, can do smaller print runs, and quick turnaround
Got Print   www.gotprint.com
Overnight Prints   www.overnightprints.com
Blurb   www.blurb.com
IndigoInkPrint   www.indigoinkprint.com

Offset Printers
Modern Postcard   www.modernpostcard.com
PrintPlace   www.printplace.com
Bang Printing   www.bangprinting.com

POD printers
Lulu   www.lulu.com
CreateSpace (Amazon)   www.createspace.com

Conventions
Comics and Pop Culture
San Diego Comiccon, WonderCon, APE   www.comic-con.org
Wizard World Comiccons   www.wizardworld.com
New York Comiccon   www.newyorkcomiccon.com
Comikaze   www.comikazeexpo.com
Star Wars Celebration   www.starwarscelebration.eu
Creation Conventions (Star Trek, Twilight, Xena, more)   www.creationent.com

Fantasy Art
Illuxcon www.illuxcon.com
Spectrum Live http://spectrumfantasticartlive.com

Gaming
Gencon www.gencon.com
Origins Game Fair www.originsgamefair.com
DragonCon www.dragoncon.com
SPIEL/Essen Game Fair www.internationalespieltage.de

Job Fairs, Trade Shows
Siggraph http://s2013.siggraph.org Has speaker panels, an art show you can submit to, animation screenings, and major companies collecting resumes like a job fair.

GDC (Game Developer's Conference) www.gdconf.com. Video game industry pro conference where new games are being debuted, industry pros share tools, technology, knowledge, and news.

E3 www.e3expo.com Video game industry, similar to GDC

Gama www.gamatradeshow.com Focused on RPG, CCG, minis, and other board games

New York International Gift Fair (or The Gift Show) www.nyigf.com Largest licensing and gift show

MAGIC Market Week www.magiconline.com Huge Las Vegas licensing and gift show focused on apparel

Book Expo America (BEA) www.bookexpoamerica.com huge expo

Legal Advice
Art Talk www.theispot.com/arttalk
California Lawyers for the Arts www.calawyersforthearts.org
Comic Book Legal Defense Fund http://cbldf.org

Art Supplies
www.jerrysartarama.com

Source Books and Directories
Workbook www.workbook.com
Directory of Illustration www.directoryofillustration.com
Play www.playillustration.com

Portfolio Sites
Free
DeviantArt www.deviantart.com
ConceptArt www.ConceptArt.org
CGHub www.CGHub.com

Paid
Ispot www.theispot.com
Workbook www.workbook.com
ChildrensIllustrators.com www.childrensillustrators.com
Picture Book http://picture-book.com

Submission Guidelines
Wizards of the Coast guidelines artdrop@wizards.com
http://www.wizards.com/Magic/Magazine/Article.aspx?x=contactinfo/art submission
Wizards of the Coast's Dungeons and Dragons art test page (from 2013)
http://www.wizards.com/dnd/feature.aspx?x=dnd/feature/dndarttest

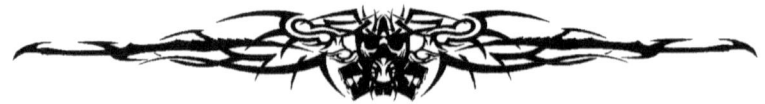

Appendix B: Baxa's Bio

The following bio is a chronology of some of the key milestones in my 25+ year career so far. And there're greater things yet to come!

The Early Days

I grew up in the west suburbs of Chicago, Illinois. At a young age, I loved getting lost in imagination and drawing all kinds of fantastic creatures inspired by characters I saw in Marvel Comics, Universal Monsters films, and KISS posters. I had an aptitude for rendering what I saw and my interest in art grew.

I was so fortunate that my local public high school had a highly developed art curriculum, which even back then was quite rare, and I took as many art classes in acrylic painting, watercolor, and drawing that I could.

1984-88 College

When I got to college at Northern Illinois University, I was well ahead of the curve and continued to take art classes. NIU was a state school, not a fancy design college, but I found out that a pro comic artist was on the faculty, so I had to go there. I majored in illustration, and was fortunate enough to be mentored by Mark A. Nelson, who continues to inspire me with his creativity and draftsmanship.

Mark helped guide me and develop a strong foundation in drawing to launch my career. He also generously had me ink backgrounds for some of his comic work and opened the door for me at TSR, the creators of *Dungeons & Dragons*. But as he always says, you can open a door for someone, but they have to have the chops to get the job.

1988 Freelancing

In 1988, fresh out of college with a Bachelor's Degree in Illustration, I began my freelance career **inking comics** for indie comic companies and doing the occasional spot illo for *Dragon* **magazine**. I also freelanced for other role-playing game companies.

By 1991, I was doing tons of black and white ink drawings for *Dragon* magazine and interior illustrations for *D&D*, most notably a long run on **Monstrous Compendiums** and the **Dark Sun** campaign setting. I did a few acrylic covers here and there, but my big foray into color illustration came when I joined the team at **FASA as a staff illustrator** in 1994.

1994 FASA

My time at FASA was a time of great creative exploration and growth. I worked primarily on **Shadowrun and Earthdawn**, whose universes where rich playgrounds for creating all kinds of interesting and visceral characters. To his credit, the art director and lead artist, Jim Nelson, fought for diversity of ideas and imagery from a wide range of artists giving the FASA product lines a great look that fans loved. While at FASA I was given free rein to experiment, including painting with oils. It was a blast.

I had showed my artwork at GenCon, the largest RPG gaming convention in the world, and continued to do so with FASA, meeting players, doing portfolio reviews, and showcasing my artwork.

1997 Magic: the Gathering

Since I was an employee of FASA's, and they considered Wizards of the Coast a direct competitor, I was not allowed to work for them. But in 1997, FASA changed their policy and I did my first cards for **Magic: the Gathering**.

I continued as a staff artist for FASA and started doing more and more Magic cards. Wizards of the Coast was always very artist friendly and did a lot to support and promote their contributing artists. I have been fortunate enough to be part of the Magic phenomenon and do artist signings at their Pro Tour Events, where you get to travel and meet the players who are out there enjoying your art on the game they love. I continue to do so to this day.

1999 Video Games

In mid 1998 I left Fasa and continued my freelance career. But I was looking for new adventures and I found them in video games. In 1999 I moved out to Southern California and began working at **Westwood Studios/Electronic Arts as a concept artist**.

I was pretty new to computers at the time, so I learned a ton about doing art on the computer, production cycles, video game asset creation and even 3D modeling. The hands on education I got there was invaluable. I worked on the shipped titles **Nox, Nox Quest**, and **Red Alert: Yuri's Revenge**.

Although I was still doing some freelance illustration while at Westwood, I was anxious to return to freelancing full time, so I left Westwood in late 2001. I moved from Orange County to Los Angeles proper to pursue work in the film industry, a much harder nut to crack than gaming.

2002 Concept Art for Films

Yet another milestone in my freelance career was **my first concept art job on a movie**. The film was *Van Helsing*, and the client was the special effects house **Greg Cannom's Captive Audience**. I'd always loved movie make-up so it was great fun being in the studio amongst sculptors and other artists surrounded by life sized creatures from all the films they worked on. What a fun gig. I was thirsty for more.

I also did some concept art for entertainment advertising companies as well. Not glamorous work, but it pays well and it was interesting to experience the inner workings of a high profile advertising firm. Another great learning experience.

Around this same time I was starting to shift my focus somewhat and I wanted to **start developing my own ideas and intellectual properties (IPs)**, so I decided to stick with my current list of clients and devote the time it would take to generate new clients to the pursuit of my own IPs.

I also supplemented my income and raised visibility by doing more appearances at Magic tournaments and conventions like GenCon and San Diego ComicCon.

2006 World of Warcraft tcg

Blizzard decided to license the World of Warcraft for a collectable card game and I did cards for most sets since the beginning.

2006 Licensing

I had been developing a line of zombified fairy characters called Wicked Fairies® in a series of paintings with the express purpose of licensing the images on merchandise. I was fortunate to land a t-shirt deal with a prominent company in that space.

The thing about your own IPs is that they take a long time to develop, and to try to get sold, and it takes a tremendous amount of time marketing them and your brand. I spend a large portion of my days doing just that. But it's worth it because it's very rewarding to work hard at building your own business and creative ideas. Some of my exciting projects have yet to see the light of day – but they will soon! And I continue to develop new ones all the time.

2008 Gnomon Dvd

The Gnomon Workshop has an excellent reputation as the leader in instructional dvds. Together we produced one of their few traditional art dvds *Dynamic Fantasy Painting With Tom Baxa*. This was an opportunity for me to do a large painting with a complete composition and discuss a lot of the things I consider make a successful fantasy painting.

2010 Blood Rituals

I heard about this new website called Kickstarter and saw the potential in it to fund self published works. At the time, almost no one in the fantasy field was using it, unlike today. I used Kickstarter to successfully crowd fund my very first art book *Blood Rituals: The Art of Tom Baxa*.

Also in 2010, I was the Artist Guest of Honor at GenCon. It was a privilege to be recognized for my years of work in the RPG industry and a chance to do GenCon in style with *Blood Rituals* in hand.

2013 And Beyond

To this day I continue to freelance as a fantasy illustrator and concept artist for a wide variety of high profile clients. I still work in oils and gouache, and also enjoy painting digitally and photo montage. I continue to work tirelessly to develop my own projects, including writing a novel, exploring new ideas in my artwork, and growing the BaxaArt brand with its newest addition **BaxaArt Academy**.

Check out my website www.BaxaArt.com for great art, merchandise, prints, paintings for sale and updates about what I'm up to. My blog is full of helpful information, stories about my life as an artist, cool art by me and my friends and much more: http://baxaart.blogspot.com.

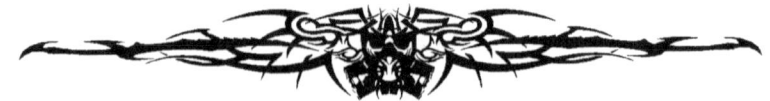

BaxaArt Gallery

Appendix C: BaxaArt Gallery

For full color versions of this artwork: visit www.BaxaArt.com.

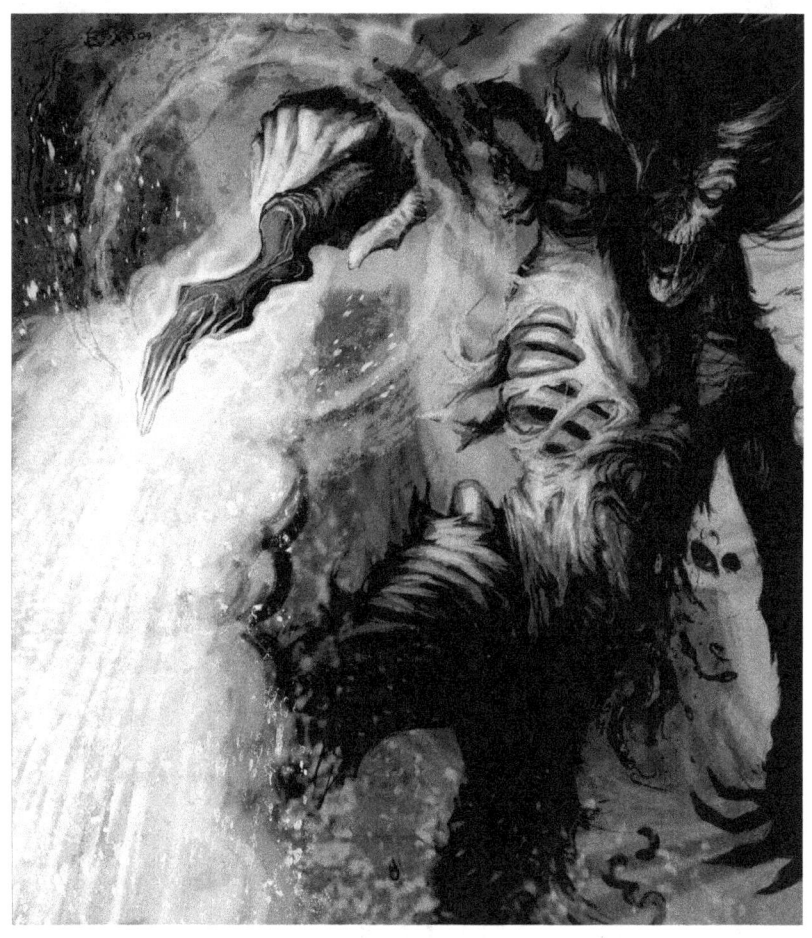

Encrusted Zombie Finger Image used by permission
© 2013 Blizzard Entertainment Inc.

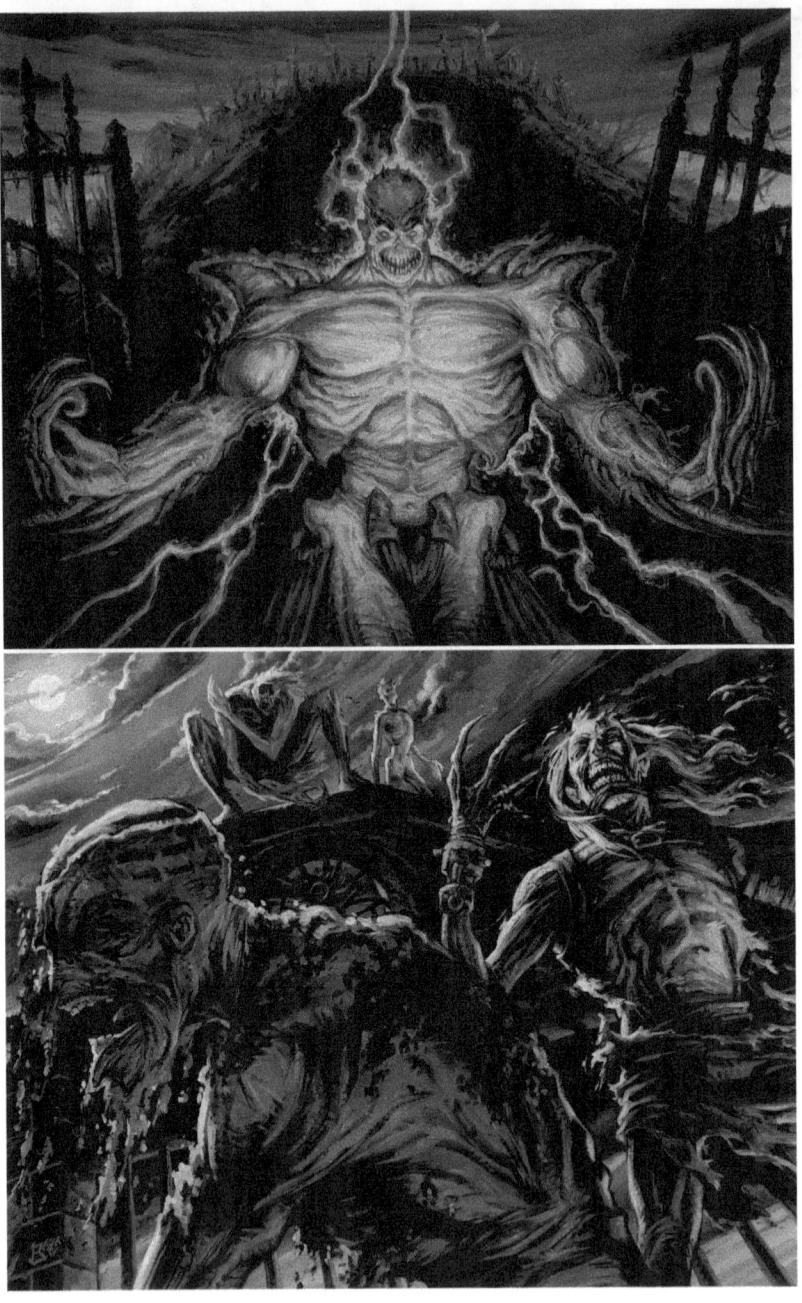

Soulless One + Zombie Infestation © Wizards of the Coast 2002

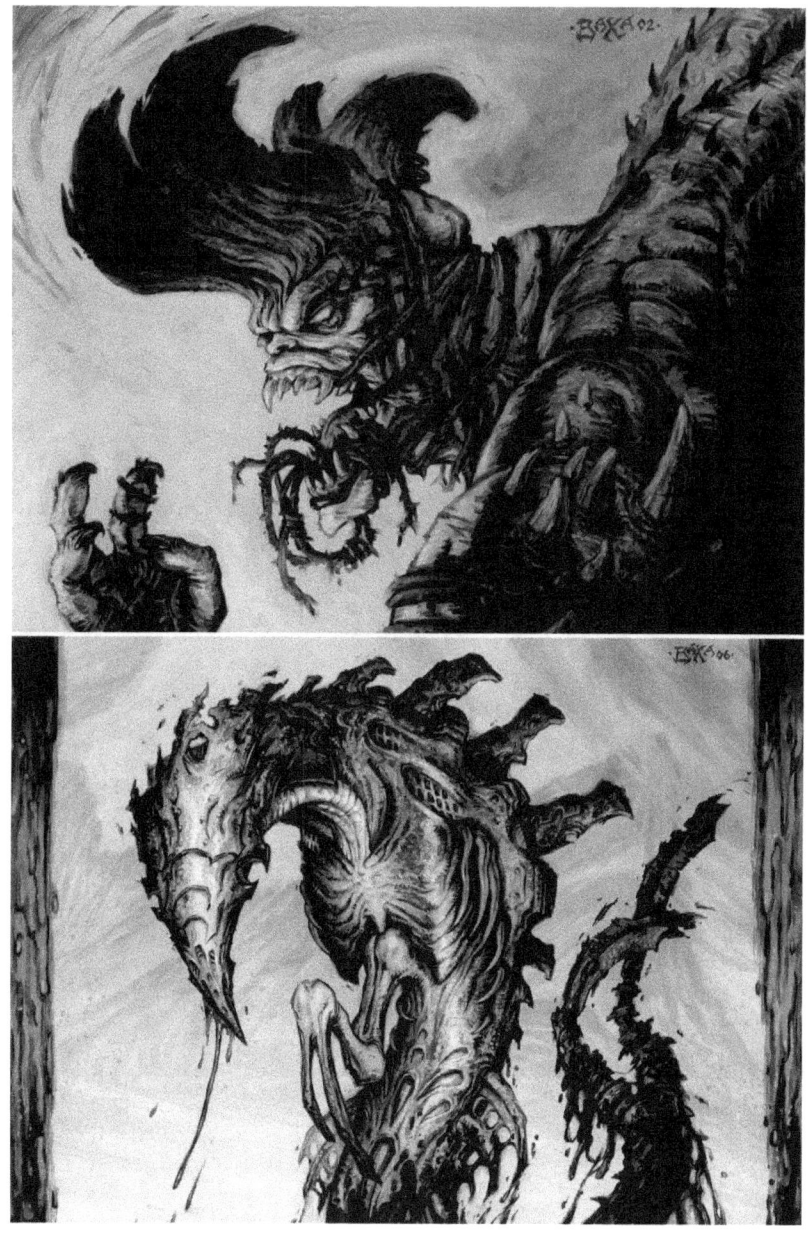

Havoc Demon + Vampiric Sliver © Wizards of the Coast 2002 + 2006

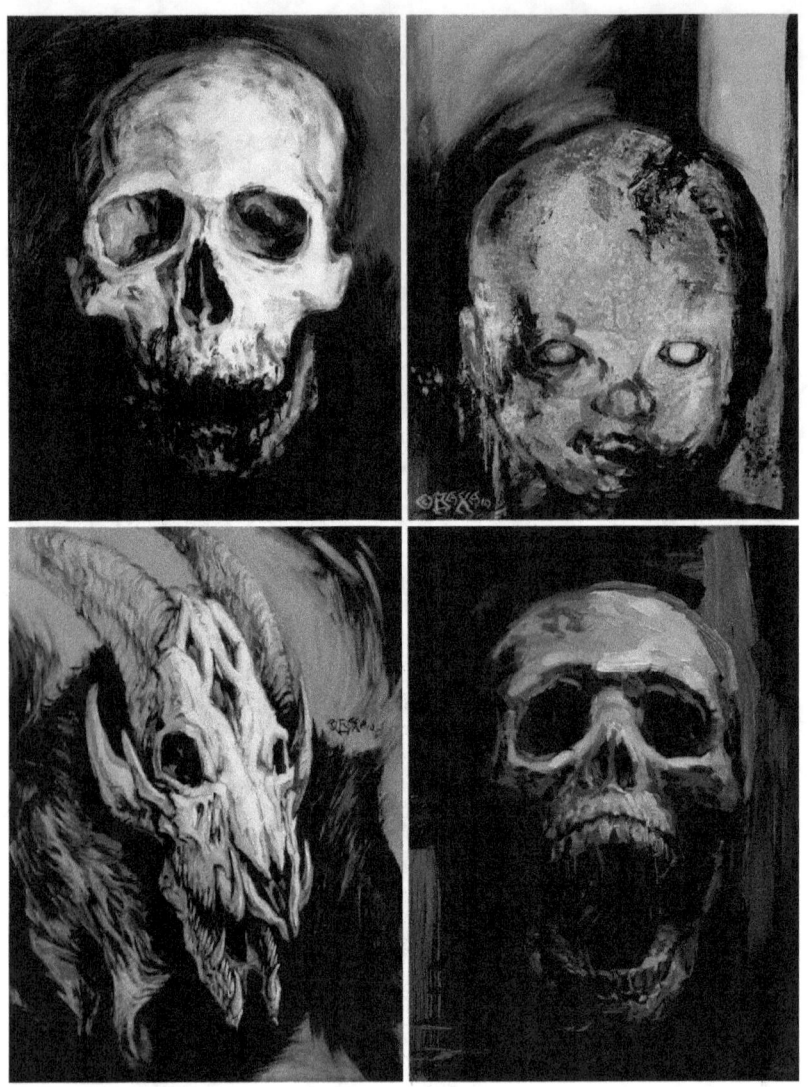

Rot Mouth Skull, Baby Crusty, HellHog Demon, Red Skull
© Thomas M. Baxa 2010

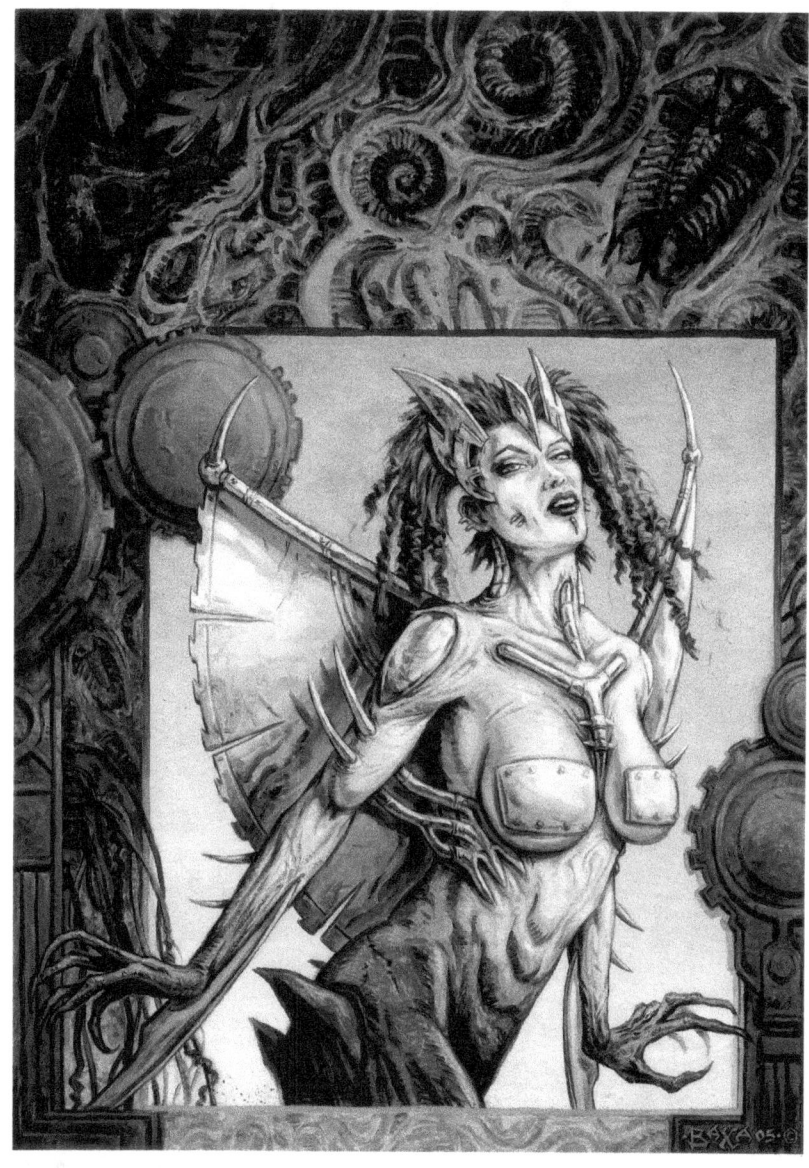

Infused Allure © Thomas M. Baxa 2005

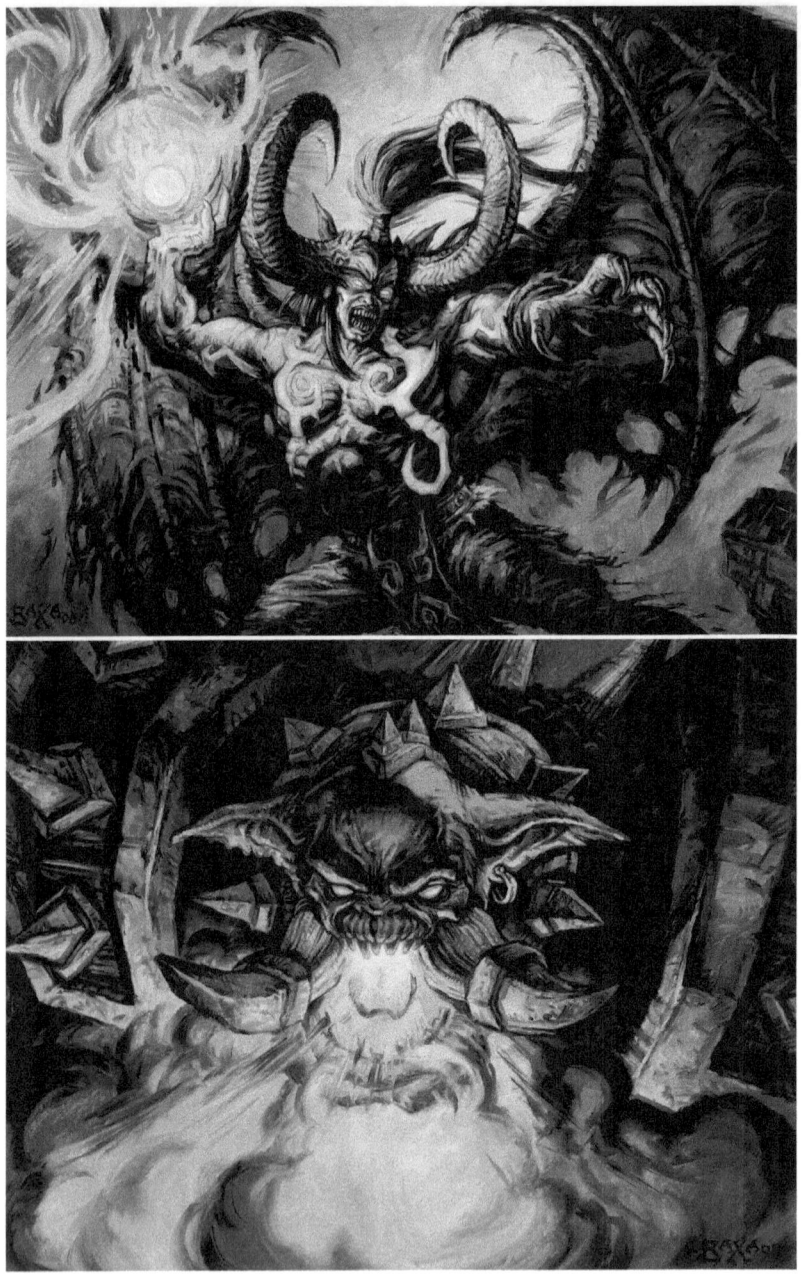

Illidan + Fel Acid Breath © 2013 Blizzard Entertainment Inc.

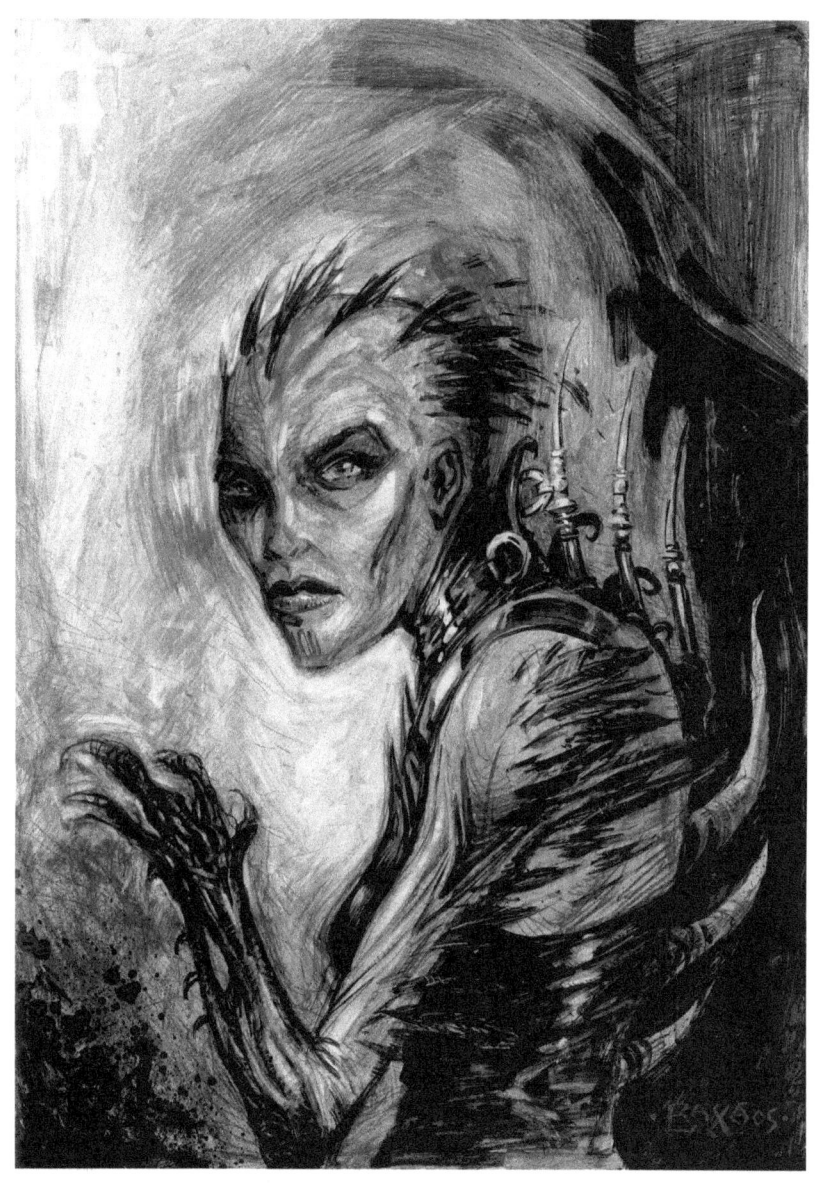

Feather Girl © Thomas M. Baxa 2005

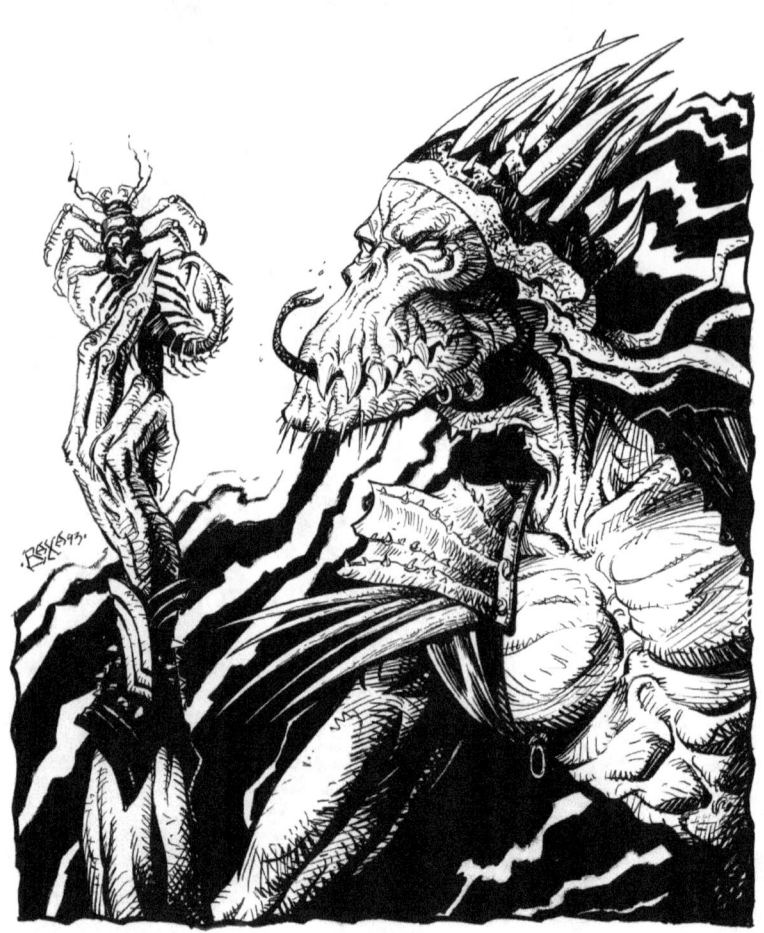

Gith © Wizards of the Coast 1993

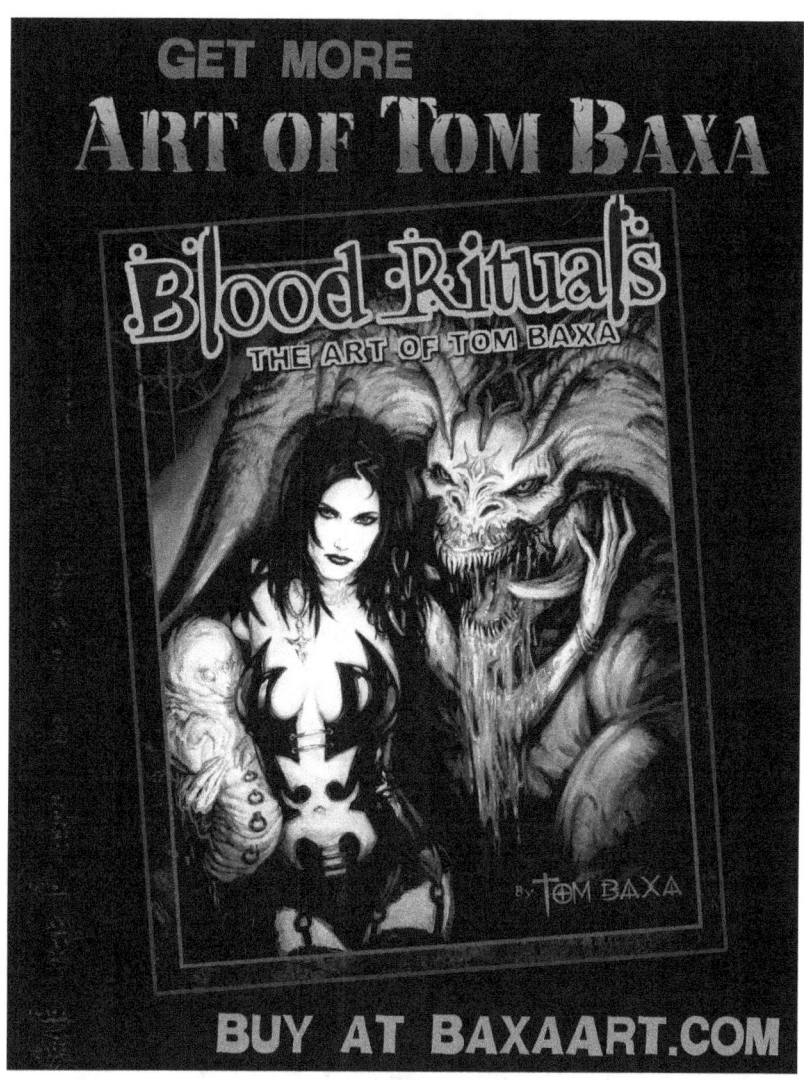

Blood Rituals: The Art of Tom Baxa
Full color art book spanning 25 years of Fantasy Illustration!
www.baxaart.com/Blood_Rituals_Index.htm

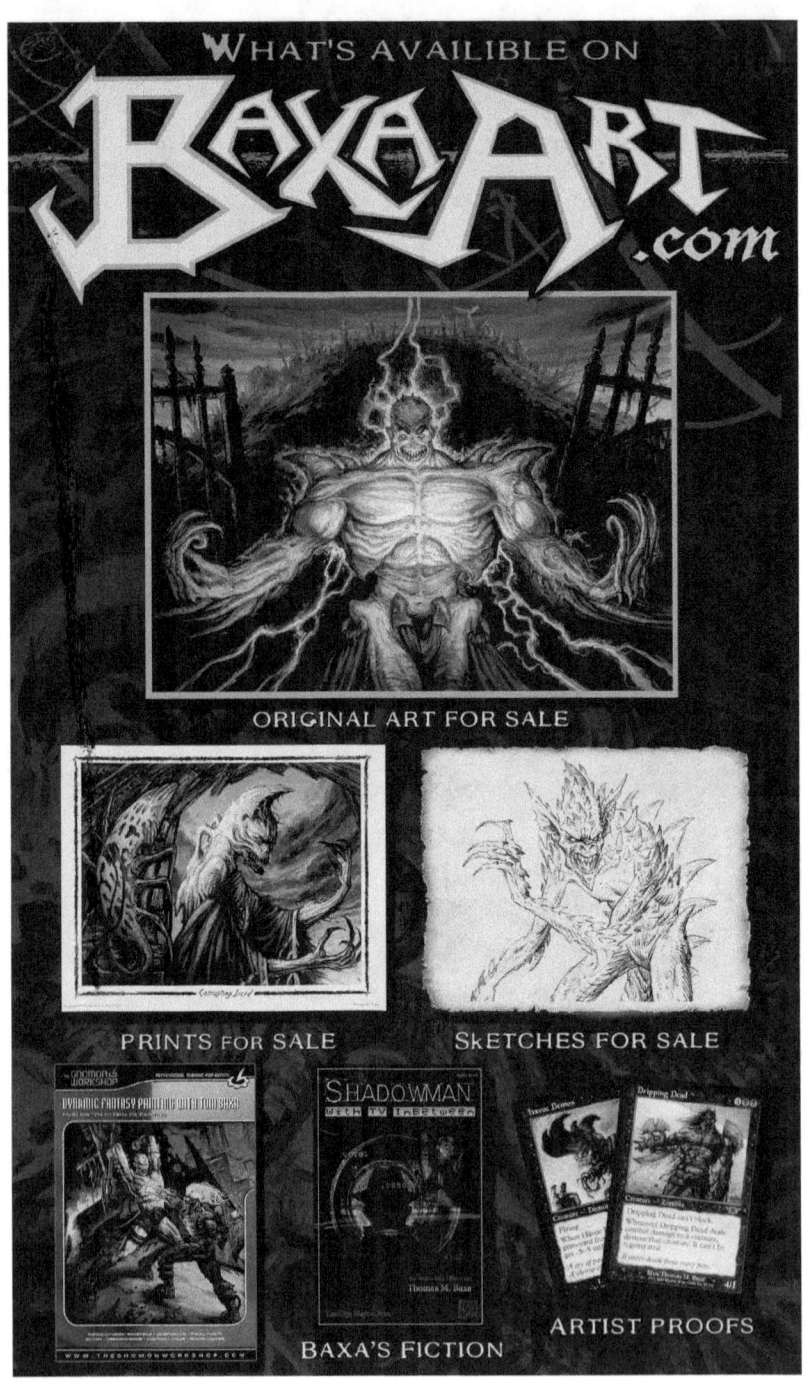

www.BaxaArt.com